SCHOLARSHIP AND THE GYPSY STRUGGLE

Commitment in Romani Studies

SCHOLARSHIP AND THE GYPSY STRUGGLE

Commitment in Romani Studies

A collection of papers and poems to celebrate
Donald Kenrick's seventieth year.

EDITED BY
THOMAS ACTON
Professor of Romani Studies
University of Greenwich

PUBLISHED BY THE
UNIVERSITY OF HERTFORDSHIRE PRESS

First published in 2000 in Great Britain by
University of Hertfordshire Press
Learning and Information Services
College Lane
Hatfield
Hertfordshire
AL10 9AB

The right of the authors to be identified as authors of this work has been asserted by them in accordance with the Copyright, Designs and Patents Act 1988.

All rights reserved. No part of this book may be reproduced or utilized in any form or by any means, electronic or mechanical, including photocopying, recording or by any information storage and retrieval system, without permission in writing from the Hertfordshire University Press.

A catalogue record for this book is available from the British Library.

ISBN 1 902806 01 8

Designed by Geoff Green Book Design, Cambridge CB4 5RA
Printed by J. W. Arrowsmith Ltd., Bristol BS3 2NT

CONTENTS

	A word for Donald – *Barikano Lav Donaldoske* VALDEMAR KALININ	ix
	Introduction: the life and times of Donald Simon Kenrick THOMAS ACTON	ix
	A champion ELI FRANKHAM	xxxiii
1	The emergence of Romani as a Koïné outside of India IAN HANCOCK	1
2	The genesis of 'Angloromani' PETER BAKKER	14
3	Proclamation or preservation? The Bible and Minority Languages PAUL ELLINGWORTH	32
4	The Celtic languages in the twenty-first century: a partisan review ANTHONY P. GRANT	40
5	"'Anti Gypyism' is not a new phenomenon". Anti-Gypsyism research: the creation of a new field of study HERBERT HEUSS	52
6	"My name in the Third Reich was Z:5742": the political art of the Austrian Rom, Karl Stojka SUSAN TEBBUTT	69
7	Myth as process ELENA MARUSHIAKOVA AND VESSELIN POPOV	81
8	The Romani movement: rebirth and the First World Romani Congress in retrospect GRATTAN PUXON	94

9	Gypsies and planning policy DIANA ALLEN	114
10	The blond bandit Arthur Thesleff – committed scholarship in early Finnish Romani Studies and today GUNILLA LUNDGREN	129
11	"Oh this Russian spirit abides everywhere": a dialogue of the imagination with Dr Donald Kenrick about the 'Russian spirit' VALDEMAR KALININ	140
12	Donald Kenrick as polyglot: could he be replaced by a machine? ERIK V. GUNNEMARK	150
13	To eat is to honour God MILENA HUBSCHMANNOVA	155
	A summary bibliography of works by Donald Kenrick THOMAS ACTON	171
	Donald CHARLES SMITH	177
	Brief notes on contributors	179

Barikano Lav Donaldoske – *A word for Donald*

VALDEMAR KALININ

Prastal dzhiipe, phare-dyveseskiro,
Dykhen, syr rat sylaly chakirela amen,
Te ná javel kamiben da bare manusheskiro,
So Romanichalsy ashty te keren?

Roma ná mek nadieja dro ilo peskiro,
Mek uchalyn kedalepe kaly,
Kerasa patyv ke ilo leskiro,
Janasa Donaldoske vága bari.

Bashaven pe gitary, Polskone-themeskire,
Khelen prijomenca, Romale sare,
Bagan xory, xachkirde-ileskire,
Roma Rasiejattyr pe svenko javen.

Eftadesha bersh pe drom leskiro,
Lylyvaria syr chiriklia peske gniazdy kheren,
Parne bala syr chergenia dudeskire,
Romany baxt sare tugatyr chakiren.

Hard days like cold nights
Cover us up as life runs by – look and believe!
Without the passion of this great man
You Romanichals, what could you achieve?

You Roma! You need not rely on your own heart alone.
Let the shadows gather round as dark as they may,
We acknowledge his spirit, kindred to ours,
Donald, your heart merits the respect we pay.

Play your guitars, you Travellers from Poland!
Roma from everywhere, dance like the wind!
Sing from the depths of your hot-blooded hearts,
You Roma from Russia, stay close behind!

Seventy years on the road of his life, bedecked
With books, as birds build their nests;
His silver hair flows like starlight,
Protecting Roma from all harm and unrest.

INTRODUCTION

THE LIFE AND TIMES OF DONALD SIMON KENRICK

Thomas Acton

DONALD KENRICK was born on 6 June 1929 in Hackney to where his orthodox Jewish family had moved from Poland. His grandfather became a British citizen shortly before the First World War. As family fortunes improved they moved to Highgate. Donald spent the period of the Second World War blitz in Cambridge. More fortunate than many war time evacuee children, he was placed at the Perse School, an historic public school with a grammar school tradition of assimilating intellectual lower- and middle-class boys to the establishment. As to safety, however, the school received a direct hit from a German bomb.

He was a bright and successful schoolboy, making the kind of contacts that could have led to a much more conventional career. He acted alongside Peter Hall, later Director of the National Theatre, and, as editor of his house magazine, *The Orient*, published the first poem by John Gross, who later edited the *Times Literary Supplement*. The three enduring themes of his life that were established at school, however, were his love of languages, folk music, and his left-wing politics.

The Perse school had always had a rather un-English commitment to effectiveness in language teaching. The great classifier of Indian languages, who had consolidated the position of Romani among them, R.L.Turner, had been a pupil there, and it is one of the few British secondary schools ever to have offered Sanskrit as an option. Ancient languages as well as modern were taught by the direct method, that is in classes where the pupils and the teachers spoke only in the language being taught. Languages were not seen as dry intellectual exercises, or crossword puzzles to be unpicked, but as being able to be mastered only as living systems of communication between real people.

So the young Kenrick found himself being taught Latin by the direct method by a teacher who wore purple socks and was a member of the Common Wealth Party. This was a socialist party led by Sir Richard Acland formed to defy the war time political truce between the Labour, Conservative and Liberal parties not to contest by-elections. Acland, son of a Liberal MP, had inherited a large estate in Somerset, but gave it to the National Trust, along with money for its upkeep, and devoted his time, as he had his wealth, to the cause of the common people (Prynn 1972: 169, Calder, 1971: 631 ff).

The people's war against fascism had engendered the most progressive political climate the country had ever known. Within the coalition government Conservative and Labour politicians like Butler and Attlee vied to encourage the tax-and-spend policies of Liberal intellectuals like Beveridge and Keynes and began to implement them even before the end of the war. But the general public blamed the Conservatives for the pre-war depression. How could it be, they asked, that in wartime when the government also bore the cost of fighting the war, that poverty, malnutrition and unemployment actually vanished? And was it unreasonable to expect the same of peacetime? The Common Wealth Party gave popular expression to this mood and won a number of Conservative seats in by-elections and gave left-wingers determined to build a better world after the war a standard around which to coalesce.

The Common Wealth Party had, in effect, picked up the baton of the 1930s Popular Front. This had been discredited by the 1939 Hitler-Stalin non-aggression pact which had also effectively ended the hope of the British Communist party of enjoying mass support. The Communist party had followed Stalin's line and, in the process, had to accept the resignation of its general secretary, Harry Pollitt, who was unable to stomach it, despite his public loyalty to 'the line' that he privately opposed. In fact, this proved a stroke of luck for the Communist party, as they were able to bring Pollitt back after the German assault on the Soviet Union, where he was able to combine loyalty with a certain proven integrity, and reinstate the policy of co-operation on the left (McMahon, 1976: 252, 269).

So left-wing Labour and Communist party members were also active in Common Wealth party campaigns. The young Kenrick had matriculated at the age of fifteen, then had to spend three years in the sixth form taking the Higher Certificate. As a sixth former he was allowed more freedom, including the right to choose his own barber. He took advantage of visits to a barber in Cambridge to visit a bookshop run by a Spanish Civil War veteran and joined the Young Communist League. The school never found out that he was amongst those daubing the slogan "Second Front Now!" around the town.

In the 1945 General Election all the assorted left-wingers finally got the chance to throw their weight into a campaign against the Conservatives, whose reliance on the popularity of their wartime leader, Sir Winston Churchill, proved inadequate. In his own seat, unopposed by Liberal and Labour, Churchill none the less conceded over 10,000 votes to an independent (Childs, 1979). In seats where the Conservatives had no chance, Communist or Common Wealth candidates stood against Labour and sometimes won. In all other seats they threw their weight behind Labour, hoping that after the war the kind of broad left-wing electoral alliance would emerge that did occur in France and Italy.

In Cambridge the Communists supported Labour to win the town and the county seats, and the socialist writer J.B. Priestley won the Cambridge University seat. The

Labour committee room in which Kenrick worked was staffed entirely by Communist volunteers. Locally and nationally there was a political landslide to the Labour party nearly as great as that which was to happen half a century later in 1997.

Any idea, however, that this meant the triumph of "Popular Front" ideas was quickly disabused. The Labour Party made it very clear that it would not accept either the Common Wealth Party or the Communist Party as affiliates. Individuals from those parties who wished to join Labour had to denounce them. Those suspected of maintaining secret contacts with them were eventually expelled. Meanwhile, the beginning of the Cold War from Churchill's 1946 denunciation of the Iron Curtain, (cited in Watson, 1989) and the exposure of Stalinist atrocities, which to some extent had been hushed up while the Russians were our war time allies, punctured the balloon of respectability the Left had enjoyed under Churchill's first government. In 1945 Pollitt had missed election in the Rhondda by a mere 972 votes. In 1950 he lost to Labour by 22,182 votes in the same seat.

Their increasing isolation made left-wingers, for a time at least, more not less active. Kenrick's last year at school was 1946–7. With his full university scholarship secured, and his exams already passed he had little to do and so threw himself into the work of the Young Communist League and its campaigns such as the London Squatters' movement which took over flats in Kensington for the homeless of West

Eventually the Communist party came round to Donald Kenrick's views. Here Communist Party General Secretary Harry Pollitt addresses a rally in Upper St. Martin's Lane opposing British military intervention in Greece – the line that a few months earlier he had cracked down on young communist Donald Kenrick for taking.

London. Kenrick's father became so concerned that he might give up an academic career for one of political agitation that he wrote to Harry Pollitt. Pollitt replied gravely that all comrades were to be encouraged to realise their full educational potential and that Donald should certainly take up his university place. Thoughtfully he copied the letter to Donald.

Donald Kenrick was to meet Pollitt personally early in 1947 at the national conference of the Young Communist League. On behalf of the Cambridge branch he moved a motion calling for an end to conscription (compulsory military service). Despite outrage at the use of British soldiers to crush communists in the Greek civil war, the party leaders were still to cling for a few more months to the illusion that they might yet form part of the governing consensus and defended the idea of the 'people's army'. Years later Kenrick recalled the occasion, "Everyone in the hall supported me. People were cheering, and we would have won the vote – if Harry Pollitt hadn't spoken on the other side!"

As a dutiful communist, however, he accepted the line, withdrew the motion, danced with Harry Pollitt's daughter at the Squatters' Ball the same evening, and later in the year trooped off to do his own National Service. He opted to join the Cameron Highlanders, in hopes of visiting Scotland. Once he had done his basic training, and having already decided to study Arabic, he volunteered for duty in the Middle East. Rejecting officer training, he spent the years 1947–9 as a corporal in the British Forces Broadcasting Service in the Egyptian Canal Zone.

During 1948 as the cold war intensified, the order went out that no communists should be allowed to serve abroad in the British Forces. Kenrick, bored with Egypt, immediately reported himself to his Commanding Officer, hoping to be sent home but he was told that his radio work was too valuable for him to be let go. Only in 1949 did he return to go to university. Rejecting the élitism of Oxford and Cambridge, he enrolled at the School of Oriental and African Studies in the University of London to do Linguistics, majoring in Arabic and Hebrew.

He left the Communist party, however, in his second year. Part of his reason for studying linguistics had been to develop the ideas of the Soviet Academician Y.N. Marr (cited in Stalin 1954, 1972). It became apparent to him, however, that the work of Marr, who had died in 1934 was mistaken on important points, and the elaboration of it by Soviet linguists therafter, encouraged by Stalin, was in fact deeply fraudulent. At the end of his life, in a letter to Pravda in June 1950 (cited in Kolakowski 1978, p.141), Stalin actually made some common sense criticisms of Marr, and on a symposium on his work that had been reported in Pravda the previous month, but without acknowledging his own role in promoting the errors he now criticised. In fact, Stalin's late interventions served to highlight that Marr's pre-eminence in Russian linguistics could only have been sustained by indefensible manipulation by the Soviet government and party. It hardly helped that at that time also the anti-Semitism of Stalin's last years was becoming apparent.

Kenrick was to remain a socialist, but found it hard thereafter to join a party. The Labour Party seemed to him to reproduce the bureaucracy of the Communist Party, but with rather less substance, while the Communist Party's programme of the 1950s, 'The British Road to Socialism' seemed a pointless toning down of communist idealism. The scholastic fanaticism of the various Trotskyist groups was equally unattractive. Eventually, during the revival of the Left in the 1970s he joined the group Big Flame, the British equivalent of the Italian autonomists Lotta Continua, with which he remained active as long as it was. He has also joined the Jewish Socialist Group. The moral basis of his life remained the often-quoted words of the Russian writer Nikolai Ostrovsky (1934) that one "should so live that, in dying one can say 'All my life and all my strength were devoted to one cause – the liberation of humanity.'" This statement was so often quoted in the Young Communists that by the late 1940s it was often attributed in error to Lenin, and may be seen, unattributed, on the tombstones of defiant old socialists who died in the cold war era. For Donald, this liberatory socialism was a faith by which to live and die. As scholarship asserted its own values, parallel to those of politics, he came across another epigram in his Sanskrit reading. This was in the Hitopadeša, a reworking by the sage, Narayana, of the lost Sanskrit classic, the *Panchatantra*, which presents moral fables, like those of Aesop, within the framework of lessons given by an elderly teacher to young princes. The teacher advises one of the princes: "A man should act as though this is his last day on earth, but study as though he is going to live for ever." (Kale 1967, Narayana 1998).

Kenrick's disillusion in 1951 was not merely with communist linguistics but with the project of a science of language in general. Henceforth his interest was to be in the practical use of languages to their speakers, rather than in languages as empirical examples of some higher truth. By the time he had left school he was already able to speak around ten languages, including German, Italian, Esperanto and Russian having been encouraged by an enthusiastic teacher named Hardcastle. By the time he left university this had risen to about twenty. In the summer of 1952 he graduated with First Class Honours and faced the problem of what to do next.

His commitment to Arabic jostled with a long-standing interest in Celtic languages, which had arisen from his interest in Scottish and Irish country dancing. His awareness of the factors making for their long-term decline, as outlined by Grant in this volume, however, were overborne by his conviction, that whether or not academic and voluntary action should succeed in reversing the decline, it was right to make the attempt. He applied for several positions, including one as an English Assistant at the Lycée Charles Gouroud in Morocco and a scholarship in a Scottish University to study and teach Celtic languages including Welsh, Irish, Gaelic and Cornish. Both were very slow to answer and when he was offered the Moroccan position he accepted it. Immediately afterwards he received an offer from Scotland, which specified, however, that he should teach Manx, a language he had not yet learnt. Unfazed by this, he was profoundly attracted by this offer, which would have set him on the path to a high-flying academic career to match the brilliance of his degree, without committing him to conventional linguistics. His conscience would not, however, let him break his commitment to the Lycée Charles Gouroud. He therefore asked the Scottish university if it would defer his scholarship for a year, by which time he would certainly have mastered Manx, and, he promised, Berber as well. They refused, and he went to Morocco. In time he came to be glad of this decision, partly because he came to believe that he could serve the cause of the liberation of humanity more effectively within schools and adult education than inside the universities, and partly because keeping commitments came to seem to him the foundation of personal integrity.

In Morocco he was teaching mainly Arab and Berber pupils, officially through the medium of French. French colonial rule was then in its final throes, and while Kenrick was a supporter of decolonisation, the feudal autocracy that was to replace the French was a somewhat ambiguous liberation. Like some of his pupils he hoped that a Berber republic might be carved out of the south of the kingdom but was distrustful of the covert British support for this. His classes were frequently disrupted by riots which prevented his pupils attending school. At the end of the school year the French finally withdrew from Morocco, the school was closing, and Kenrick returned to London in the summer of 1953 unsure as ever of politics and where he wanted to work but with a new-found commitment to teaching as a profession.

Back in London he applied to the University of London Institute of Education to take a Postgraduate Certificate of Education, but the course was already full and so he had to defer for a year. Again he found himself at the University Appointments Bureau, looking for work. One interview they arranged for him was for "government work" with an un-named branch of the security services. As much from curiosity as anything he met the interviewer at a gentlemen's club in London and found himself discussing the possibility of overseas intelligence work. Whether, however, he used the wrong fork at lunch, or displayed the wrong attitudes, he never heard from them again. Instead he went off to teach in Switzerland for a year, at the Rosehill (formerly Rosenberg) Institute, an international private secondary school in St Gall. He returned to take his Postgraduate Certificate of Education in the autumn of 1954.

After succeeding, he taught for two years in a London school. Before he started, however, he spent the summer of 1955 teaching at a Danish school in London after which he met his future wife, Bente. In the spring of 1956 Bente decided to become Jewish before the birth of their only child, Timna. Donald himself taught Bente the Hebrew prayers necessary for her formal conversion. Together they were to embark on a mutual exploration of their cultural identities.

They began to circulate to friends a monthly listing of Scandinavian – related events in London. This developed into a small magazine *Odin – The London Scandinavian Monthly* which they edited. Donald's articles in *Odin* were to be the basis of his MA dissertation on *The Portrayal of the Jew in Scandinavian Fiction and Drama (1700–1940)* which he finally passed at University College, London in 1965.

This took a long time partly because his supervisors insisted he demonstrate degree level competence in Norwegian, Danish and Swedish, in order to qualify for an MA in Scandinavian studies. Partly, however, it was because new interests had continued to flood into his life.

In 1957 Donald moved to Pitman's College to take up the post of Head of Languages and Supervisor of Studies. In this private sector post he began to use what was then the newest technology for language teaching, and import the novel idea of the language laboratory from France. He joined the Audio-Visual Language Association (AVLA) a ginger group which had been set up in opposition to the more conservative Modern Languages Association, and organised a conference. The young language teachers made a crusade of insisting that language instruction should be linked to the broadest appreciation of culture supported by the best available modern technology, rather than stuck forever in ossified rituals derived from the pseudo-scientific and inaccurate grammatical approximations originally derived from the teaching of Latin to medieval Europeans. This brought him into contact with the Language Department at Ealing College, then seen by many as at the cutting edge in language instruction. In 1961 he left Pitman's to join the staff at Ealing.

While he was still at Pitman's, however, he had been able to lead numerous student parties abroad on foreign trips which, in turn, enabled him to indulge his passion for folk dance. He had grown up with Jewish dance, and took to Scottish dancing during his army service. When he returned to become a student he had visited Cecil Sharp House, where the young princesses Elizabeth and Margaret Rose were aficionados of American square dancing, and joined the Society for International Folkdance. He demonstrated at dance weekends for the International Branch of the Youth Hostels Association, bringing some dances to England from European countries for the first time.

To help with his Irish dancing he had learnt Irish, which was then the language used during *ceilidhs*. This led to him being co-opted for a time as treasurer of the Committee for Irish Education in London, after Brendan Mulcare was impressed by Donald's proficiency in taking the money at the door of their first benefit dance, even from the musicians' friends and relations. This work eventually led to the start of Irish Studies at the Polytechnic (now University) of North London.

Most important of the new cultures he encountered through folk dance was that of Bulgaria. Eventually Donald became so enamoured of the work of promoting English-Bulgarian cultural exchange, that in 1963 he decided to take a job teaching in a school in Bulgaria. At first Bente had accompanied him on some of his overseas trips, especially before the birth of their daughter in 1958. Bente began work for a prestigious architectural practice and the relentless pace of their lives placed the marriage under increasing stress. Donald's decamping to Bulgaria came to seem a relief. Originally it had been planned that Bente would follow Donald to Bulgaria but, in spite of a family holiday in Dubrovnik, the marriage was effectively over. Bente took a flat at 61,

Blenheim Crescent and although Donald was to return to London to stay at, and eventually take over that flat, and make it the intellectual centre of Romani Studies in Britain for the last thirty years, Bente was to seek and find the security she needed elsewhere.

In Bulgaria Donald found, however, that some of those with whom he had hoped to collaborate had taken on other commitments. To some extent he had stranded himself in Bulgaria, unable to accomplish what he had hoped, at a period of emotional vulnerability. He found, however, a renewed faith in socialism in Bulgaria, not in the ruling institutions of the communist party, but in the basic willingness of people in a poor society to help and support one another in the struggles of daily life. He once remarked that the self-criticism sessions of the teachers' group in the school where he worked were among the most personally helpful experiences of his life. This may seem bizarre to some in the individualistic West, who see the intrusion into personal lives of communist society only as an affront, the basis of the distrust between individuals which poisoned civil society in central European societies.

Yet, while the end of communism has brought advantages to East Germany, Poland, Hungary, the Czech and Baltic Republics, where the communist party was essentially the instrument of Stalinist imperialism, few sensible people would now argue that the ending of communism has improved life for the majority of citizens of the former Soviet Union, the former Yugoslavia or Bulgaria. In those countries, for all their faults, and despite their failure to modify more than slightly the lack of religious and intellectual freedom of preceding regimes, the communist parties, the result of indigenous revolutionary movements, were the way in which ordinary people worked together to improve their lot. What Kenrick found in Bulgaria was a society where, despite poverty and shortage, altruism and unselfish service were not regarded as a daft personal eccentricity, and where personal honesty and safety could be taken almost for granted. The personal networks of loyalties between individuals who trusted each other – the institution of *vraski* – was able to circumvent the inflexibilities of the bureaucracy and keep the system running.

That is not to say that the structures of government did not contain the normal share of insecure manipulators, paranoid authoritarians and greedy chancers. But the ending of the communist system hardly marked the defeat of those individuals: rather, it set them free from all restraint to commandeer the emergent capitalism and seize the wealth of the country for themselves, resorting to extreme nationalism, anti-Semitism and anti-Gypsyism to camouflage and legitimate their activities, whipping the middle classes into line through the fear of a crime wave of which, in private, they are often the chief sponsors.

Kenrick's reaffirmation of socialism did not therefore mark any re-adoption of the role of *apparatchik*; indeed he frequently circumvented the laws of East European countries by bringing in books to individuals, staying with dissenters secretly in their homes. He worked, and still works happily with many East European intellectuals whose opposition to and sometimes suffering at the hand of communist authoritarianism blinded them to the inequalities and unfreedoms of the capitalist West. Sometimes such a commitment to moral activism has been caricatured (in Kenrick's case, notably by Lady Plowden) as mere do-goodery. Kenrick has always responded that the alternative, of leaving the do-badders to get on with it, was not an option for him.

Socialist Bulgaria, therefore, provided a retreat for Kenrick and friends who helped him for the time being to discipline his energies and priorities. He also found there the interest that was to be the most significant of his life: the Romani people. While attending an International Esperanto Conference he went with friends to a café near Sliven where some musicians were singing in what was obviously not a Slav language. Kenrick's Bulgarian friends told him the language was probably Turkish but when he was introduced to the musicians, they told him they were singing in Romani.

Ajvaz, Donald Kenrick's first teacher of Romani, playing for Donald and his daughter Timna in a restaurant in Brussels.

Fascinated, he took lessons from one of the musicians and also met Demeter Golemanov, a young Romani headteacher who spoke a similar dialect. Golemanov was also a balalaika virtuoso who had studied to become a teacher of Russian in Moscow and had made records of Romani song there – a fact that perhaps helped to protect him against the repression of the Romani language which had begun in Bulgaria ever since the Gypsy newspaper *Nov Put* had been forbidden to use it at the beginning of the 1960s. Golemanov's father had been a hero of the Communist resistance to fascism before and during the Second World War, and Demeter's own openness, integrity and unfeigned socialist idealism put his support for the regime beyond serious question even when he started entertaining foreign visitors (even Romani evangelists from France, although he had to answer some police questions after that). Like Kenrick he spent hours organising groups for folk music; his idealism was in fact a mirror of Kenrick's own. In the summer of 1970 Golemanov received unprecedented permission to spend the whole summer school holiday as Donald's guest in England.

Something of the flavour of being Donald's summer guest at that time is conveyed by Lundgren's paper in this book – a whirlwind of visits to encampments, caravan schools and Romani leaders. I myself hosted Golemanov's stay at the illegal encampment in Ripple Road, Barking, and drove him up to Birmingham with the local Gypsy leader, Harry Smith, and Gypsy Council secretary, Grattan Puxon, to back up the legendary Johnny Connors in successful resistance to an eviction. I still have the tape-recording of dust and stones falling off the mechanical digger which the bailiffs drove at us to try to scare us away from standing in front of the caravans. In the caravan where we stayed the night before Golemanov wrote and played a song for us by candlelight (Golemanov 1971) – and found that this made him welcome anywhere. In fact, in Oxford, English Gypsies took up a collection for him. Driving him around was my first opportunity to use the inflected Romani that I had been learning from the correspondence course run by Donald Kenrick and Ronald Lee (and we talked and talked). Although Golemanov was denied permission to attend the World Romani Congress in 1971, he was allowed to go to the second Congress in Geneva in 1979 and remained an enthusiastic supporter until his health began to fail at the end of the 1980s. Sadly, many of the new generation of Romani activists of the 1990s saw him as too much of an old communist and at his death he was on the margin of events. Twenty-five years before, however, full of energy, talent and hope he was to go back to Bulgaria to tell how he had "lived the Romani revolution" in England.

It is important to understanding Kenrick's subsequent trajectory that one of his first colleagues in Romani Studies was himself a Rom, equal to Donald in education, intellect and passion. Kenrick was never tempted to consider Roma as mere objects of research. There was, however, a traditional establishment in Romani Studies in the form of the Gypsy Lore Society based in Liverpool. This had been founded by Victorian linguists and folklorists in 1888. They had sponsored the work of a young autodidact linguist, John Sampson, who wrote one of the most important dictionaries of Romani (Sampson 1926). Although lacking a university education himself, Sampson was "found" a position as librarian of the new University College at Liverpool, and bolstered by honorary degrees, including, ultimately, one from Oxford, and became the centre of a group of non-Gypsy disciples, one of whom, Dora Yates, took over as secretary, and editor of the Journal of the Gypsy Lore Society (Sampson 1997: 176, Wade 1973). In 1965 she was still in this position in her eighty-fifth year with another eight years to go before she would die in harness. She urged Kenrick to publish in the Journal any Romani songs he recorded and introduced him to the equally elderly Bernard Gilliatt-Smith (1883–1973) who, after learning Romani from Lalere Sinte in Germany in 1902, had published widely on Bulgarian and other Romani dialects during his time as a British diplomat in Eastern Europe (Murray, 1973). He sent tables of verbs to Kenrick and introduced him to the Bulgarian scholar, Kiril Kostov, who lent him his unpublished doctoral thesis on the Romani dialect of Sofia (Kostov, 1963). In 1965 Kenrick had to return to London to present his MA thesis finally, if only because without doing so, he could not embark on the PhD thesis he now planned, a Chomskian generative grammar of the Drindari Romani dialect of Kotel. He eventually completed this in 1969 at the University of London's School of Oriental and African Studies.

Back in London, a chance meeting in a bookshop put Kenrick also in the way of

Thomas Acton teaching children on a disused airfield in Hornchurch in 1967.
The two girls are the daughters of John Brazil who coined the title "Gypsy Council".

Thirty years on, Thomas Acton, Professor of Romani Studies at the University of Greenwich

Gypsies in England. He happened to be in Probsthain's antiquarian bookshop, near the British Museum, enquiring whether there were any Romani texts, when Arthur Probsthain introduced him to the Austrian folk singer, John Brune, who happened to be looking for books on Gypsies in the shop at the same time. John Brune was one of the small group of sympathisers in England who were working with Fred Wood, Jasper Smith, John Brazil, Soli Brown, Brian Richardson, Tom O'Doherty and others to help Grattan Puxon set up a Gypsy Council in England, as Puxon describes in this volume. Brune took Kenrick off to North Wales to meet descendants of Sampson's informants, and also introduced him to Puxon, who immediately corralled him into active community work with English Gypsies in London, supporting the group resisting eviction in Canning Town. There he began to take notes on the mixed English-Romani dialect of the Romanichals. As Bakker observes in this volume, Donald Kenrick and Ian Hancock were the first linguists to treat this dialect as a language in its own right. He was also able to act as an interpreter for foreign Roma visiting England – notably at the formal foundation of the Gypsy Council in December 1966 – and then to act as a courier for the Comité International Tzigane on visits to Eastern Europe.

I met Kenrick for the first time a year later just before Christmas 1967 when the Gypsy Council held a rally in Bethnal Green. I had been running the Gypsy Council's first school project on a disused RAF airfield at Hornchurch in Essex, and Puxon asked Kenrick to take a coach down to bring myself, the local leader John Brazil, and as many of the families as possible. To Kenrick's surprise, we filled the coach. A couple of hundred English Gypsies and Irish Travellers were addressed and entertained among others by Grattan Puxon, Vanko Rouda, the President of the Comité International Tsigane, the Welsh Romani broadcaster, Derek Tipler, Charles Reinhardt (cousin of the jazz musician Django Reinhardt), the evangelist Oscar Lycke, and Richard Hauser, the psychologist brother-in-law of Yehudi Menuhin (Acton, 1974:171). In the bar afterwards John Brazil demonstrated stepdancing and introduced me to 'old' Tom Wilson, father of the Romani evangelical leader of the same name, who was to collaborate with Kenrick on a modern dictionary of English Romani. (Kenrick and Acton, 1984d). With him was Koka Petalo, the Dutch Lovari Rom leader. On the coach back to Hornchurch we sang the whole way.

By this time Kenrick had re-established himself in London. After a period as a supply teacher, he had gained a position as lecturer with Gravesend Adult Education College. He found that adult education gave him a great deal of freedom in the long run. He could teach anything of his own inclination – such as 'The novels of Ngugi wa Thiongo' or 'Alma Mahler and her Three Husbands' or 'Kentish Dialect Poetry' – for which he could recruit a class, a task which grew easier as his reputation spread. At the same time, he could set up classes to meet any local needs he could spot and he could often find casual lecturing work for out-of-work friends in popular subjects like French and sociology. He started English as a second language and other classes for the Punjabi community in Gravesend. He also began long-term adult literacy work on the nearby Bean Gypsy caravan site (c.f. Kenrick 1974b). After eight years at Gravesend (by now renamed Thameside Adult Education Centre) and reaching the post of Vice-Principal, he was offered the post of Principal but declined, because of his wish to continue teaching. His managers, however, did not want to lose him and appointed him Adult Literacy Co-ordinator for the whole of the county of Kent for a year, and followed this by recommending him for a further year to the national government sponsored Adult Literacy Basic Studies Unit (ALBSU). Eventually he resolved the conflict between the demands of management and the desire to teach by accepting a position at Hackney Adult Education College which was nearer his home in Notting Hill. This job allowed for at least two half-days a week to be spent on educational activities with local Travellers, as well as the other range of teaching. There he was to remain until his retirement in 1991 – and in fact even later, as he continued, a most reluctant pensioner, to do part-time sessional teaching as long as the regulations permitted.

The legacy of Kenrick's work in adult education and adult literacy does not show up clearly in the bibliography of his work. He would tell friends working in universities: "You're judged by the number of books and papers you write; in adult education we're judged by the number of conferences and courses we run or go to." More than many areas of expertise, the cutting edge of pedagogical practice is mediated in practice itself; it resists its formalisation in the text. Pedagogical literature is largely written with student teachers in mind, and with a few exceptions is a summary simplification of current practice, rather than a stimulus to its change. Of course, university teachers of subjects other than pedagogy and nursing even resist training altogether, and are shame-faced about the way they pick up lecturing techniques from colleagues, as though it were a kind of admission of weakness. It is perhaps, therefore, not too surprising, that the textual residue of Kenrick's educational career is lost in the minutes and collective reports of a dozen committees and a hundred conferences rather than in any clear statement of policy – which would be out of date almost as soon as it was written (which is what teachers always say about any books on teaching). But also, right from the start of Kenrick's career in adult education he was drawn into other research and writing which were to make his most international and lasting impact.

After the foundation of the Gypsy Council in 1966, Kenrick began to help Grattan Puxon and Leulea Rouda (the brother of Vanko) assemble evidence for individual reparations claims for Roma who had survived the Nazi concentration camps. Early in 1967 he spotted an advertisement in the *New Statesman* from the Wiener Library offering grant-aid for research on modern history. He made a successful joint application with Puxon. Between them they not only covered all the material in the Wiener Library but made research visits to Hungary, where Kenrick met the linguist Gyorgy Meszaros and others, and in Czechoslovakia he met the social anthropologist Milena Hubschmannova, as she details in her paper in this volume. Such scholars, of course, each had their own cultural and linguistic agenda, to which Kenrick contributed unstintingly. In addition he was taking a great deal of time to meet the emergent political leaders, as Puxon shows.

By the beginning of 1970 Kenrick and Puxon had compiled a preliminary report which was to be the basis of the work of the War Crimes Commission of the World Romani Congress and also came to the attention of Norman Cohn at the University of Sussex's new Columbus Centre which was publishing a series of studies in the dynamics of persecution and extermination. The report was revised into a book, published in 1972, entitled *The Destiny of Europe's Gypsies.* Translated into French, German, Italian, Japanese and Romani (twice) in its first edition, and also Spanish, Portuguese and Bulgarian in its second, this book still forms the starting point for the scholarly study of the *porraimos*, the Romani Holocaust, which is meticulously detailed in the book. This is not to say there had been no previous work, and even writing by Romani survivors; but all of these were in obscure journals or languishing unpublished in archives, totalling no more than 150 pages in all, marginal curiosities like the Gypsies themselves. Until *Destiny* there was no overall scholarly study which showed that both the fate of the Roma in Europe, and the Holocaust itself can be only understood by confronting this episode of European history. Much work has since been carried out. The papers by Tebbutt and by Heuss in this volume show how we must consider the impact both on society and on individuals, and are notable for the width of scholarly literature upon which they can draw. The fact that such a field of study exists, as a distinct area of study, rather as a series of footnotes upon other problematics is largely due to the pioneering work of Kenrick and Puxon, and Kenrick's continuing engagement with an ever-widening debate. The standard history of the Romani people (Fraser, 1995) both acknowledges this contribution, and follows it in making the explanation of this genocide a focal point for understanding the overall development of Romani history.

While they were writing this book, however, Puxon and Kenrick were between them also carrying the main organisational burden of the Gypsy Council. In 1968 the Caravan Sites Act was passed, and although Part II of it, relating to the duty of local authorities to provide caravan sites for Travelling Gypsies was not implemented until 1970, the pace of resistance to eviction hotted up considerably, and with it the campaign to provide voluntary education for Gypsy children not allowed into schools. Kenrick gradually became Puxon's secretarial mainstay especially after 1969, when the latter stayed with Kenrick for a while after the end of his partnership with Venice Manley. Those of us fighting evictions in the provinces were constantly ringing for advice and the stress began to tell on his health. In 1968 he developed a stomach ulcer and began to take Roter tablets which have since been restricted because of their hallucinatory side effects. To be researching the endless tales of horror of the war time genocide of Roma, while at the same time dealing on a daily base with the mean-spirited racism of English persecution of Gypsies, as well as coping with a full-time job would be enough to unsettle any mind, and it is hardly surprising, that sooner or later both men needed help. For Puxon this came in the form of an engagement with the Primal Therapy movement while living in California in the 1980s. For Kenrick the crisis came

Donald Kenrick at a Gypsy Council demonstration in Whitehall.

Three Irish Traveller children from a 1972 summer school stand by the steps of Donald Kenrick's house.

earlier, when he was hospitalised for a week early in 1970, coming out just before the foundation meeting of the National Gypsy Education Council at the Whitfield Memorial Church in Tottenham Court Road.

Being forced to stop and take stock was probably necessary. To the untutored eye he was as hyperactive at the NGEC foundation meeting as he had been a few weeks earlier at the Gypsy Council celebration at a roadside camp in Dunstable of the implementation day for the Caravan Sites Act Part II. But he had been made aware of the need to consider himself, to take three meals a day, eight hours sleep, a night and regular exercise; to make more careful plans and order his priorities, to care for friends even though they had no connection with his work. He realised at last he had to live in the light of his own mortality. Puxon moved out to a new Gypsy Council headquarters at Blake Hall Crescent in Wanstead. Among other considerations, Kenrick was expecting a visit from his daughter, Timna, who after her parents' divorce had gone to live with her Mother in America. Eventually, she chose to spend most her time with her father and go to Holland Park Comprehensive school, spending only summers in America. It is from 1970 on we find Kenrick's mature work and the bulk of his publications.

He was to need all his new-found strength and stability during 1971 first during the World Romani Congress (described by Puxon in this volume) and a few weeks after the Congress when Puxon moved to the former Yugoslavia, and Kenrick took over as secretary of the Gypsy Council. He worked with two local Gypsy leaders, Tom Lee from Newham and Roy Wells from Wandsworth, who moved the Gypsy Council office to

385, The Strand, in central London. There was also a part-time secretary, Linda Shampan, who had volunteered through the counter-cultural Uncareers Service.

His relations with Shampan became gradually closer and in 1973 they began living together. Shampan became something between a stepmother, and an elder sister to Timna during her adolescence, and a supporter of Donald's causes. With him she joined the socialist group Big Flame, and participated in the West London community newspaper *Bush News*. Together, both left-wing, non-Zionist Jews, they supported the Palestinian cause, while able to oppose anti-semitism and assert that they too had a share in the contemporary Jewish identity and cultural heritage. She played a role in educational and community work with the then small East European Kalderash Rom community in West London, and then made a journey to India, where she made contact with Indian Gypsy (Ghor or Banjara) organisations and leaders, including Ranjit Naik, Ram Bhanawat Singh and Shyamala Devi, which led to their sending a delegation to the second World Romani Congress in 1979.

Sadly, however, they were to grow apart as Shampan followed her own vocation through social work and nursing training. But even though Kenrick never had a shortage of male or female friends, Shampan's advice and support has remained a crucial fund of common sense for him in community politics and also for Timna, who followed her example in training as a social worker, and worked at Chiswick Women's Refuge. Kenrick has remained a family man, with an ever-present commitment to his four grandchildren and their parents.

During 1972 the political divisions within the Gypsy Council and the National Gypsy Education Council grew and between 1972 and 1974 three major factions were to emerge, each with educational and political wings. Kenrick was unable to bridge the gaps.

The tensions first appeared in 1972 as arguments over money were exploited by Lady Plowden. She encouraged Tom Lee to break away from the Gypsy Council to create a more 'moderate' group, the Romani Guild, which did not believe in the international links and Romani nationalism of the Gypsy Council. The following year, in April 1973, Tom Lee and Lady Plowden quit the National Gypsy Education Council, carrying 11 of its 20 committee members with them and set up the Advisory Council for the Education of Romanies

When Grattan Puxon returned to London in 1972 after having been expelled from Yugoslavia, he took up residence in the attic flat above Kenrick's at 61 Blenheim Crescent with his new wife, Sanije Ibrahim. In 1973 Grattan Puxon became secretary of what was left of the National Gypsy Education Council, Hughie Smith became Chair and I became treasurer. During 1973 Grattan Puxon tried, in vain, to rally the movement around opposition to "designation" (the provision of the 1968 Caravan Sites Act which gave councils the right to move on "surplus" Gypsies once they had provided sites at a minimum level). At the end of 1973 Kenrick resigned from the secretaryship of the Gypsy Council hoping that a new secretary, Elizabeth Easton, herself a Gypsy would keep together what was left of the Gypsy Council and National Gypsy Education Council after Lady Plowden and Tom Lee had denounced them.

It did not work. The full details of these splits are too complicated to explain here and indeed are difficult to write about because the issues are often still raw from the perspective of those involved. Differences between the London leadership of Roy Wells and Eddie Gentle and the northern leadership of Hughie Smith and Tom O'Doherty led to the latter taking over the Gypsy Council on a narrow, fairly conservative platform. Hughie Smith then resigned the chair of the National Gypsy Education Council, in 1974 and Kenrick was elected in his place. I took over the role of secretary - and indeed the attic flat at 61 Blenheim Crescent, when Grattan and Sanije were able to return to Yugoslavia later the same year.

The overall effect was that by 1974 the group which had coalesced around Roy Wells' Southern Gypsy Council and the rump National Gypsy Education Council was the smallest of the three factions in English Romani politics. It was democratic and Romani internationationalist in outlook and led by Roy Wells, supported by Donald Kenrick, Eddie Gentle, and myself. It was sandwiched between two highly competitive rivals. On one hand there was the educationalist authoritarianism of Lady Plowden and her new Advisory Council for the Education of Romanies supported by Tom Lee's Romani Guild. On the other side was the inward-looking Gypsy-ist authoritarianism of Hughie Smith.

We were unabashed. We were convinced that we stood for principles of Romani self-determination, open debate and organisation, accountability of elected officers and democracy. Puxon's paper, describing the years up to the first World Romani Congress tells of a time when we were young and giants walked the land and we were convinced that the injustices of the ages were about to be put right.

Indeed at the beginning of the 1970s, we thought we had made our case, won the argument, and that the battle was all over bar the shouting. We had much to learn then about the tenacity and structural rootedness of racism but the vision of transcending it was not something that anyone could abandon in the face of setbacks. The open and democratic structure of the National Gypsy Education Council made it a welcoming refuge to those who became bruised in the factional struggles which continued in the other organisations. By 1977 both Tom Lee and Tom O'Doherty had rejoined it, and it had become the largest, rather than the smallest of the factions, and its leaders included a number of Romanichals, like Peter Mercer, Nathan Lee, Eli Frankham and later the young Charlie Smith who had not been involved in the squabbles of 1972–3. In 1979 Kenrick was able to act as translator for a delegation to the second World Romani Congress which drew members from several Romani organisations but which was essentially organised by the National Gypsy Education Council; and the same occurred at the third and fourth Congresses of 1981 and 1990. The National Gypsy Education Council eventually re-named itself the Gypsy Council for Education, Culture, Welfare and Civil Rights (GCECWCR) and elected Kenrick an honorary life vice-president.

Second World Romani Congress, Geneva 1978.

As more Gypsies took over the organisational work, Kenrick was able to give more time to work with the Romani language. At a conference in Oxford in 1971, timed to happen just before the first World Romani Congress (Acton, 1971) he held a debate with Ian Hancock on the history and role of the English Romani dialect, the seminal role of which is discussed by Bakker in this volume. Working with Tom Wilson, he prepared the first modern dictionary of the dialect and co-edited an overall study of it (Kenrick and Acton, 1984). At the same time he was also collaborating on the development of the international dialect, acting as the first secretary of the World Romani Congress Language Commission and helping to prepare the alphabet finally adopted at the second Congress in 1979. Over many years, working with the *Atlas Linguarum Europae*, he has, literally, put Romani on the map of Europe. Hancock's paper in this volume demonstrates how crucial our understanding of the development of Romani is to our understanding of Romani identity itself.

In 1990 at the fourth Congress, Kenrick was to be the only linguist present who refused to sign up to the adoption of the new alphabet, not so much because he objected in principle to its morpho-phonemism, but because he was unhappy that a relatively small number of linguists had taken a decision in the name of a whole people without adequate discussion of the details of the proposal. Nonetheless, after being added to the official list of candidates by nomination from the floor, he continued to be

Peter Mercer, Chairman of National Gypsy Education Council, with Hungarian Romani cultural worker, Dr. Agnes Daroczi, at the Third World Romani Congress, 1981.
Photograph by David Altheer

elected to the Language Commission and to the Encyclopaedia Commission, one of a very few non-Roma to continue to hold any office in the International Romani Union.

During the last thirty years Kenrick has made himself available, selflessly and unstintingly, to help those producing literature in the Romani language. Although a declared atheist, religious translators of all kinds have found him a sympathetic but rigorous editor of their work, concerned not only with details, but with the kind of spirit of communication that Ellingworth grapples with in this volume. For many years until retirement (when Anthony Grant took over the work) he acted as a formal consultant on Romani to the United Bible Societies. He has befriended each of the first three Roma to undertake translation of the entire bible, editing the work of Mateo Maximoff, encouraging that of Sulyo Metkov, and still debating that of Valdemar Kalinin, whose poem and paper in this volume perhaps show how it is that this sometimes irascible man, who never resiles from his own opinions, yet can win not merely the respect, but also the affection of religious fellow-workers who disagree with those opinions.

Passing the task of organisation to others has also not lessened Kenrick's commitment to case work with individuals. In 1982 for the first time he helped a Romani family who could not afford professional advice to make an appeal against the refusal of planning permission to live in caravans on land they owned. Other families in the same position also sought his help, and somewhat to his, and their surprise, he won some of their appeals. As his expertise in the field grew, he began to be regarded as a planning consultant on a par with qualified town planners and lawyers working in the field, winning their respect and exchanging case notes with them. Diana Allen's paper in this volume shows the importance of this area of work. The struggle for the right to stop on their own land has also radicalised many individual Gypsy activists, from Yui Burton and Rabbie Boswell in the 1970s down to Sylvia Dunn and Hester Hedges in the 1990s. The valiant Sylvia Dunn began by working with Donald Kenrick at the start of an epic battle to gain her own planning permission, and went on to found the National Association of Gypsy Women. Allen, Hedges and Dunn, like Kenrick, are key supporters of the Traveller Law Reform Campaign currently seeking fresh legislation to help Travellers in Britain (c.f. Kenrick, 1999e).

Donald Kenrick is 70 now. Still cycling, still a dancer (and promoter of folk bands), still an Esperantist, still translating, writing on languages, on history, still standing up before planning inspectors and judges, still living in two rooms at 61 Blenheim Crescent, ascetically disciplining his possessions to the space, throwing out old books as he acquires new ones. Still inspiring, still teaching, still the very model of committed scholarship. All of us acknowledge his influence. His own work weaves its way through all of these papers, looming larger in some than others, but all of them are offered to him as responses to the kinds of questions he has been asking throughout his life. We salute him.

References

Acton T. ed. 1971 *Current changes amongst British Gypsies and their place in International Patterns of Development* National Gypsy Education Council, Oxford.
Acton T. 1974 *Gypsy Politics and Social Change* Routledge and Kegan Paul, London.
Childs D. 1979 *Britain Since 1945 – A Political History* Benn, London.
Churchill W. 1946 speech to conference in Fulton, Missouri, in March, cited in Watson, 1989.
Fraser, Sir A. 1995 (2nd ed.) *The Gypsies* Blackwell, Oxford.
Golemanov D. 1971, "Ilo, Ilo" in Acton T., Denaro R. and Hurley B., *The Romano Drom Song Book*, Romanestan Publications, Oxford.
Kale M.R. 1967 (6th ed.) The *Hitopadeša of Narayana, edited with a Sanskrit commentary and notes in English* Motilal Banarsidass, Delhi.
Kolakowski L. 1978 *Main Currents of Marxism, Vol. II: The Breakdown* Clarendon Press, Oxford.

Kostov K. 1963 *Grammatik der Zigeunersprache Bulgariens: Phonetik und Morphologie* Ph.D. Dissertation, Humboldt University, Berlin.

Mahon J. 1976 *Harry Pollitt, A Biography* Lawrence and Wishart, London.

Maximoff M. 1995 *E Nevi Viasta* Société Biblique Française/United Bible Society, Paris.

Metkov S. 1995 *O Neevo Zavyeti* Seventh Day Adventist Church in Bulgaria, Sofia.

Murray, H. 1973 "Bernard Joseph Leo Gilliat-Smith" *Journal of the Gypsy Lore Society*, Series III, pp. 108–116.

Narayana 1998 *Hitopadeša* South Asia Books, New York.

Ostrovsky N. 1934 *How the Steel was Tempered* Foreign Languages Publishing House, Moscow (n.b. translation of the quotation in the text is in part new).

Prynn D.L. 1972 "Common Wealth – A British "Third Party" of the 1940s" *Journal of Contemporary History* Vol.7 (1–2).

Sampson, A. 1997 *The Scholar Gypsy: The Quest for a Family Secret* John Murray, London.

Sampson, J. 1926 *The Dialect of the Gypsies of Wales* Clarendon Press, Oxford.

Wade, R.A.R. 1973 "Dora Esther Yates, Litt.D., M.A." *Journal of the Gypsy Lore Society*, Series III, pp. 99–108.

Watson J. 1989 *World History since 1945* John Murray, London.

A Champion

ELI FRANKENHAM

We have a champ, make no mistake;
He will always punch his weight.
He will fight with determination
To do his best for the Gypsy nation.
He's always there, to right a wrong,
Some battles hard, some battles long.
Not just in Britain, but around the world,
The Gypsy flag he's unfurled.
Discrimination! – He wants to end it:
That man's name is Donald Kenrick.

CHAPTER ONE

THE EMERGENCE OF ROMANI AS A KOÏNÉ OUTSIDE OF INDIA

Ian Hancock

Premise

THE PRESENT hypothesis rests upon the supposition that the ancestors of the Roma were members of the Kśiattriya or military caste, who left India with their camp followers during the first quarter century of the second millennium in response to a series of Islamic invasions led by Mahmud of Ghazni. Linguistic and historical arguments in support of this position are found in Hancock (1999), and are summarised below.

It is maintained that together with Urdu, Romani developed from a contact language (of the type known as a *koïné*, and for which I employ here the term *Rajputic*) over a millennium ago, from a levelling of the medley of languages spoken on the battlefields of north-western India. While the speech of those troops who remained in India subsequently normalised in the direction of the surrounding local Indian languages, those who moved away from the area and became linguistically isolated from it, experienced no such metropolitanising factor, their speech and linguistic behaviour, as well as their social patterns, developing differently as a result. I also demonstrate that rather than being an isolated case, language contact situations are typical in India, and propose that the Domari and the Ghorbati languages, as well as others, emerged from the same type of sociolinguistic framework.

Koïnéization

Nida and Fehderau (1970) were probably the first linguists to establish the *koïné* as a typological category. They saw it as a language of wider communication typified by "modifications in the direction of simplification of morphological and syntactic structure [... but which] presents no such structural break as is clearly present in the case of pidgins" (1970: 147), and which is "always mutually intelligible with at least some forms of the standard language" (1970: 152). The definition most usually relied upon these days, however, is Siegel's (1985: 375-376):

Koineization is the process which leads to mixing of linguistic subsystems, that is, of language varieties which either are mutually intelligible or share the same genetically related superimposed language. It occurs in the context of increased interaction among speakers of these varieties. A koine is the stabilised composite variety that results from this process. Formally, a koine is characterised by a mixture of features from the contributing varieties, and at an early stage of development, is often reduced or simplified in comparison to any of these varieties. Functionally, a koine serves as a lingua franca among speakers of the different varieties. It may also become the primary language of amalgamated communities of these speakers.

Although they are not subject to the drastic restructuring essential in the definition of a pidgin, koïnés do share with the latter the fact of being native to no one; thus every speaker of a koïnéised (or pidginised) variety of a language speaks another language or dialect natively. The particular status of such linguistic systems "that stand between 'normal' primary languages... and pidgin and creole languages" has been addressed in a theoretical framework by Whinnom (1981), and is becoming a specialised area of typological study (e.g. Jahr, 1992; Siegel, 1985 and 1993, Bakker and Mous, 1994); in Reinecke's (1937:80) earlier ground breaking study of the classification of different kinds of contact language, he deals with Hindustani briefly in his category of 'lingua francas'.

Koïnés may also be characterised by extensive lexical adoption, *i.e.* their mixed-source vocabularies, either drawn from other languages, or reflecting different dialects of the same language, a process known as levelling. Also – because of their non-native status – they are typified by the lack of certain registers, such as formal style or baby talk. In some cases they may in time acquire some measure of official standardisation and status and may be referred to as 'Union' languages; Union Dyula, spoken in West Africa, is one such example. When this happens, a koïné can, in the course of time, lose its identity as an auxiliary dialect, and become a first language, thereby developing all of the characteristics associated with the same: socially- and gender-determined registers, proverbs, a folklore and so on. The best-known koïné, that which emerged from various Ancient Hellenic dialects, became the basis for Modern Standard Greek (Comrie, 1990:412). The word itself is from that language: ἡ κοϊνή διάλεκτοξ "the common dialect."

Because for its speakers a koïné lacks the emotional rootedness of a first language, it is more readily susceptible to linguistic modification and adaptation than other languages, and its speakers are generally more tolerant of variability within it, in pronunciation, and in grammatical and lexical selection. With multiple inputs contributing to its initial emergence, it remains open to ongoing modification as long as it continues to exist as an adjunct linguistic system.

Rajputic was a such a koïné and was, therefore, able to adapt to its changing linguistic environments. Those speakers who returned to, or remained in, India, accommodated accordingly. In Islamic areas, Rajputic continued to be modified by pressure

An Indian dance troupe with delegates at the Third World Romani Congress in Göttingen, 1981. *Photograph by David Altheer*

from Persian and Arabic, eventually giving rise to Urdu, the official language of Pakistan and the state language of Jammu and Kashmir in India. In Hindu areas, the modifying influence was Sanskrit, giving rise to Hindi, the official language of India, by the fourteenth century (Khullar, 1995).

India and language contact

Because of its tremendous linguistic diversity, India has long been recognised as a part of the world where language contact has produced numbers of hybridised and restructured languages – meriting a section of its own in the *Bibliography of Pidgin and Creole Languages* (Reinecke, 1975:632–5). While the specific case of Rajputic was one of koïnéisation rather than pidginisation, Southworth (1971:270–1) at least "assumes that pidginisation took place throughout the Indo-Aryan area, but that its long-range linguistic effects were tempered or reinforced by other social factors [...which] have led, at the extreme end of the spectrum, to a result that is similar to the classic modern cases of pidginization known from the Caribbean and the Pacific." He discusses the Marathi language in particular, which is also dealt with in the same framework by Gumperz and Wilson in the same volume.

In wording hardly acceptable today, Petersen (1912:421–32) was the first to discuss this as a phenomenon dating from the very beginnings of Aryan-non-Aryan contact:

> As the old Aryans invaded the Indian peninsula and conquered certain aboriginal tribes, they would impose their language upon those whom they enslaved and which consequently formed a part of their society. But since these black aborigines had organs of speech as well as linguistic habits that differed widely from those of the Aryan invaders, they were unable to learn the language in the same form as the one in which it was spoken by their conquerors, and it was modified to suit their own characteristics in much the same way as the American negro has modified the English language through his own physiological and mental peculiarities. And just as many peculiarities of the negro dialect are common to the whole large area of the South or his original American home, since the peculiarities which cause these aberrations are common to the whole race, just so a number of phonetic changes in Prakrit were common to all of the widely scattered areas where these popular dialects were spoken, since here also common racial peculiarities would cause common effects... and it is therefore not surprising that Prakrit and Vedic should have been virtually coexistent not only from the beginning of the transmission, but ever since the Aryans first invaded India and began enslaving the aborigines.

The first to bring attention to this specifically in the context of contact phenomena was James Clough well over a century ago, in his book *On the Existence of Mixed Languages*. In it, he explains the emergence of Hindustani as a two-stage process: firstly that the Uzbeks (or "Uzbek Tatars", as he called them) from the north of Kabul invaded Persia in the fifth century, adopting the dialect of the Persian court (*Zeban Deri*) as their language of administration – rather than any regional vernacular (*Zeban Parsi*) and then, some centuries later, that they went on to conquer India during the reign of Mahmud of Ghazni (AD 997–1028). Mahmud's administrators in India

> ... experienced some difficulty in communicating with their new subjects. A lingua franca was composed, consisting principally of corrupt Persian and Hindí, and this was known under the name of *Urdú Zebán*, or camp language, to distinguish it from the court language, but the poets called it *Rekhta*, or 'scattered,' on account of the variety of elements composing it (Clough, 1876:15).

It was in fact the Huns, a nomadic Turkic-speaking people (Baskakov, 1969; Maenchen-Heffen, 1973), rather than the Uzbeks who invaded Persia and north-western India in the fifth century, and it was Mahmud himself who invaded India rather than the Huns, as Clough intimates. Kachru's (1990:470–1) more modern (and more accurate) account tells some of the same story, maintaining that Hindi itself originated in this contact situation:

> Hindi as a language is said to have emerged from the patois of the market place and army camps during the period of repeated Islamic invasions and establishment of Muslim rule in the north of India between the eighth and tenth centuries AD. The speech of the area

around Delhi, known as *kharī bholī*, was adopted by the Afghans, Persians and Turks as a common language of interaction with the local population. In time, it developed a variety called *urdū* (from Turkish *ordu*, 'camp'). This variety, naturally, had a preponderance of borrowings from Arabic and Persian. Consequently, it was also known as *rextā* 'mixed language'.

Ketalaer's grammar of Hindustani, dating from the late seventeenth century, describes a clearly koïnéised variety of that language, as does that of Lebedeff published in 1801, and reduced varieties of Hindi continue to be spoken in India and elsewhere today, indicating that this process is an old and ongoing one (c.f. Chatterji 1931, Khubchandani 1963, Zograf 1963, Kelley 1966, Abbas 1969 and Mesthrie, 1993).

Both Clough's and Kachru's accounts make reference to Urdu's being a military lingua franca, although neither elaborates on this. In Turkish, its primary dictionary entry is in fact "army" (Alderson and İz 1959:259). Its use by non-Indians is reflected in its two non-Indian names: Urdu (from Turkish) and Rekhta (from Persian).

The Rājpūts

Among the Hindu soldiers involved throughout the early period of Indian conflict with Islam were the Rājpūts, who were a conglomerate force conscripted from many ethnic and linguistic populations in India, including the Ahirs, the Gujjars, the Lohars, the Lobhanas, the Saudagars, the Siddhis and the Tandas; in this way they were "welded out of different non-Aryan material into a martial society" Watson (1988:88). According to Thakar (1969:227), "Most authorities accept the view that the Rājpūt clans were either descended from the Huns settled in northern and western India or from those tribes and peoples who had entered India together with the Hun invaders." Collectively, all foreigners entering India were called (in Sanskrit) *mlechchha*, or "impure," a status gradually lost by those who became assimilated over time. By the ninth and tenth centuries, during the height of the period of Islamic expansion, the Rājpūts had come to wield considerable political power and had achieved warrior caste status. They were divided into a number of clans, four of which had special status: the Pratiharas, the Chauhans, the Solankis and the Pawars. In being given royal lineage by the Brahmins (their name *Rājpūts* means "sons of princes"), they were also allowed to display emblems signifying their descent from the Sun and the Moon as military insignia.

The Rājpūts were not originally a single ethnic population but a conglomerate, professional one drawn from many distinct peoples. Today, however, numbers of distinct ethnic populations have emerged in India over the past thousand years, who trace their descent to them. Those associated particularly with Roma, both in their own tradition and according to the consensus of many western scholars, are the Ghor, or Banjaras. In addition to those cited here, other sources on the Banjara include Thurston and Rangachari (1909), Rathod (1988) and Isaac (1984).

The Banjara

Banjara tradition maintains that during the Ghaznavid period, some Rājpūts left India through the Himalayan passes never to return. "The Khyber, most famous of the passes, has been an immemorial trade-link with Central Asian and Mediterranean communications. South of the Khyber the main routes from the Iranian Plateau are by the Gomal and the Bolan passes, and finally along the Makran coast" (Watson, 1988:12). Rathore (1997:2) gives the names of several Banjara and other historians who have written about Ghor history, and about the Rathore and Chauhan Rājpūts who left Rājpūtana in response to the Ghaznavid invasions, spreading out to the four points of the compass. Naik (1978:5) writes of the Rājpūts who "about 1,000 years ago, during the invasion of Mohammed Ghori and Mohammed Ghazni into Greater Panjab... fled through the Khyber and Bolan Passes and went to Central Asia and moved further into Europe...[they] came to be known as Gypsies, and another group remained in India in jungles and Chambal Khore, a valley in Rajasthan, and came to be known as Lamans or Banjaras." Western historians too, acknowledge this:

> Some Rājpūt clans, or portions of them, after offering fierce resistance to various Muslim armies – tales of these exploits are also part of widespread folk tradition – drifted north or south into the mountainous regions of Central India or the Himalayas, and some may have gone as far as Nepal. Many of them remained in north India (Minturn and Hitchcock, 1966:11).

The fact that Rājpūt communities in twenty-one out of the thirty-one states throughout India speak varieties of the same language (in two distinct dialect divisions), is indicative of their having dispersed from a single area at an earlier time. Grierson (1907:*ix*:56) says:

> Banjārī falls into two main dialects – that of the Panjab and Gujarat, and that of elsewhere (of which we may take the Labhānī of Berar as the standard). All these different dialects are ultimately to be referred to as the language of western Rājpūtana. The Labhānī of Berar possesses the characteristics of an old form of speech, which has been preserved unchanged for some centuries. It may be said to be based partly on Mārwārī and partly on northern Gujārāti.

Grierson goes on to say that the Banjari language of southern India is mixed with the surrounding Dravidian languages. This is what we would expect, given the social and linguistic history of the population; an almost identical situation exists among the Seminoles, with whom the Banjara may be compared: over the past three centuries they have become a single Native American ethnic people, but in fact they descend from fugitives from the British colonists who represented some twenty or more quite separate language groups, both Indian and African, who were able to find refuge in Spanish Florida. Their very name is from Spanish *cimarrones*, which means "fugitives," and they maintain two mutually unintelligible languages, Muskogee and Mikasuki, amongst themselves in their community today (Hancock, 1980).

Romani

In order to accept the hypothesis that Romani emerged from a military koïné, it must first be established that the ancestors of the Roma were indeed a military force at this time and place in history. In Hancock (1999) I assemble linguistic, historical and cultural evidence to support this position, which I summarise here:

1. The linguistic features of Romani identify it as a new-Indic language rather than an old-Indic language, which dates its time of separation from India at no earlier than ca. AD 1000.
2. The Romani language cannot be traced to any single Prakritic branch of the Indic languages, but has features from several of them, although it is most like those of the Central group. The language closest to Romani is Western Hindi, which itself emerged from Rajputic.
3. Romani includes a substantial Dardic component (particularly from Phālua) and items from Burushaski, a language-isolate spoken in the Pamir and nowhere else. This, and other linguistic evidence, points to an exodus through this particular area – the same area through which the Ghaznavids moved into India.
4. The various Romani terms for non-Romani peoples suggest a military-non-military relationship; thus gadžo is traceable to an original Sanskrit form (gajjha) which means "civilian," das and goro both mean "slave, enemy, captive," and gomi means "one who has surrendered."
5. Romani has a military vocabulary of Indian origin, including the words for "soldier", "sword," "spear," "trident," "battlecry" and "gaiters." Most of its (for example) metalworking or agricultural vocabulary, on the other hand, consists of words not brought from India.
6. Some Roma groups in Europe today maintain the emblems of the Sun and the Moon, as did the Rājpūts, as identifying insignia. Tod (1920:*i*:69) traces this to the Mongols.
7. Cultural practices of some Roma groups in Europe today resemble elements of Shaktism or goddess-worship, as in the Rājpūts' worship of the warrior goddess Parvati, another name for Kali-Durga. Although the figure of St. Sara in Saintes-Maries comes from an older local myth, and "black" Madonnas and other statues of dark-coloured wood are hardly uncommon in Europe, the European pre-eminence of Les Saintes-Maries among such festivals may be taken to indicate a certain cultural affinity (Fraser, 1995:313). Much as the ancient Romans rediscovered Jupiter in the Greek Zeus, so the Indian goddess Kali may be rediscovered in the Romani Sara-Kali in France today. Her statue is immersed in the Mediterranean just as it is in the Ganges once a year in India.

8. Throughout the earliest fifteenth and sixteenth century written records we find that Roma told their largely uncomprehending western interlocutors that they had been defeated after conflict with Islamic forces (Fraser, 1995: 72,83). We should recall that the period after the Muslim invasion of India was also a period in which Byzantines, Crusaders and Armenians sustained a patchwork of anti-Islamic military resistance in Anatolia, with the last Armenian principality being reduced by Ottomans only in 1361. The oral tradition of some Roma groups in Europe includes stories of a conflict with Islam leading to the original migration West.

9. The mixed linguistic nature of Romani is evident from the numbers of synonyms of Indic origin in modern Romani, e.g. the multiple words for 'wash,' 'burn,' 'awaken,' 'back,' 'dog,' 'fight,' 'belt,' 'give,' 'birth,' 'arise,' 'bracelet,' 'cold,' 'comb,' 'day,' 'excreta,' 'fear,' 'food,' 'heel,' 'leave,' 'man,' 'move,' 'non-Rom,' 'open,' 'pay,' 'sing,' 'straw,' 'thin,' 'tomorrow,' 'raw,' 'wet'.

If we hypothesise that Rajputic, the military lingua franca of the army camps a thousand years ago, became reshaped differently as its speakers separated, and moved into different areas, we can account for its Islamisation in Muslim areas, where it became the Persian- (and increasingly Arabic-) influenced Urdu (written in Arabic script), and its Hinduisation in Hindu areas, where it became Sanskritised (and written in Devanagri script). But some Rajputic speakers "remained in jungles and Chambal Khore, a valley in Rajasthan, [and] came to be known as Lamans or Banjaras ... the group which fled to the forests and remained there are the present-day hill-tribes called the Banjaras" (Naik, 1978:5). Under such circumstances, their original Rajputic did not develop into either Hindi or Urdu, but emerged into a distinct but related new language – Ghorbati (also called Ghorboli, Lamani or Banjari). The speech of those Ghor (Banjaras) who subsequently left Rajasthan for other parts of India to the South underwent further change in the direction of the surrounding languages, as Grierson noted.

The movement out of India by those Rājpūts who were the ancestors of the Roma is accounted for in Banjara history; less easily explained is why they did not return to India. Possibly they continued to maintain themselves as a mercenary military force, engaging in conflicts with the Muslims along the Silk Road and the Caspian littoral; the linguistic evidence points to this as their route to the West. Soulis (1961:163) suggests that Seljuk raids in the area at the end of the eleventh century were a factor. Marushiakova and Popov (1997:63) attribute their eventual movement into Europe to the twelfth and thirteenth century Ottoman invasions. Significantly, and as further support of their original profession as (besides soldiers) *shiviranuchara* or camp followers they document those early Roma as "servants in the auxiliary detachments or as craftsmen servicing the army."

Their separation from India caused something of a linguistic and social trauma.

Even within India, the Rājpūts were able to maintain a distinctiveness from the surrounding peoples but lacking even that normalising factor, the ancestors of the Roma were left completely isolated with their language and mixed ethnic identity, becoming increasingly remote from their homeland. As with the Rājpūts before them, the sense of being a composite population on one level, but a distinct and "special" population on another, came in time to characterise a distinctively Romani world view which permitted the Roma to continue to accept new people into their number, providing they took on Roma identity, and a Romani linguistic trait which allowed the language to incorporate and assimilate new grammatical and lexical material. This capacity to absorb and modify, socially as well as linguistically, represents a continuum from the time of the creation of the Rājpūts, and remains an integrally defining aspect of Romani identity.

Domari

In Hancock (1995), I demonstrated that, contrary to the established belief, Romani and Domari have distinct and unrelated histories, separated by over five hundred years. It was possible to show this by examining the Iranic lexical content of both, and concluding that the percentage of shared items was far too low if both languages had been part of the same migration through Persia. If the third member of the conventional trilogy comprising this theory is included – Lomavren, spoken in Armenia – then there is *no* single Iranic item shared by all three branches. It is clearly of an old-Indic type, and differs significantly from Romani in its phonology, grammar and lexicon.

While it can be demonstrated that Domari, spoken in several dialects throughout the Middle East, but particularly in Syria, is not related to Romani (other than that they are both Indian languages – which could equally well be said about Romani and Sinhalese), accounting for its origin presents a different problem.

The movement of the ancestors of the Roma out of India has traditionally been explained by looking to Firdausi's account of the gift of several thousand musicians in the fifth century from the Indian king Shankal to the Sassanid shah of Persia. That such an episode occurred is quite likely, since it has been documented in a number of places (Hancock, 1999). But it does not hold up linguistically, since the musicians were "Sindhian," from the north-western Prakritic area, and Domari shows much closer lexical similarities with languages of the Central group (Nseir, 1998). According to "*The Encyclopedia of Islam*" (Minorsky:V: 818), there is a group which identifies itself as Kurdish east of Bohtān in Persia, "which bears the suggestive name *Sindī* or *Sindiyān* (the *Sindhis*)."

Instead, the presence of the Dom (Domari speakers) as well as of other 'Gypsy' populations in the Middle East such as the Karači, whose linguistic affiliation has still to be determined (Kenrick, 1976 c,d) might well be accounted for using the same theoretical framework as that proposed here for Romani, i.e. composite military troops

Ian Hancock with Donald Kenrick

moving westwards out of India. Like Roma, the Dom also refer to non-Dom as *kājjă* "civilians." To justify this, it must be shown that there was an invasion of India in this area at this time, and that Indian troops left India to engage them.

This proves to be the coming of the Turkic-speaking Huns who, starting from Bactria, eventually occupied other parts of Persia and India, but who were defeated and driven back by the Persians in the sixth century (Thapar, 1966: 142), and who were gradually absorbed into the local population in India by the end of the millennium. While their cultural impact was not extensive, the linguistic consequences of their invasion were far-reaching:

> Prakrit is of linguistic interest as illustrative of the linguistic evolution from Prakrit to Apabhramsha (literally 'falling down'). Apabhramsha, a corrupt form of Prakrit dialect, is believed to have originated in the north-west and travelled from that region with the migrations of people who scattered and settled in central and western India after the Hun invasions (Thapar, 1966:257).

There are accounts of the invasion of the Huns, and references to their being "pushed back" in a "brave defence" by King Skanda Gupta who, "for the duration of his twelve-year reign ... was obliged to ward off their predatory assaults" (Wolpert, 1977: 94):

From the middle of the fifth century a new barbarian invader, the Hun, made his ominous appearance, as his kindred were doing in Europe. For a generation or so the Guptas succeeded in holding off this menace from the northwest. But toward the close of the century it reappeared in the persons of Toramana and Mihirakula, the latter holding Kashmir, western India and part of the Gangetic basin. In fifty years the Huns were pushed back to Kashmir and parts of the northwest, and they never again became a threat, losing their identity among the Rājpūt clans of later fame." (Wright, 1969: 301; see also Thapar, 1966:140).

> The White Huns, or Ephthalites, or as the Indians called them, Hunas, were barbarians in the sense most painful to settled societies... While Attila's Huns streamed across Eastern Europe to attack Italy in the mid-fifth century, a southward wave overwhelmed the Sassanid Empire in Persia and the Kushan remnants of the Indian northwest. Skanda Gupta (455–470) is credited with a brave defence of his western frontiers in face of this irruption, but by about 500 a Hun chieftain was recorded as far south as Ujjain ...The Gupta dynasty is taken to extend, though interrupted in the fifth century by Hun invasions, from 320 to about 450... [the Buddhist university city of] Taxila, beyond the Gupta boundaries, [was] in the fifth century devastated by the Huns (Watson, 1988: 60, 62, 66).

There are also some references to the possibility that the Indians who moved out to confront the Huns at this time were from Kabul rather than Sindh, and that the two events have been confused over time. Harriot (1830:524–5) reported that a Persian historian, Fateh Ali Khān, told him that Firdausi's musicians were from Kabul, not Sindh, and Gobineau's Kauli informants in Persia in the 1850s assured him that their ancestors were from Kabul, not Sindh, and that their name was originally *Kabuli* (1857: 690). At the time of the Hun invasions, Kabul was not just the city it is today, but an entire Hindu kingdom (also called *Kapisha*) which extended from the Kabul River Valley to the Hindu Kush. Siraiki, Multani and some other languages transitional between the central and northwestern groups are now spoken in this area, though we need to reconstruct the linguistic situation as it was there fifteen centuries ago.

Conclusion

The mixed nature of Romani, and the social and linguistic clues evident in an examination of (particularly) its lexicon, make a strong case for its having taken its initial form as a military koïné which left India with its speakers, subsequently developing outside of its homeland. Work begun on an examination of its historical phonology and grammar also supports the fact of its multi-source origins. The identity of its first speakers, and the circumstances of its emergence, established a sociolinguistic 'character' which continues to typify the Romani people and language.

The same type of military historical scenario may also explain the presence of Indian languages and peoples such as the Domari throughout the Middle East.

References

Abbas, Khwaja A., 1969 "A link language for the common man," *Language and society in India*, 1969:29–36.
Alderson, A.D., and Fahir İz, eds., 1959 *The Concise Oxford Turkish Dictionary*, The Clarendon Press, Oxford.
Bakker, Peter, and Maarten Mous, eds., 1994 *Mixed languages: 15 case studies in language intertwining* IFOTT, Amsterdam
Baskakov, N.A., 1969 *Vedenie v izuchenie Tjukskix jazykov*, Vysshaya Skola, Moscow.
Bright, William, ed., 1966 *Sociolinguistics*, Mouton, The Hague
Chatterji, Suniti K., 1931 "Calcutta Hindustani: A study of a jargon dialect," *Indian linguistics*, 1(2–4):177–234.
Clough, James Cresswell, 1876 *On the Existence of Mixed Languages*, Longmans, Green and Co. London.
Comrie, Bernard, ed., 1990 *The World's Major Languages*, The University Press, Oxford.
Fraser, A., 1995 (2nd ed.) *The Gypsies*, Blackwell, Oxford.
Gobineau, Count Joseph de, 1857 "Persische Studien I: Die Wanderstämme persiens," *Zeitschrift der Deutschen Morgenländischen Gesellschafft*, 11:689–699.
Gumperz, John J., and Robert Wilson, 1971 "Convergence and creolization: A case from the Indo-Aryan/Dravidian border in India," *in* Hymes, 1971:150–167.
Hancock, Ian, 1980 *The Language of the Texas Afro-Seminoles*, Publication of the Seminole Negro Scout Historical Association, Brackettville.
Hancock, Ian F., 1995 "On the migration and affiliation of the Rom, Dom and Lom Gypsies," *in* Matras, 1995:29–59.
Hancock, Ian F., 1999 *The Origins and Westward Migration of the Romani People* Occasional Paper of the International Romani Archives, No. 5, 675, 989.
Harriot, John, 1830 "Observations on the oriental origin of the Romanichal, or tribe miscalled Gipsey or Bohemian," *Transactions of the Royal Asiatic Society*, 2:518–88.
Hymes, Dell, ed., 1971 *Pidginization and Creolization of Languages*, Cambridge University Press, Cambridge.
Isaac, Jeanette, 1984 "The Banjara: Nomads of time," *Swagat Magazine*, July, pp. 52–9.
Jahr, Ernst Håkon, ed., 1992 *Language Contact: Theoretical and Empirical Studies*, Mouton De Gruyter, Amsterdam.
Kachru, Yamuna, 1990 "Hindi-Urdu," *in* Comrie, 1990:470–89.
Kelley, Gerald, 1966 "The status of Hindi as a lingua franca," *in* Bright, 1966:299–308.
Ketalaer, Josua, *ca.* 1698 [1743] [Grammatical description of Hindustani] private, Leiden.
Khubchandani, Lachman M., 1963 *The Acculturation of Indian Sindhi to Hindi, a Study of Language in Contact*, Unpublished doctoral dissertation, The University of Pennsylvania.
Khullar, K.K., 1995 "Urdu, the language of national unity," *India Perspectives*, March, pp. 21–25.
Maenchen-Heffen, J. Otto, 1973 *The World of the Hun*, The University of California Press, Berkeley.
Marushiakova, E., and Vesselin Popov, 1997 "The Romanies in the Balkans during the Ottoman Empire," *Roma*, 47:63–72.
Matras, Yaron, ed., 1995 *Romani in Contact: The History, Sociology and Structure of a Language* Amsterdam: John Benjamins
Mesthrie, Rajend, 1993 "Koineization in the Bhojpuri-Hindi diaspora, with special reference to South Africa," *in* Siegel, 1993:25–44.

Minorski, V., 1954 "Luri" in *The Encyclopedia of Islam* Leiden University Press, Leiden.

Minturn, Leigh, and John T. Hitchcock, 1966 *The Rājpūts of Khalapur, India*, Wiley, New York.

Naik, Ranjit, 1978 *Banjara (Indian Roma) from Barothan*, Report presented at the Second World Romani Congress, Geneva, April 8–11.

Nida, Eugene A. and Harold W. Fehderau, 1970 "Indigenous pidgins and koinés," *International Journal of American Linguistics*, 36:146–155.

Nseir, Amjad ibn, 1998 *The subgrouping of Domari within the Aryan languages: A morphosyntactic analysis* Research Paper, Department of Linguistics, The University of Texas at Austin.

Petersen, Walter (1912) "Vedic, Sanskrit and Prakrit," *Journal of the American Oriental Society*, 32:414–28.

Rathod, Jasvantsinh N., 1988 *Report on the Survey of Banjara Castes*, Tribal Research and Training Centre, Ahmedabad.

Rathore, B. Shyamala Devi, 1997. "Gypsy Music" Paper presented at the Conference on Romani Studies, University of Greenwich, London.

Reinecke, John, 1937 *Marginal Languages: A Sociological Survey of the Creole Languages and Trade Jargons*, Unpublished doctoral dissertation, Yale University.

Reinecke, John, Stanley Tsuzaki, David DeCamp, Ian Hancock and Richard Wood, eds., 1975 *A Bibliography of Pidgin and Creole Languages* The University of Hawaii Press, Honolulu.

Siegel, Jeff, 1985 "Koines and koineization," *Language in Society*, 14(3):357–78.

Siegel, Jeff, ed., 1993 *Koines and Koineization* (as *International Journal of the Socioloogy of Language*, Special Issue, No.99) Mouton de Gruyter, Berlin.

Soulis, George C., 1961 "Gypsies in the Byzantine Empire and the Balkans in the late Middle Ages," *Dumbarton Oaks Papers*, 15:142–65.

Southworth, Franklin C., 1971 "Detecting prior creolization: An analysis of the historical origins of Marathi," *in* Hymes, 1971:255–73.

Thapar, Romila, 1966 *A History of India*, Two vols., Pelican Books, London.

Thurston, Edgar, and K. Rangachari, 1909 "Lambādi," in their *Castes and Tribes of Southern India*, The Government Press, Madras, vol. 4.

Tod, James, 1920 *Annals and Antiquities of Rajasthan, or the Central and Western Rājpūt States of India* Three vols., The University Press, Oxford.

Watson, Francis, 1988 *A Concise History of India*, Thames and Hudson, London.

Whinnom, Keith, 1981 Non-primary types of language," *Logos Semantikos*, 5:227–41.

Wolpert, Stanley, 1977 *A New History of India* Oxford University Press, Oxford.

Wright, Desmond, 1969 *History of the World: Prehistory to the Renaissance*, Two vols., Hamlyn. London.

Zograf, G.A., 1963 "Kalkutsij xindustani knotsa," *Kratkii Soobshchenija Instituta Narodov Azhii*, 61:142–53.

CHAPTER TWO

THE GENESIS OF ANGLO-ROMANI

Peter Bakker

DONALD KENRICK was one of the first to deal with Anglo-Romani as a language in its own right, and not a decayed form of another language. Anglo-Romani was the name given by the Gypsylorists to the language of the English Romanichal Gypsies, (which they themselves call simply 'Romanes') of which the grammatical system comes from English and the vocabulary in part from Romani. Kenrick was also one of the major authors on the functions of Anglo-Romani and, by implication, other similar languages as well. Further, he was one of the first to ponder the question of the genesis of languages of the Anglo-Romani type: it is no longer the same language as the Romani language as spoken throughout Europe, such as its closest relative Welsh Romani. It has become a different language. Anglo-Romani roughly combines a colloquial English structure with a Romani lexicon. For this reason Kenrick prefers the term 'Romani English'. This same type of mixture of a Romani lexicon with another language is known from in various areas of Europe. Several generalising terms have been proposed for this type or class of languages: creolised (e.g. Acton 1989), intertwined, "pogadised", and Para-Romani (c.f. Bakker and Cortiade 1991) for this class. I am honoured to be able to dedicate this essay to Donald. His work on Romani and Anglo-Romani has been an important source of inspiration for me and many others in the field.

This paper deals with the history of Anglo-Romani. This was the subject of a debate between Ian Hancock and Donald Kenrick in 1971. Since then more research has been done, and it may be an appropriate time to take up the discussion again. It will appear that I do not agree with the Master (or actually, both Masters) in many points, but without Donald Kenrick we would not even have been aware of the matter. My inspiration comes from Donald's claim that Anglo-Romani developed gradually from a type of Romani such as Welsh Romani. His arguments for this claim are based on a thorough knowledge of modern Anglo-Romani, some study of early sources, and acquaintance with parallel developments in Finland where, according to him, the same thing is going on right now. Although space does not permit discussion of all the available early sources on Romani in England, I have examined them to provide some empirical material for a conclusion which appears to differ from Kenrick's.

Kenrick versus Hancock

In the early 1970s Donald Kenrick (1971a) and Ian Hancock (1971) debated the origin of the Anglo-Romani language. Kenrick believed that Romani in Britain "gradually lost its distinctive syntax, phonology and morphology – in that order – during five hundred years of contact with the host language." (Kenrick 1979a: 112; 1984: 80).

His arguments for gradual development are twofold. On the one hand he points to developments in contemporary Finnish Romani, which is observed as taking over Finnish phonology. On the other hand he points to the older sources of Anglo-Romani, which show more Romani elements than the present-day language, both in the grammatical system (sounds or phonology, word structure or morphology, word order or syntax) and in the vocabulary. Romani words and structures documented in the nineteenth century are no longer known today. Kenrick pointed to the fact that

The linguist Marcel Cortiade, organiser of the Fourth World Romani Congress, making a point about *Pogadi Jib*.

> "the extensive records of Gypsy speech in England in the nineteenth century show that the middle-aged informants spoke a mixture of English and Romani in the way that many young Finnish Roms mix Finnish and Romani today. Some informants [in Borrow 1874, P.B.] still spoke the inflected language (...) but the same writer quotes many sentences which have English syntax and morphology, and I would class them as Romani English." (Kenrick 1979a: 113; 1984: 81).

Other sources, such as Leland (1874) and Smart and Crofton (1875) show a form of Romani with only some Romani grammatical inflection surviving, according to Kenrick. Kenrick (1979a: 114; 1984d: 82) also quotes one of Smart and Crofton's Anglo-Romani teachers, who said that "all the old people spoke real old Romani words" when he was a young man. Although this man clearly refers to *words*, Kenrick interprets this as though the informant "thought that the last speakers to use Romani *morphology* [my emphasis, P.B.] in England (...) died at the beginning of the nineteenth century."

Hancock (1971) did not agree with Kenrick. He claimed that Anglo-Romani was created in the sixteenth century, in a pact of Cant speakers and Romani speakers. This language contact situation is in a way reminiscent of the situation in which pidgins and creole languages come about. His arguments were most clearly expressed in Hancock (1984), where he also quotes contemporary sources describing such contacts (p.90-1). Hancock explicitly states that the Romani elements are retained, not intrusions into English.

The controversy boils down to three main points: the time of genesis of Anglo-Romani – in the nineteenth century (Kenrick) or in the sixteenth century (Hancock); the pace – a gradual (Kenrick) or sudden (Hancock) genesis of the language and finally, whether Anglo-Romani came about as a conscious creation (Hancock) or not (Kenrick).

The question

How can we resolve this controversy? In this paper I will base my argument on the study of the earliest sources of the Romani language in England. For a full picture, one should also take historical data on English Gypsies into account, as well as anthropological and social data, but that is not feasible here.

The question is: what can we deduce from early sources regarding the evolution of a form of Romani of the Welsh Romani type (with a syntactic, morphological and phonological system like continental Romani) toward the type of Anglo-Romani, which has a similar lexicon to Welsh Romani, but the grammatical system of colloquial English? Did this happen slowly (as claimed by Kenrick) or abruptly (as claimed by Hancock)? Was it, as Hancock claims, the result of close contacts with English people without a fixed abode, and the Gypsies, in the sixteenth century, or did it happen in the nineteenth century, as claimed by Kenrick?

Diachrony of the sources

One of the ways of solving this problem is by looking at all the early material that we have on Romani in the British isles, and see what these can tell us about the history, and perhaps also the genesis, of Anglo-Romani. When did Romani evolve from the language as it is spoken in many parts of the world, into the characteristic language as is spoken today on the British Isles, called by its speakers "Pogadi Jib" (which translates as "broken language" – a label I don't agree with)?

The very first source of Romani from the British Isles (or from anywhere in the world) is the much discussed text by Andrew Borde of the mid-sixteenth century (see Fraser 1992: 11 for a facsimile reprint, and Hancock 1984 for an analysis). It is a kind of

Romani that does not show the influence of English yet (except marginally), and it must be the kind of Romani that evolved into Pogadi Jib. It was probably close to the variety of Romani spoken in Wales which was documented magnificently 350 years later by John Sampson (1926a).

The next oldest source for Anglo-Romani is a recently discovered manuscript from the early seventeenth century, which provides some key information. I will come back to this important source below. After this, there is a long gap to the middle of the eighteenth century, the reasons for which have been explained by Acton as the result of a pervasive negative attitude against Gypsies during that period.

In 1753 one James Poulter alias Baxter published his autobiography. Poulter mentions the language of the Gypsies ("Romney"), which he distinguishes from Cant. He quotes only very few 'Gypsy' words, all of which are unmistakably Romani: *cauney* "fowl, chicken" (Romani *kahni*, Welsh Romani *kåni*, Anglo-Romani *ka:ni*), *bucket-chats* "sheep" (Romani *bakro*, Welsh Romani *bakichò* 'lamb' or *bakarō* 'sheep', Anglo-Romani *ba:kro*) and *john* "to know" (Romani *dzhan*, Welsh Romani) *dzhun*, Anglo-Romani *dzhin*). Welsh Romani forms here and in the rest of the paper are all quoted from Sampson (1926a) with some typographical modification reflecting technical constraints.

After the 1780s more or less continuous series of Romani material is collected in the British Isles and published by a range of people. Marsden (1785) may have been the first. It is not clear, however, whether any of the few words he quotes were collected from English Gypsies. Furthermore, it is impossible to conclude anything about the nature and origin of his material, if at all from England.

Jacob Bryant did field work with Gypsies in Windsor in the 1770s, and he published some of his material, inspired by Marsden's article, in 1784. It is hard to conclude anything definite on the basis of so little material (six sentences and some unconnected words). These phrases contain a number of pronouns with case markers and some clitics, which suggest a Welsh Romani type of dialect. On the other hand, in the six adjective-noun combinations that we find, three (*fainī pū* , *bauro panee*, *bitū thēm*) show gender agreement, but *fainō wokli*, *bauro charrie* and *moloo georgee* combine masculine adjectives with feminine nouns. This is normal in Anglo-Romani, but not in Welsh Romani. For further analysis, see Sampson (1910–11).

In 1796 John Cragg of Threekingham, Lincolnshire, conversed with some Gypsies and wrote down a few words of their language, to be more precise nine words and two short sentences (published 1907–08 by William A. Cragg). This material could just as well relate to a variety of the Welsh Romani type as one of the Pogadi Jib type.

The next source, material collected by Reverend Walter Whiter from Norfolk, is much more extensive. Whiter had a strong interest in languages and in 1822–25 he also published *Etymologicon Universale; Or, Universal Etymological Dictionary*, in which he compares many languages. One of the languages is Romani. Apparently he had collected the material himself in England. Apart from the words in this book, there was also earlier material, collected before 1800. Some of it was published in Whiter (1800) but a manuscript called *Lingua Cingariana* was lost.

The phonological and lexical features of the Romani elements leave no doubt, first, that the material is original, and second, that it was collected from English Romanichal Gypsies. My discussion is based on the studies on Whiter's Anglo-Romani material (Groome 1888, Grosvenor 1908-09). Whiter's Romani material is quite extensive: almost 500 entries in Grosvenor 1908-09, and some 150 of these are phrases and sentences. Grosvenor (1908-09: 167 n. 1) provides evidence that his material was collected between 1787 and 1800.

The syntax in Whiter's material is clearly Romani, only slightly influenced by English. The phonology seems English or close to English, since the Whiter material does not seem to distinguish the Romani sound /x/, the two distinct types of /r/, or aspirated consonants. Considering his multi-lingualism he could not have missed all of these. Morphology, if present, is as in Romani. In some case, however, the appropriate endings are lacking. Some examples, two of the Welsh Romani type, one intermediate and two of the Anglo-Romani type are given here. In these and the following sentences, all non-Romani elements are italicised and Romani elements are in normal type. Numbers here refer to Grosvenor's system.

1. beshto s'o kam
   sit.PARTICIPLE is-the sun
   "The sun is set" (39)
   (Welsh Romani *beštó o k 'am* "the sun has set", Sampson 1926a: 35)
2. keri j'ovva
   home I go
   "I am going [home]" (7)
   (Welsh Romani *k'here* "home", Welsh Romani *dzhava* "I go")
3. avree se yog
   out is fire
   "The fire is out" (49)
   (Welsh Romani *avri* "out", *si* "is", *yåg* "fire")
4. ga te soto, ga te vodros
   "go to sleep, go to bed"
   (Welsh Romani *jå* "go"?, *te* "to", *suto* "slept", *vodros* "bed")
5. klitsen de woder
   "Lock the door."
   (Welsh Romani klizinisar "to lock", klizin "lock", hudar "door")

If one looks at all this material, we can easily notice the use of some English elements, but overall the language remains Romani. Example (3) shows Romani word order, but English semantics: English "is out" is literally translated into Romani. In the last example we see the English article "the". In short, this is a form of Romani slightly influenced by English.

The nineteenth century

The material from the eighteenth century and before therefore does not provide evidence that the language was "pogadised". The first nineteenth century source, however, clearly shows an English grammatical system.

Francis Irvine, when travelling to India in 1805 on the *Preston East Indiaman*, made acquaintance with a Romanichal called John Lee, from whom he learned some Romani. Irvine published 140 words in total and about fifteen phrases fourteen years later in an Indian magazine, drawing parallels with Hindustani (Irvine 1819). Irvine's view of the language is one "of a tongue gradually obliterating ..." (Irvine 1819:69). Lee and Irvine may also have been the first to try and explain the origin of the language. It is suggested here that the grammatical elements of Romani were gradually lost and then borrowed from English, reminiscent of Kenrick's view:

"Long before the roots of a language are lost, its construction and idiom, with all particles used for connexion and government, are usually forgotten: – as the English Gipsies borrow from the English a great number of the former, much more should we expect them to avail themselves of the latter in use amongst the English." (Irvine 1819:67)

In the sentences cited from Lee, there are phrases like:

6. *Can you* roku Roomus *and play upon the* bosh?
   "Can you speak Gipsy and play upon the fiddle?" (p. 61)
   (Welsh Romani *raker-* "speak", *Romanes* "Romani language", *bašav-* "make music" – actually the first sentence of a widespread Anglo-Romani song)
7. Ry *of the* Roomdichil
   King of the Gypsies (p. 61)
   (Welsh Romani *rai* "gentleman", Romani (not Welsh Romani) *Romanichal* "(Northern) Gypsy")
8. mar *di* gojoo
9. koor *di* gojoo
   "beat the non-Gypsy!"
   (R. *mar-* "to kill, hit", R. *kur-* "to hit, beat")
   (Irvine: "signifying a battle amongst them"; p. 64)

These are remarkably close to modern Pogadi Jib. There is no doubt it was, as there is nothing which points to something like the Welsh Romani type. This may, by the way, also be the oldest attestation of the name 'Romanichal' for the Gypsies of England.

David Copsey of Braintree, inspired by the appearance of Hoyland's book on the Gypsies in 1816, conversed with a group of Gypsies of the Lovell family travelling through his native town of Braintree in Essex, not far from London. The Lovells readily supplied him with Romani words, forty-three in all and, more interestingly, seventeen brief sentences. These sentences mostly seem to be of the Welsh Romani type, even though English words are also used in the four sentences quoted here (Copsey 1818, Axon 1907):

10. *Very* dooster shum
    Very well
    (Welsh Romani *dosta* "enough", *sum/šum* "I am")
11. *How* dóevee ánkee devús
    How far have your travelled to-day?
    (Welsh Romani *dur* "far", *'vián* "you came", *kadivés* "today")
12. Pen *your* naave
    "What is your name?" (lit. "say your name")
    (Welsh Romani *phen* "say", *nav* "name")
13. *I go* káta kongrée
    "I go to church"
    (Welsh Romani *katè*, *kat'* "towards", *kangeri* "church")

It is not obvious how to interpret the English elements in these sentences. They do not seem to be prototypical borrowings and neither do these reflect typical codeswitching patterns, as they violate most proposed constraints. Neither are these sentences of the Anglo-Romani type.

Bright (1818) collected material on British Romani and other dialects. He worked with Gypsies in Norwood. Their language appeared to be very close to what he had collected in Hungary. The Caló material that he also published shows a variety of the Anglo-Romani type: Romani vocabulary, but here combined with a Spanish grammatical system (his Caló material has been reprinted in Bakker 1995). Bright considered the material he collected in Britain closer to the Hungarian material than the Caló (Spanish Para-Romani) material that he had from Spain. This was due to "intercourse with the people of the country, which must be instrumental in contaminating their language, as well as their character, more than either the Gypsey of England, or the Hungarian Cygani." (Bright 1818 as quoted in Russell 1915-16: 167).

Nevertheless, Bright's Anglo-Romani shows significant influence from English. Its phonological system is close to or identical with that of English. Case marking is no longer used (except occasionally in pronouns and some fossilised expressions). Romani verb endings are regularly used, but occasionally uninflected verbs show up as well. Word order is close to that of English, and only seldom more like Romani. Despite this pervasive influence from English, the language is not Anglo-Romani or Pogadi Jib.

14. Mai mang tut del mande wai   (Bright's Romani)

me mang tu-t d-el m-an lové
1-NOM ask-Ø you-ACC give-3 me money   (morphemic)
"I pray you, give me that which I have deserved"   (B's English)
(Welsh Romani *mè* "I", *mande* "at me", *mang-* "beg, ask" *tut* "you" (accusative),
del(a) "he gives", *lové* "money").

In this example, the verbal ending of *mang* is missing. The word *del*, in Welsh Romani "he gives", is used for a command. This verb form *del* can be used in Pogadi Jib in all functions, including commands.

Stow Fair in Gloucestershire where Angloromani is used all day in horse dealing.

In the next example, we encounter the English adverb *away*. The word for horse is case-marked, but from a Welsh Romani perspective the case is somewhat odd. Finally, one could have expected a vocative form in the last word, but it is nominative.

15. Le o giv, *away*, gresti, chi   (Anglo-Romani,)
    take.the wheat away horse-PREP girl
    Take the oats away from the horse, wife (literally)
    "Take the oats from the horse wife"   (Bright's English)
    (Welsh Romani *lè* "take!", *o giv* "the corn/rye", *gresti* "at the horse", *chai* "girl")

In the final last example we have a sentence with a word order impossible in English, but common in Welsh Romani (cf. example 1).

16 Pre si o kam   (Bright's Romani)
    opre si o kham
    up be-3 the sun
    "The sun is up"
    (Welsh Romani *oprè* "up", *si* "is", *o kham* "sun")

The next source is from the 1830s. The Reverend Samuel Fox collected words and sentences from Gypsies in Derbyshire in 1832 and 1833 (Thompson 1924: 161). His material was published in Sampson (1926b). He worked with itinerant Gypsy families, whose route passed by Morley and/or Smalley in Derbyshire. Fox's material totals a few hundred words, including some short phrases, and eighteen sentences. In the vocabulary the number of English words is small: *dīpō* "deep", *fōkī* "people", *hilō* "hill", *grand* "big", *sɔmɔrus* "summer" (the word *fainī* "fine" is from Bryant). Strikingly, these English words are all given in combinations of at least two words. This may mean that single English words are omitted from the list on purpose, and that the vocabulary contains fewer lexical items from English than were actually used. This practice has been repeated by many others as well.

In the sentences, there is a striking difference between the first seven and the final eleven sentences: the first part contains no English syllable at all, whereas the other eleven sentences all have at least one English word or morpheme. There are even sentences with only one or two Romani elements:

17. *Who do you* dowker *to*   (Fox Anglo-Romani)
    Who do you dùker to   (Sampson interpretation)
    Who do you tell fortunes to?   (Fox English translation)
    (Welsh Romani *dūrker-* "tell fortunes")

18. *I am very* poroo   (Fox Anglo-Romani)
    I am very poru   (Sampson interpretation)
    I am very old   (Fox English translation)
    (Welsh Romani *phurō*)

In the sentences we find two Romani prepositions (*chee/kī* "to", *vry* "from") and one case marker (*chavinga/chaving* = *chhavenge* "for the children", with dative ending), and six English prepositions (three times *to*, twice *for* and once *fran*, a dialect form for "from"). In the vocabulary, we only have Romani prepositions.

The syntax is thoroughly English: subject-verb rather than verb-subject as in:

19. Yec raunee weller   (Fox Anglo-Romani)
    yek rɔnì 'wela   (Sampson interpretation)
    one lady comes   (Sampson "literally")
    "The lady is coming"   (Fox English translation)
    (Welsh Romani *yekh* "one", *rånì* "lady", *'vela* "comes")

There are further complex English constructions like stranded prepositions:

20. Kievy an *fran* (Fox Anglo-Romani)
   kai 'vīan fran? (Sampson interpretation)
   where you came from
   Where do you come from? (Fox English translation)
   (Welsh Romani *kai* "where", *'vīán* "you came")
21. So jassee cheeo gave *for* (Fox Anglo-Romani)
   sō jasə kī ō gav for (Sampson interpretation)
   what you.go to.the town for
   what goest thou to the town for? (Sampson "literally")
   What are you going to the village for? (Fox English translation)

The question words are mostly from Romani (*šar* [Welsh Romani *sar*] "how", *kai* "where", *sō* "what", *savə* "which"), but there are also *who* and *how* from English.

As for the verbs, there are some verbs inflected as in Romani, such as in:

22. *I* dowker our (Fox Anglo-Romani)
   I dūkeráua (Sampson interpretation)
   I tell fortunes

Fox's texts point to the following facts: in this group in 1832, the gender distinction in adjectives was lost, the syntax was completely English, possessive relations had to be expressed in the way of English. Many things were expressed with both English and Romani expressions, such as question words, personal pronouns and probably (low) numerals. Nevertheless, the word list shows that Romani words were used for many actions, objects and concepts, and also grammatical function words such as demonstratives, locative adverbs, prepositions and articles.

Smart

The first systematic study of Anglo-Romani, beyond the collection of words and sundry sentences is the work of Bath C. Smart.

The language that Smart (1862-63) describes retains quite a few Romani grammatical features, such as the definite articles *o* and *i* (written "y"), although "the definite article is often left out altogether" (p. 12). The Romani indefinite article is not used, as they "invariably use the English Indefinite Article" (p. 12). The Romani plural marker *-a* or *-ja* is used, written "yor" or "or". But they "often use the English plural in *s*" (p. 13), or a combination of the two. The Romani gender endings in adjectives are preserved, as well as the comparative ending in *-der*, written "-dair". The Romani pronouns are partly preserved (nominative, oblique/accusative, prepositional), and the other cases are replaced by English prepositions, with prepositional case endings used on pronouns (e.g. *from mandy* "from me"). Further a number of Romani prepositions are used. Demonstratives, possessive pronouns, question words and other pronouns from Romani are frequent. Verb conjugation follows the English pattern. Often the Romani third person form functions as the root to which English endings are added. The preterite ending *-as* is occasionally used. The past participle form is *-do* or *-o* seems to be productive, and inflected forms of the verb "to be" are regularly used. Word order appears to be like English, with rare exceptions like *tatcho see doovo*, lit. "true is that". This summarises Smart's grammatical sketch. As an appendix to his article Smart gives three texts, which corroborate what he stated in his sketch.

Discussion

This is the last source I discuss, since the 1870s mark a change. On the one hand, the study of Anglo-Romani becomes more systematic, and collaboration between the Romanichals and outsiders increases. Three books on the language were published within a few years: Leland (1874), Borrow (1874) and Smart and Crofton (1875). On the other hand, students of the language start to make increasing use of previous work, which may make it in a sense less reliable than the work of their naive predecessors. These scholars may also have filtered out things they do not consider correct. Therefore I will stop here with the discussion of the older sources – of which I have not used all. Table 1 summarises the data, including some I have not discussed above.

If we look at the Table, it may seem that Kenrick is right: the phonology has been exclusively or primarily English since the earliest documentation after Borde. The free grammatical morphemes, such as demonstratives, articles, pronouns are exclusively Romani in the earliest documents, then there is a long period where Romani elements are more common than English elements, and finally English and Romani are equally used (the only exception is Lee-Irvine of 1805). The productive morphology gradually becomes almost exclusively English after 1850. Syntax is mostly or exclusively Romani until around 1818. Then English starts to dominate, and after 1850 it is exclusively English. Lee-Irvine of 1805, however, does not fit the picture for neither syntax, free grammatical morphemes nor morphology and it is clearly more anglicised than most later sources.

This Table seems to illustrate what Kenrick claims: first phonology and syntax, then morphology – even though Kenrick claimed that loss of distinctive syntax would precede phonology. However, this does not prove that the development was gradual. From some sources we get very little material. Also, the Romanichals came from different regions in England, and there may have been regional differences. The developments may have happened at different times in different regions. Further, the methods of data-collecting may have varied, yielding dissimilar results. Therefore one would wish to have more older material and this has surfaced a few years ago. It contains the most devastating counter-evidence against gradual development.

A recently discovered Anglo-Romani word list from Winchester is dated 1619 (McGowan 1996). It is a list of words from the confession of one Walter Hindes, who

Table 1: Sources of phonology, syntax, morphology and free grammatical morphemes in some pre-1870 sources of English Romani

		PHO	SYN	MOR	FGM
1542	Borde	R?	R	R	R
1776	Bryant	E>R	?	R	R
1790s	Whiter	E	R	R>0	R
1796	Cragg	?	?	?	?
1798	N.N.-Sampson 1930	R,E	R>E	R>E,0	R>E
1805	Lee/Irvine	E	E?	E	E
1818	Copsey/Axon	E	R	R>E	R,E
1818	Bright	E	E>R	R>0	R>E
1832–3	Fox	E	E	R	R,E
1836	Roberts	E>R	E>R?	R>E	R>E
1850s	Taylor	E	E	E	R,E
1862	Smart	E	E	E>R	R,E
1865	Sinclair	E	E	E,R,0	R>E
1872	Sanderson	E	E	E>R	E,R

Meanings of abbreviations and symbols:
Column headings: PHO = phonology; MOR = morphology; FGM = free grammatical markers (e.g. pronouns, articles, demonstratives, prepositions); SYN = syntax.
In columns: E = English; R = Romani; 0 = neither; in the columns: E>R : English used more than Romani [this does not suggest a diachronic path]; E,R : English and Romani used roughly equally.

was apprehended in the company of Gypsies and put into jail in Winchester. He had met the group in London. All the material shows English syntax throughout, the English plural morpheme *-s*, and no adjectival agreement (*trickney ruckey* "little girl" beside *trickney ruckelo* "little boy" – both have a feminine adjectival ending). All but two of the 130 or so words can be found in Sampson (1926a). Everything in the material is of the Anglo-Romani type, and nothing of the Welsh Romani type. Some example phrases:

23. swisht *with a* sayster *in the end*
    lance? with a iron in the end
    "staff with a pike" (Welsh Romani *sastārn* "iron")

(Even though Welsh Romani deviates from the 1615 form, the form in the list is identical to the more general Romani form *saster*. I am not able to provide an etymology for the word *swisht*, unless it is the same root as *schümije* "lance" in the van Euwsum material (Kluyver 1910-11), a root extinct everywhere except in Finnish Romani *hummi/xummi*.)

24. coore *the* gorife
    kūr the guruv
    "go beat the cow"

This provides incontrovertible proof that a dialect of the Welsh Romani type had developed into Anglo-Romani already by 1619. But does that prove that Kenrick is wrong and Hancock is right? Not necessarily. The material discussed above provides three arguments against Hancock's view that Cant speakers and Romani speakers made a pact to combine their languages. One argument against Hancock is the fact that several Cant speakers, who were interviewed in the Winchester Records, claim that they do not know the language of the Gypsies.

A second argument is that throughout the centuries people distinguish strictly between Cant and Romani. The Winchester records of the 1610s show a strict separation between Cant and the 'Gypsy' language: among the Cant words quoted there is no Romani, or the other way around. The second example is the Cant speaker Poulter. He gives some Cant phrases, and he explicitly distinguishes Cant from Romani, as in the following quotation (as given in Winstedt 1910-11): "Gypsies are a People that talk *Romney*, that is a *Cant* that nobody understands but themselves." This clearly indicates that the language of the Romanichals is not understood by Cant speakers. The third witness is Marsden. He too said that Cant and the language of the Gypsies were unjustly equated. He discusses Gypsies as "obscure, despised, and wretched *people in England, whose language has been considered as a fabricated gibberish, and confounded with a cant* [my emphasis]".

Other arguments against Hancock's claim that the 'sturdy beggars' and Gypsies combined their languages into one "jargon", are the following additional facts:

(1) There is hardly any influence from Romani in Cant. If the "lawless" would indeed have learned Romani (even if only the lexicon), one would expect more Romani words in Cant than are actually attested, especially in post-1550 sources, since speakers of this type of language look for constant lexical renewal (cf. Matras 1998a, 1998b).
(2) There is a continuous confusion of Romani and Cant among early writers. Many early vocabularies and songs are Cant rather than Romani, although authors called it "Gypsy" (cf. Leland 1889: xxi-xxii). The contents are never, or very little, mixed, however.
(3) It is sometimes claimed that Cant words were purposely left out of writings on Romani. This is not likely for the naive pre-1870 writings. Nevertheless, the amount of Cant is negligible or absent.
(4) Inflected Romani was still used in England in the nineteenth century and even into the twentieth century. It is unlikely that the two languages would have survived side by side for four centuries, especially since they did not have different functions.

In short, even though Anglo-Romani must have come about in the sixteenth century (in any case it was an established language in 1619), there is no indication that there was indeed this pact as claimed in some early source.

Are the nineteenthn century sources reliable?

In my choice of data I have focused on those which precede the wave in publications on Anglo-Romani from the 1870s. The books published by Leland, Smart and Crofton and Borrow in 1874 and 1875, show a type of Anglo-Romani which contains more Romani in most sentences than what we apparently hear in everyday speech today. Some students of the language have claimed that these older texts were therefore not reliable.

Kenrick and Acton (1984d: 10) estimate that "only about 20 per cent of the words are from the special Romani vocabulary" in "spontaneous 'Romani' speech by English Gypsies" in modern days. Even a cursory look at older sources shows that these indeed contain many more Romani elements, and therefore these authors find that there are differences between "Romani sentences which sound unnatural (like some of those laboriously built up by Smart and Crofton's collaborators in "How the Petalengro jelled adré mi-Duvvel's Ker (...) and those which sound like spontaneous utterances. (Kenrick and Acton 1984d: 10). They go on to argue that Smart and Crofton "worked over their long prose texts intensively with their informants, 'improving' them (i.e. making them more Romani) at each revision. (Kenrick and Acton 1984d: 11). The same is said to be true for Borrow's Anglo-Romani. Actually none of these early authors claim they did this, so these must be conjectures based on language-internal evidence. But one can also ask: why should the spontaneous spoken language of the 1870s have been the same as in the 1970s?

This static view does not seem to leave open the possibility that the language changed in the intervening 100 years. And this is most likely the case: Anglo-Romani has been under 100 more years of pressure of English, and a strong influence, notably on the vocabulary (more Romani words have fallen in disuse) and also on the grammatical remnants, is exactly what one would expect.

My arguments are briefly that, even though the different texts were written or dictated at different times and by different people, they do show many similarities and therefore they can be considered reliable. Furthermore, all authors of the 1870s use variant forms of demonstratives, pronouns and question words – here from Romani, there from English. If these students of the language, or the speakers themselves, really wanted to make the texts as much Romani as possible, they would have dropped all these English elements and have replaced them with their Romani equivalents, since they were apparently known to them. But all of them use them side by side, often in the same text. Therefore I think there are enough internal indications that the prose texts are reliable as documents of Anglo-Romani of that time – including

Leland's texts, even though it has been proven that he is an impostor with his Chinese Pidgin English and his Micmac-Algonquian texts (his Romani song book is a clear fabrication as well).

In short, the comparison between Anglo-Romani in the 1870s and in the 1980s shows differences because the language changed. Not surprisingly, it changed in the direction of English, a language used by all Anglo-Romani speakers on a daily basis.

So how did Anglo-Romani come into being? I am convinced that the change from the Welsh Romani type to the Anglo-Romani type must have occurred suddenly, say within a generation of speakers. The motives for the change may have been a combination of the desire, on the part of the speakers, to rescue a disappearing language, which they wanted to preserve because of its usefulness in secret communication and as one of the markers of their Gypsy identity. After being crystallised as an Anglo-Romani language, the knowledge of residual Romani patterns gradually disappeared. Uncommon words also gradually fell into disuse. Romani elements were replaced by English patterns. The latter can be proven with the fact that there are no recordings of a transitory stage: utterances are either Welsh Romani or Anglo-Romani. Even in sources that seem to combine a Welsh Romani type and an Anglo-Romani type, we never find them combined in a single utterance. (This is also true for Derek Tipler's data collected around 1950 (Tipler 1957), which discusses both Welsh Romani utterances and Anglo-Romani utterances, but they were apparently never used in combination. The only exception that I know of are Norwood's fieldnotes as quoted in Matras (1988a: 13). Romani speakers who knew both (like Sylvester Boswell in Smart and Crofton 1875), always keep the two languages apart.

Conclusion

In the preceding sections I have discussed the oldest documented sources for the language called Anglo-Romani. More important than its origin is its current status. Let me first say that I consider Anglo-Romani a real, normal language in all senses of the word, even if it is not the first language acquired by the young Romanichals, and even if it cannot exist without the availability of English, and even if it is used only for special purposes, not for everyday communication.

All languages change, and languages change faster when they are in contact with other languages. If we compare the European languages as to their rate of change, the two extremes are Icelandic and English. Both are spoken on islands. Iceland was never invaded, and Iceland has been an essentially monolingual society since its settlers arrived. Icelanders today can understand the Edda saga of more than 750 years ago without any special study of the old language, whereas Chaucer's work written 150 years later requires a special study of early English. Old English changed rapidly and radically under the influence of Scandinavian and especially French. The main reason for this difference is the social fact that Icelandic was not in contact with other languages, and there was no significant immigration to Iceland, in contrast to Britain, and neither was Iceland a colonial power. Languages change faster in multilingual societies.

British Romani has been under the influence of different dialects of English since the arrival of the Gypsies in Britain. Virtually all Romanichals must have been bilinguals throughout their lives. Therefore it is not surprising that Romani as spoken in England has changed. It has changed in two ways. First, from a language of the Welsh Romani type to a language that has so strong an English influence that it can no longer be considered the same language. I have argued above that it happened rapidly and in the sixteenth century for the first time. Thomas Acton has proposed to call Anglo-Romani a "daughter language" of Romani of the Welsh Romani type. This term might have been appropriate if this was not already an existing term with a rather different meaning in historical linguistics (where Italian is called a daughter language of Latin). Whatever the label, it makes no sense to consider Welsh Romani and Anglo-Romani the same language: they have grown apart to become two different languages altogether, and not dialects of the same language. The fact that both are called Romanes by their speakers points to their common origin, not to their being identical. Both are normal languages. But neither of them must be considered 'proper Romani' - nor should any other variety of Romani be called thus. Any variety of Romani and Anglo-Romani is a proper language.

The second cluster of changes are those that took place after the crystallisation of Anglo-Romani. It continued to evolve under the influence of English, so that Kenrick's label "Romani English" can be justified today. Remnants of Romani grammar and uncommon words were lost in that period.

The lesson from historical linguistics is that all languages change, especially in situations of language contact, and that all languages are equal, no matter what the extent they have changed. Using some language as a standard to which other languages have to be compared is a dangerous form of normative behaviour. The speakers of the languages are the main victims. If considered the same language, speakers may feel that they are not proficient in the language that they use every day. Anglo-Romani, and other languages of the Anglo-Romani type, must therefore not be equated with Romani. The languages are distinct. And this is something of which Donald Kenrick has always been aware. Scholars can take him as an example, both in his engagement and in taking the language of Gypsies seriously, especially an unclassifiable language such as Anglo-Romani.

References

Acton, Thomas, 1989 "The Value of 'creolized' dialects of Romani" In: M. Shipka, ed. *Language and Culture of the Romanies*, Svjetlost, Sarajevo.

Acton, Thomas and Kenrick, Donald, 1984, *Romani Rokkeripen To-Divvus. The English Romani dialect and its contemporary social, educational and linguistic standing* Romanestan Publications, London.

Acton, Thomas and Donald Kenrick, 1984a. "General introduction" in Acton and Kenrick (eds.) 1984.

Axon, William E.A., 1907 "The English Gypsies in 1818" *The Antiquary: A Magazine Devoted to the Study of the Past* 43: 181-4.

Bakker, Peter, 1995, "Notes on the genesis of Caló and other Iberian Para-Romani varieties" in Yaron Matras (ed.) *Romani in Contact. The History, Structure and Sociology of a Language*. J. Benjamins, Amsterdam 125-50.

Bakker, Peter, and Cortiade, Marcel, 1991, *In the Margins of Romani* Publications of the Institute for General Linguistics, Nr 58, University of Amsterdam.

Borrow, George, 1874, *Romano Lavo-Lil. Word-Book of the Romany or, English Gypsy Language*, [Reprint 1982: Alan Sutton, Gloucester].

Bright, Richard, 1818 *Travels from Vienna through Lower Hungary*, Private, London.

Bryant, Jacob, 1785 "Collections on the Zingara or Gypsey Language, obligingly transmitted by Mr. Bryant" *Archaeologia* 7 (1785), Also in *Annual Register* 1785.

Copsey, D., 1818 (Letter to) *Monthly Magazine*, October 22.

Cragg, William A. 1907-1908 "Gypsy words, 1796." *Journal of the Gypsy Lore Society* 2nd series 1: 187.

Fraser, Angus. 1992 *The Gypsies*. Oxford: Blackwell.

Groome, Frances Hindes, 1888 "Anglo-Romany gleanings." *Journal of the Gypsy Lore Society*, 1st Series, 1(1): 102-3.

Grosvenor, Lady Arthur, 1908-09 "Whiter's 'Lingua Cingariana' " *Journal of the Gypsy Lore Society* New Series, 2: 161-79.

Hancock, Ian, 1971 "Comment on Kenrick" in: Thomas Acton (ed.) *Current Changes among British Gypsies and their Place in International Patterns of Development*. Oxford: NGEC, pp. 15-18.

Hancock, Ian. 1984 "The social and linguistic development of Anglo-Romani." in: Acton and Kenrick (eds.) p. 89-134.

Irvine, Francis, 1819 "On the similitude between the Gipsy and Hindoostanee languages." *Transactions of the Literary Society of Bombay* 1: 57-70.

Kluyver, A., 1910-11 "Un glossaire tsigane du seizième siècle" *Journal of the Gypsy Lore Society* New Series. 4: 131-42.

Leland, Charles G., 1874 *The English Gypsies and their Language* Trübner and Co., London.

McGowan, Alan, 1996 *The Winchester confessions 1615-1616. Depositions of travellers, Gypsies, fraudsters, and makers of counterfeit documents, including a vocabulary of the Romany language* Romany and Traveller Family History Society, South Chailey, East Sussex.

Marsden, William, 1785 "Observations on the language of the people commonly called Gypsies" *Annual Register* 27, pp. 382-6.

Matras, Yaron, 1998a "Para-Romani revisited" in Yaron Matras (ed.) *The Romani element in Non-Standard Speech*, Harrassowitz, Wiesbaden, 1-27.

Matras, Yaron, 1998b "The Romani element in German secret languages: Jenisch and Rotwelsch" in Yaron Matras (ed.) *The Romani element in Non-Standard Speech*,: Harrassowitz, Wiesbaden, 193-230.

Poulter, John, 1753 *The Discoveries of John Poulter, alias Baxter*. Private, Sherborne (apparently second edition).

Russell, Alexander, 1915-16 "Bright's Anglo-Romani vocabulary" *Journal of the Gypsy Lore Society* 2nd Series, 9: 165-85.

Sampson, John, 1907/08 "English Gypsies in 1818" *Journal of the Gypsy Lore Society* New Series 1: 183-5.

Sampson, John, 1910-11 "Jacob Bryant: Being an analysis of his Anglo-Romani vocabulary, with a discussion of the place and date of collection and an attempt to show that Bryant, not Rüdiger, was the earliest discoverer of the Indian origin of the Gypsies" *Journal of the Gypsy Lore Society* 2nd Series, 4: 162-94.

Sampson, John, 1926a [1968] *The Dialect of the Gypsies of Wales*, Clarendon Press, Oxford.

Sampson, John, 1926b "The dialect of the Derbyshire Gypsies, Compiled in the parish of Smalley by the Rev. Samuel Fox 1832-1833" *Journal of the Gypsy Lore Society* 3rd series 5(4): 62-94.

Sampson, John, 1930 "An East Anglian Romani vocabulary of 1798." *Journal of the Gypsy Lore Society* 3rd series 9(3)

Smart, Bath, C., 1862-63 "The dialect of the English Gypsies" Appendix to the *Transactions of the Philological Society* 1862-63: 3-87.

Smart, B.C. and Crofton H.D., 1875 *The dialect of the English Gypsies*, Asher and Co., London. [1875 is "second edition. Revised and greatly enlarged"]

Thompson, T.W., 1924, 1925 "Samuel Fox and the Derbyshire Boswells" *Journal of the Gypsy Lore Society* 3rd series 3: 158-179; 3rd series 4 (1925): 11-37.

Tipler, Derek, 1957 "Specimens of modern Welsh Romani" *Journal of the Gypsy Lore Society* 3rd Series, 36(1/2): 9-24.

Whiter, Walter, 1800 *Etymologicon Magnum, or, Universal Etymological Dictionary*, F.Hodson, Cambridge.

Whiter, Walter, 1822-25 *Etymologicon Universale; or, Universal Etymological Dictionary. On a new plan. (...). With illustrations drawn from various languages: The Teutonic Dialects (...) Greek, Latin, French, French, Italian, Spanish. - The Celtic Dialects (...) Sclavonic, Russian, etc. - The Eastern Languages, Hebrew, Arabic, Persian, Sanscrit, Gipsey, Coptic, etc. By the Rev. Walter Whiter, M.A., Rector of Hardingham, in the County of Norfolk, and late Fellow of Clare Hall*, 3 Vols., Cambridge University Press, Cambridge.

Winstedt, E.O., 1910-11 "An early mention of the language 'Romney'" *Journal of the Gypsy Lore Society* 5: 78-9.

CHAPTER THREE

PROCLAMATION OR PRESERVATION?
THE BIBLE AND MINORITY LANGUAGES

Paul Ellingworth

MY ONLY FORMAL qualifications for contributing to this Festschrift are, first, a period of increasingly close collaboration and friendship with Donald Kenrick going back over twenty-five years, and, second, admiration for a linguistic achievement that I could never emulate, let alone equal. Colleagues more eminent than I are happy to salute Donald as *il miglior fabbro*.

My informal qualifications for writing about minority languages are however, perhaps stronger than might at first appear, and provide an excuse for a page of reminiscences. As a native speaker of English, I am the linguistic equivalent of blood group O (to which, incidentally, I also belong). Nothing could be less remarkable; nothing more likely to reinforce the British preconception that the English language is normal and others are odd.

If I have been to any extent liberated from this prejudice, it has been through finding myself, through no merit of my own, in a series of minority situations. For my first few years I was brought up in Yorkshire by a primary school teacher mother from whom I learned to speak what the kinder members of the surrounding population called "nicely". After a couple of years in Monmouthshire, where I was disappointed not to hear, let alone have to learn, Welsh, we moved to Somerset. There, on the one hand, my RP accent was fine-tuned: "uz" became "us", and the stressed vowel of "basket" was lowered and lengthened, though "oxshn" never became "awkshn". On the other hand, however, my school's liberal linguistic policy was bidialectal: the majority who wanted could speak Zummerzet in the playground on condition that they used more or less standard English in the classroom.

This was good basic training for belonging to minorities later on: for a year, one of four native English speakers in a French town of 13,000 inhabitants; a boy from a country grammar school in a university still dominated by products of the English public schools; a foreigner in Germany for another year; a white man based for ten years in black Africa; and for the last twenty-four years an Englishman in an increasingly nationalist Scotland, where in an England v. Iran football match, it is the Saddamites who would be cheered. All this may not have completely eradicated from my subconscious the "patriotic prejudice" that "The English, the English, the English are best," (Flanders and Swann 1959) but it has permanently inoculated me against taking it seriously.

It is however my work as a translation consultant with the United Bible Societies, and in particular my colleagueship with Donald Kenrick, that have enabled me to become a participant observer, a guest, in a wide range of minority communities: especially Romani groups from Romania and Belarus to France and the United Kingdom (where the editor of this volume has given invaluable guidance in Romani English or Anglo-Romani), and from Finland and Sweden to Italy and Spain; but also with Kurds (that other, very different, nation without a homeland) in Turkey and Germany, Catalans in Spain, and Gaels in Scotland.

This has not been a one-man initiative, though it has sometimes felt like it: in addition to Donald's essential polyglot input, I pay tribute to the concern and support, in these and other minority languages, of the United Bible Societies and several of its member national Bible societies, and some other bodies, notably the Co-operative Baptist Fellowship. It is a matter of mixed pride and amusement that when Donald and I retired from our part-time involvement in Romani Scripture translation projects, our work load was distributed between ten other colleagues.

The title of this contribution is taken, not from the area of our Romani work, but from a lecture (to be published as one of the Warrack Lectures on Preaching) and a sermon delivered in October 1998 by my friend Donald Meek, Professor of Celtic in the University of Aberdeen. He was referring to two contrasting views of language, both espoused in different periods by the Scottish Society for the Propagation of Christian Knowledge (SSPCK) in its Gaelic work (Meek 1993: 701ff.). On the one hand is a functional, broadly Aristotelian, view of language as a means to the end of communication. This view is often asserted or presupposed by churches and Bible societies when they treat language in general as a means to the end of effective *proclamation* of Christianity. On the other hand is what one might call an ontological or Platonic view of a given language as, if not quite an end in itself, at least something of irreducible value, inseparable from the community of its speakers and their distinctive culture, and thus at all costs deserving *preservation*.

The functional view of language bears particularly hard on minority language communities when it asserts or implies that, if languages in general are no more than tools for communication, then *a fortiori* minority languages are likely to be inferior tools for that purpose.

"How, " I have often been asked, "can primitive, uneducated 'gipsies' translate the Bible?" One answer might run: "If I, like one Gypsy Bible translator I know, could speak Romanes, Romanian and Hungarian with equal fluency, and German and Russian too, I would not call myself primitive or uneducated." In any case, formal education is not to be equated with intelligence.

"But," questioners tend to continue, "these primitive languages have no words for biblical concepts like ... I dunno ... covenant, or propitiation." Leaving aside the question of how far these English terms effectively communicate to native English speakers the meaning of *berith* or *hilastérion*, it is true that speakers of minority languages frequently struggle to translate these and other, less 'technical', expressions in ways which their intended readers will understand.

The situation is often complicated by hesitation in choosing between an old, indigenous expression which only a diminishing number of older speakers still use, and a borrowed synonym which everyone understands. Brunn (1998: 430), in an article based on experience as a New Tribes Mission translation consultant in Papua New Guinea, concludes: "... the foreign origin of any given word does not necessarily mean that it should be rejected, but the archaic nature of a word almost always does". This may well mean that the 'indigenous' vocabulary is considerably diluted. Barbara Hyde (1999: 17) asserts "... it is estimated that only 8 per cent of vocabulary items in the modern [Albanian] language derives from the original Albanian roots." But to note this does not decide the debate in any particular case.

In the course of one such discussion with Romanian Kalderash translators about words for 'gift', it appeared that the borrowed item in common use was the Romanian *kado*, itself clearly borrowed from French. In such a case, functionalists would say without hesitation: if the borrowed word communicates the meaning better than the indigenous term, then the borrowed term must be used, because we are translating for today's speakers, not yesterday's. On this level, functionalists usually have the best of the argument. Yet one can appreciate the anxiety of minority language speakers who see each fresh borrowing as a new outpost of an invading power. It would be interesting, for example, to test the hypothesis of inverse correlation between the increasing number of English borrowings into Scots Gaelic and the declining number of speakers of the language.

The functionalist view is sometimes reinforced by pragmatic considerations. A self-supporting national Bible society may feel specially responsible for minorities within its own area (the Danish Bible Society's unfailing support of Greenlandic scriptures is an outstanding example) however, international bodies such as the United Bible Societies, and those of its member societies whose work it subsidises, may tend to give priority to large printings of whole Bibles in majority languages which will sell, rather than small editions of single Gospels in minority languages for free distribution. The proof of the pudding (the pragmatic argument concludes) is in the eating: if lots of people are buying lots of Bibles, then those Bibles must be communicating. The conclusion is grossly over-simplified, but it is not wholly false.

The ontological view tends towards identifying a language with its speakers. Almost by definition, a language creates the community of its speakers. Those in the Scottish Highlands and Islands who 'have the Gaelic' are closer to one another than to those who do not – however naturally and courteously the talk may shift to English

Donald Kenrick with Leulea Rouda, then joint General Secretary of the World Romani Congress (centre), and Mateo Maximoff, first Kalderash Romani translator of the Bible (left).

when a non-Gaelic speaker calls. The comparative smallness of a minority language community fosters the preservation and transmission of a rich, often largely oral literature. Anecdotes, even if recounted in a *lingua franca* such as English or French, tend to have their 'punchline' delivered first in the vernacular, then anticlimactically translated. Family relationships are remembered or explored as a means of identifying one's place in the community. I once went round a Gypsy site in Laval with the late, lamented Romani author and Bible translator Mateo Maximoff. Within a couple of minutes, in each trailer, he had identified the diverse origins of each family and his close or more distant links with them.

It follows that the decline of a language is felt as a threat to the community of its speakers; the death of a language is seen as a tragedy closely resembling the final extinction of an endangered species, the destruction of an irreplaceable part of the creation and the human heritage. In his sermon, "Christians and Minority Languages", referred to above, Donald Meek spoke movingly of the *Times* obituary, early in 1996, of

Red Thunder Cloud, "the last person to speak the tongue of the Catawba tribe" in Massachusetts. This sense of loss is no less if, as Anthony Grant has privately informed me, commentators have questioned the extent both of Red Thunder Cloud's Catawba ancestry and his command of the language.

It is thus almost inevitable that the life of any minority language community should find political expression, interacting with the politics of the major language community or communities in which it is set (c.f. Kenrick 1989a, for Romani). Examples of such interaction, too numerous to quote, vary from attempts by the majority (or by the government in power, which outside democracies may not be the same thing) to eliminate the minority language and even its speakers by force, to positive legal and/or constitutional action for the protection of linguistic minorities, backed by the provision of adequate educational and cultural resources (Stephens 1976; *Linguistic Minorities* 1986; Clark 1994; cf. Pozarell 1983). A negative attitude to minority languages usually presupposes a functional view of language, whereas the ontological view is often a factor in a more positive approach. The situation is, however, complicated by the fact that community of language, though often a factor making for political separation, is not always coterminous with nationality.

In an area where people's deepest feelings are engaged, simple solutions are likely to be illusory. Academic discussions about ontology versus functionality tend to be drowned out by acoustic 'noise' from a history of linguistic oppression. We may, however, venture to ask how closely religious attitudes to language may approach the functional or ontological positions which we have sketched.

At first sight, the prospects for any religious consensus on the matter seem dim. On the one hand, the Jewish and Muslim traditions appear strongly to presuppose an ontological view: the Torah is by definition the Hebrew Torah; the Quran is the Arabic Quran. On the other hand, Buddhist monks in Mongolia happily translate their Scriptures from Tibetan rather than from Sanskrit, since it was through Tibet that Buddhism came to them. Similarly, English-speaking Christians have no inhibitions about referring to their translations as "the Bible". "Here in Manchester," writes David Clines, "the Bible is in English. And you can prove it by walking into any W.H. Smith's. 'Do you have a copy of the Bible?', you ask, and quick as a flash comes the reply, 'I'm sorry, sir, but no; we have no actual Bibles here. All we have are translations.'" (Clines 1997: 9).

True, the Christian tradition is not monolithically functionalist. Through most of the Church's history, most Christians have virtually canonised a particular version of their Scriptures (the Septuagint in the east, the Vulgate in the west). This apparently ontological attitude has often been transferred to versions in other languages, such as the Church Slavonic or the Authorised or King James Version. Yet, at least since the Renaissance and the Reformation, the translation of the Bible into many hundreds of vernaculars has restored and extended a mainstream Christian tradition going back to the beginning. New Testament writers unhesitatingly quoted or adapted the Hebrew

Scriptures in Greek; most astonishing of all, they freely transmitted the teaching of Jesus in Greek, preserving only a handful of expressions in the original Aramaic (Meier 1991: 265-8; Müssies 1992: 202a).

There is absolutely no evidence that such practices were considered as interim measures, comparable to the SSPCK's transitional policy of providing Gaelic Scriptures until all Gaels could read English. The eastern Mediterranean was never going to learn a politically insignificant language like Aramaic. The trend was all the other way, towards the increasing use of Greek and even Latin in Palestine itself, not to mention the Jewish diaspora. There is, however, a clear distinction between the initial impulse to provide Scriptures in the *lingua vulgata* (Latin, Slavonic etc.), and the later use of such translations as instruments of cultural or ecclesiastical imperialism.

This area is a minefield of interreligious and interdenominational conflict. Our cautious steps in it so far have proceeded on the basis that the functional/Aristotelian and ontological/Platonic views of language are irreconcilable. Yet it is sometimes the case that conceptually contradictory elements somehow co-exist within human experience: for example, sex is functionally procreative, yet it is widely associated with values which transcend the procreative function to achieve ontological value. How far can such an analogy be applied to the faculty of language? Let us propose a few theses for examination.

1. Language is *at least* a means of communication (though not the only one). If it is not a means of communication, it is difficult to say what it is.
2. Language is one of the great distinctively *human* faculties. If one may speak of language in a non-human context, it is only in a strictly limited way, or by analogy. Conversely, human beings deprived of language are impaired in their humanity.
3. The gift or faculty of language is normally the possession of *one* language as one's mother tongue: natural bilinguals or polyglots (Steiner 1975: 115-8) are privileged exceptions – more frequent in minority than in majority language communities. The mother tongue normally remains the language most deeply embedded in the subconscious, the language in which one most commonly dreams or counts or prays, the 'language of the heart'.
4. For a *community*, its common language is correspondingly "the shrine of a people's soul" (Smith 1947). This is the essential motivation for the preservation of a language, especially the endangered language of a minority community.
5. Just as language itself is an essential but imperfect means of communication, so *translation* is an imperfect but possible and often necessary procedure, notably in the case of interlingual communities such as the Christian church. *Traduttore traditore* is a half-truth: translations offer hostages to fortune, but they do not have to hand over all the keys to the citadel. There is always some loss in translation, but it is rarely total. Indeed there may even be gain. "The 'German Shakespeare' is the envy of the English," writes Honolka (1978), "simply because *the English* are forced

to perpetuate the 350-year-old petrified language of genius on their Shakespearean stage, whereas *we* have the opportunity of recreating, from generation to generation, a new and modern Shakespeare whose language remains forever young" (cited in Salevsky 1998: 212f.).

6. Whether one considers the *purpose* of translation to be that of bringing the reader to the original text (a position more friendly to the ontological view) or of bringing the text to the reader of the translation (a position more friendly to the functionalist view), in practice it is difficult to push either method to the limit without breaking the link between reader and translation, thereby nullifying the whole enterprise. For example, the forthcoming revision of the French Segond Bible is moving in practice a considerable distance from its formal-correspondence point of departure; J. Krasovec (1998) records a generally converse tendency during the development of the 1997 Slavonic Bible.

7. The analogy may perhaps be pushed a little further. Things go wrong either when, in a sexual relationship, the functional (sex) and the ontological (love) become isolated from one another. Similarly, things go wrong when a living language is either suppressed, or conversely when it is imposed (for example in a liturgy) long after it has ceased to communicate.

8. The unkindest thing one can say to a member of an endangered language community is: "*In the long run* we are all dead" (Keynes 1923); yet it is true. All languages, minority and majority alike, will one day change out of recognition and disappear, together with their speakers, and ultimately the whole human race. Yet what matters most within a human perspective is our own, our community's, and our descendants' well-being. Within this perspective, our language is non-negotiable.

References

Brunn, D., 1998 "The 'Pure' Vernacular: Are we producing a translation that is understandable today?" *Practical Papers for the Bible Translator*, Vol. 49 (4) (October), pp. 425-30.

Clark, D.J., 1994 "The Impact of Christian Scriptures in Selected Minority Languages of Thailand: A Preliminary Investigation", in H. Pavlincová and D. Papousek (eds.), *The Bible in Cultural Context*. UBS, Brno, pp. 69-79.

Clark, D.J., 1997 "Minority Language Status and Attitudes towards Bible Translation". *Technical Papers for the Bible Translator*, 48.3 (July), pp. 336-45.

Clines, D.J.A., 1997 *The Bible in the Modern World*, Sheffield Academic Press, Sheffield.

Flanders, M. and Swann, D., 1959 "Song of Patriotic Prejudice", in *At the Drop of a Hat* and *At the Drop of another Hat* Recordings of a performance at the Fortune Theatre, London, EMI, Hayes, Mddx.

Honolka, K., 1978 *Opernübersetzungen. Zur Geschichte und Kritik der Verdeutschung musiktheatralischer Texte*, Henrichshofen, Wilhelmshaven.

Hyde, B., 1999 "Albanian" in *The Guardian Weekly*, 3 January.

Jenniges, W., 1997 2nd ed. *Select Bibliography on minority languages in the European Union*, European Bureau for Lesser Used Languages, Brussels (1st ed. 1993).

Keynes, J.M., 1923 *A Tract on Monetary Reform*, ch. 3., London, quoted in *The Oxford Dictionary of Quotations*, p.395.11.

Krasovec, J., 1998 "Conceptual Schemes and the Literary Unity of Biblical Texts". Unpublished paper delivered to a United Bible Societies Forum at Arnoldshain, Frankfurt am Main., August.

Linguistic Minorities Project, 1986 *Linguistic Minorities in Countries Belonging to the European Community*, Office for Official Publications of the European Communities, Luxembourg.

Meek, D.E.M., 1993 "Scottish SPCK", in N.M. de S. Cameron et al. (eds.), *Dictionary of Scottish Church History and Theology*, T. & T. Clark, Edinburgh.

Meek, D.E.M., 1998 *Sermon*, preached in King's College Chapel, Aberdeen, 16th October, on the occasion of the Warrack Lectures on "Preaching in the Scottish Highlands".

Meier, J.P., 1991 *A. Marginal Jew: Rethinking the Historical Jesus*, Vol.1, Doubleday, New York.

Müssies, J.,1992, "Languages (Greek)", in *Anchor Bible Dictionary*, Vol. 4, Doubleday, New York, pp. 195b-203b.

Salevsky, H., 1998, "Translation Criticism: A fictitious problem of Translation Science?", in H. Salevsky, *Über die Sprache hinaus. Beiträge zur Translationswissenschaft*, (Wissenschaft, Vol. 50.) TEXTconTEXT-Verlag 1Heidelberg, pp. 99-221.

Smith, E.W.,1947 (Revised edition) *The Shrine of a People's Soul*, Friendship Press, New York (originally 1929 Livingstone Press, London).

Steiner, G., 1975 *After Babel*, Oxford University Press, London.

Stephens, M., 1976 *Linguistic Minorities in Western Europe* Gomer, Llandysul.

CHAPTER FOUR

THE CELTIC LANGUAGES IN THE TWENTY-FIRST CENTURY:
A PARTISAN REVIEW

Anthony P. Grant

I SHALL BEGIN this tribute to a thoughtful observer and scholar of Celtic languages by being brutally frank. If present population trends continue, and there is no reason to believe they will not, the future of the Celtic languages, already spoken almost exclusively by bilinguals, is almost unremittingly bleak. Excepting Welsh and possibly Breton, no Celtic language is likely to survive the twenty-first century with a body of speakers large enough to ensure its continuation. Goidelic will become the first middle-range genetic grouping in Europe to become extinct since East Germanic did so about 1800 with the death of Crimean Gothic. If we restrict ourselves to a discussion of language shift among first language speakers, then we can be pretty sure that Gaeltacht Irish will be the first to go, despite the role of the Irish as a symbol of national identity and a compulsory school subject, with Scottish Gaelic lingering in the smaller of the Western Isles for maybe a generation more. Cornish and Manx have already gone, though versions of them are being revived with some degree of success.

This is in spite of efforts by Celtic language enthusiasts, both 'insiders' such as native speakers of these languages, and more outside participants, including authors of pedagogical works such as the honoree of this collection, to try to engender interest and ability in these languages on the part of people who either speak them but don't overmuch care about them, or who did not learn them but who feel that they should do. Kenrick himself (1983c: 254) has warned against official over-estimation of the strength of Irish. The bitter irony is that these languages have speaker bases crumbling just when our understanding of the mechanics of language shift and preservation has never been more acute.

Indeed many of the factors which bedevilled the paths of these languages have been tardily mitigated or removed in the course of this century. Irish rose from being neglected by British authorities to being an official, if relatively little-used, language of a progressive Western European nation. Welsh and English co-occur on many symbols of officialdom, and even if Welsh is not co-official with English, it is certainly not despised and its speakers abused as much as it was a century ago. The official role of

Gaelic in Scotland is much less public than that of Welsh in Wales, but it can claim in parts of the Western Isles and Skye a higher proportion of native speakers than Welsh has anywhere, even in Gwynedd. Even Breton has risen in public estimation over the past fifty years, from the passing of the tepid measures of the *Loi Deixonne* in 1951 to the presence of numerous Breton-language sites on the Internet.

In addition, while Celtic languages are regarded as socially acceptable in a way which would have astounded the great-grandfathers of the present bodies of speakers, they are also coming to be more readily accepted as parts of a valid lifestyle by younger people, especially (but not only) those who exhibit a stronger traditional attachment to their home communities. As younger speakers now will be the older speakers of tomorrow, and since they may have children who will acquire these languages, this is especially significant.

The increased role of Celtic languages in domains of interest to younger people can be illustrated by a couple of examples from current popular music. The popularity of the Skye-based rock group Runrig in Scotland, who generally included some Gaelic material in their shows, was signalled by the 300,000 people who stood to listen to them in Princes Street, Edinburgh on New Year's Eve 1996. Their 1995 philosophical ballad 'An Ubhal as Airde/The Highest Apple' is still the only Celtic-language song to make the Top Twenty in the UK, and at their dissolution a couple of years ago it remained their biggest chart success, though how much this is a result of the fact that it was used in a beer commercial has not been gauged. Those who are looking for something more hard-edged might have been more attracted by the Welsh band Catatonia, whose album *International Velvet* was one of the best-selling rock albums of 1998. Its title track is entirely in Welsh except for a refrain in English about the blessings of being Welsh! However, Catatonia's nationwide singles chart successes have been entirely in English.

The prominence of Celtic languages in the media is naturally on a strictly regional level: few outside the Principality would want to watch s4c, for example, though some Welsh-language programmes have been successful formats when rendered into English (the children's programme *Superted* being the shining example). For the most part, Celtic-language TV programmes at least in Great Britain tend to be adaptations of English-language ones, or else are very much audience-specific.

This was certainly the case with my personal longitudinal research into the domains of Gaelic-language TV in northern Scotland. Three kinds of programmes accounted for the 450 minutes of Gaelic-language programming that one could see on an average week across three channels in Scotland in 1998 (the week beginning October 31 1998 was taken as a sample; Channels 4 and 5 presented no such programmes during the period of investigation). Local news programmes, including weekly news round-ups, accounted for 80 minutes, children's programmes (both original, such as *Dê-a-Nis?*, 'What Now?', and translated ones) for 200 minutes. This included an excellent children's activity competition programme, *Cleas* ('Skill'), in which teams from Scotland and Ireland – all speaking their variety of Gaelic – competed each week. Documentaries, on such diverse subjects as Scottish towns, the isle of Eriskay and the history of Celtic boxers, accounted on average for 30 minutes, and Britain's best (because least sensationalist) soap-opera, *Machair*, for 35 minutes. There were also occasional religious, sporting and other programmes in the schedule from week to week, including a fine series for learners of Gaelic, *Talking our Language*, which was screened in weekday afternoons, at an almost optimally bad time for catching potential viewers (not surprisingly, learners' programmes have long been a key component of Gaelic-language programming, both on radio and on TV). Original programmes were subtitled, translated ones generally not so. Sixty minutes of Gaelic broadcasting was on BBC2, 125 on BBC1 and 285 minutes were on Grampian TV.

While it is a good sign that there is some demand for TV programmes in Gaelic and Welsh (though the output is only a fraction of what it could be, especially now that non-terrestrial stations play such a part in TV media), it is unwise to be too sanguine about the chances of survival of these languages, simply because they are used in the most popular form of broadcasting and communication, and this is not only true in Wales and Scotland. It is true, for example, that the undated survey reported in Ó Murchú (1985) indicated that 70 per cent of Irish people occasionally watched an Irish-language TV programme and that 73 per cent believed that the revival of Irish was something that no real Irish person could object to, but these sentiments have not been translated into the reversal of language shift. In any case, many of my students at the University of St Andrews knew the lyrics to the Gaelic version of *Postman Pat*, without understanding them. All this indicates is that they watched a lot of TV in the afternoons.

I spoke earlier about lifestyle choices among users of Celtic languages. I think that it is fatal not to factor considerations of such choices into our prognostications for Celtic languages. People living on the cusp of the twenty-first century have a much wider range of choices than were available a century ago, and a much greater degree of opportunity to exercise these choices. Ever fewer people are now compelled to spend their lives on a croft or in a fishing village, living on herring and potatoes while the rain comes tumbling down. In the 1930s the Irish satirist (and Irish-speaker) Flann O'Brien used to point out in the *Cruiskeen Lawn* columns in the *Irish Times* that the choice that the Irish Government faced in funding either 'Gaelic or slums', but not both, was a false one. Unlike Gerry Adams, O'Brien knew where the bodies were buried: he was able to play linguistically with Irish very skilfully, and to ridicule the prejudices of people, especially Dubliners, who regarded Irish as what he called "bogman's backchat". Indeed the livelihoods of people living in the linguistic archipelago of the *Gaeltachtaí* have improved immensely since the 1930s, though attempts to create a Leinster Gaeltacht in Meath proved less durable. In this context the introduction of the *deontas* paid to parents of children speaking Irish in traditionally Irish-speaking areas, and the chance thereby of their acquiring home improvement and other grants, are wise and eminently sensible moves on Dublin's part.

Many of the social, educational and financial pressures which conspired against parents who would have liked to pass on their Celtic language to their children have been lifted, especially in Ireland. At the same time there has been a heightening of awareness of what the components of a national identity are, and a greater understanding of how everyone selects for themselves the components which go to form their personal and other identities. And one component which has been selected less and less is that of a distinctive language. It is much easier to wear a kilt, bezant badge or balaclava, to play the bagpipes, to bake soda bread, or to practise a certain form of dancing, than to learn a new language. More and more the use of these languages among self-consciously Celtic people (and these are middle-class rather than the overwhelmingly working-class people who actually speak Celtic languages in everyday life) is becoming emblematic rather than natural.

Jones (1998) has shown this for Breton, but this is especially the case with Cornish (or Cornic: Price 1984 and after) and Manx, the 'revived' languages whose native speakers, such as they are, are now only a handful of pre-teen children, raised with the help of playgroups such as the Cornish-language *Dalleth* ('Forward'), who also know English. Anthropologist Sue Lewis of the University of St Andrews is currently examining the construction of Manx identity, and the role of the Manx language in the formation of this identity. It appears from her research (personal communication, May 1998) that one does not have to 'have' Manx to feel truly Manx; it's all right if you simply know that someone somewhere is taking care of that side of things, and as long as there is someone around who has acquired Manx, that will satisfy the needs of many who wish to proclaim their Manx identity but who don't get beyond the usual handful of words and phrases.

Much the same can be said of Cornish, although given the spread of Cornish-language classes (decreasing in number since the heyday of the 1970s), and the occurrence of such classes elsewhere in the south of England and even in Australia, the demographic profile of the learners of the language is somewhat atypical of the inhabitants of Kernow itself. One wonders how many manual labourers or 'giro technicians' are bringing up their children to speak Cornish, and what the March 1999 attempts to have Cornish recognised by the EU bodies for Lesser-Used Languages will really amount to. But then the learning of languages outside formal schooling has always been a typically middle-class pursuit in Britain, as Celtic-language enthusiasts have observed to me, and as MacDonald (1986) graphically illustrated for Brittany and by implication for parts of Britain as well. A friend of mine, not herself a Cornish-speaker, though married to a Cornishman, once told me that she identified a 'mystery language' on a quiz show as being Cornish because the person speaking it sounded like a stockbroker's wife.

The revived languages present a host of problems of their own, and this is especially true of Cornish. There is no figure in the history of Manx comparable to that of

Robert Morton Nance (bardic name *Mordon*) in the history of Revived Cornish. Given Nance's rather ill-informed approach to Revived Cornish phonology and morphology, this may be no insurmountable handicap. In any case, Manx's chances of revival are infinitely better than those of Cornish, even though this is moot since Manx will never be revived as the first language of a community which identifies itself as ethnically Manx. Cornish was extinct for all practical purposes by 1780, while Manx survived into the 1970s or later, if one regards the Manx of the late Ewan Christian as being authentic Late Spoken Manx as acquired in early childhood (see Broderick 1984-6; it is insufficiently appreciated that Ned Maddrell, 1877-1974, the so-called last speaker of Manx, actually learned English first and acquired Manx as a young child from his monoglot aunt, Mrs Margaret Taubman or *Paaie Humman*: see the text that he gave in Jackson 1955). Our records of written Manx, produced when the language had thousands of speakers and a living, if not very vigorous, written tradition, are at least ten times as extensive as those for Cornish, and include the whole Bible and several books of the Apocrypha, bilingual Manx-English dictionaries, the Book of Common Prayer and an abridgment of *Paradise Lost*, in addition to original works such as legal pronouncements, a cookbook, volumes of reminiscences, songs and tales, and other genres which Cornish never had. They also include cylinder and tape-recorded material, although the dearth of teeth and rapidity of speech of many of the last speakers often make these hard to understand.

Putting the matter simply, we know infinitely more about every aspect of Manx than we will ever know about Cornish, even though we had no records of Manx until the seventeenth century, by which time Cornish was already in terminal decline. One of the things which mitigate against more people learning Manx, or against them getting very far with it, is the orthography, which resembles a linguistic correlate of what Philip Larkin said about parental influences in the poem which had him disbarred from any chance of the Laureate. Manx spelling has all the faults of English spelling and quite a number, such as *c-cedilla*, or dental consonants followed by 'h', which are *sui generis*. There are also some discrepancies between the pronunciation of Manx as used by its last speakers, and as dutifully recorded in Jackson 1955, and the way in which it is generally pronounced by learners nowadays, for example the realisations of the vowel written *aa* in traditional Manx orthography. Furthermore Mannin is a semi-independent state and a haven for off-shore bankers, whereas Cornwall is *de facto* simply the West Virginia of the English counties. The only thing which Cornwall has above the Isle of Man is touristic glamour in the form of surfing and palm trees. Mannin has the political power to bring about a change in official attitudes to Manx in a way of which Cornish people can only dream.

In addition there is the issue of exactly which variety of Cornish to revive. Price (1998) is an important recent paper on this, while the matter has also been discussed in Grant (1998). Any form of Cornish which is intended to be revived as a spoken language will have to be based either on Middle Cornish (c. 1250-1504), which has a greater number of texts with some literary merit, or on Late Cornish (1504 onwards), which is better attested in terms of the actual number of words (both types and tokens) which have come down to us. It is documented in the only roughly contemporary account of phonetics and grammar which we have for Cornish (namely Edward Lhuyd's *Archaeologia Britannica* of 1707), but which shows greater influence of English on morphosyntax and lexicon. (Old Cornish, attested from the tenth to the thirteenth centuries, is simply too scantily attested for consideration in this context.) Nance's work was based on Middle Cornish, though Henry Jenner, the founder of the Cornish revivalist movement, preferred Late Cornish, which indeed is the form he discussed in Jenner (1904).

A great deal of heat and remarkably little light has been generated by the debates about spelling and structure in Cornish which have long been a feature of the revivalist movement but which have proliferated since 1985, quite often in a tone of personal animosity. As Price (1998) points out, Richard Gendall, the chief proponent of Late Cornish as the mainstay of a revived Cornish, has stayed aloof from this infighting, and that in itself is in my opinion another commendation for Late Cornish. The Revived forms of these languages should be kept separate from our knowledge of the actually attested forms of Middle and Late Cornish, to which professional Celticists will refer. This distinction, especially in the case of Middle Cornish, is crucial but often blurred.

The proliferation of varieties can lead to confusion. A recent pan-Celtic phrasebook (Gunn 1993) provides words and phrases in Breton, Irish, Gaelic, Manx, Welsh and no less than three kinds of Cornish: Nance's 'Unified Cornish' (or as it is sometimes slyly known, *Mordonnek*), the modified form of this, known as *Kernewek Kemmyn* ('Common Cornish'), put forward in the mid-1980s by Dr Ken George, and the revived Late Cornish favoured by Richard Gendall and his supporters. Reading the forms of the phrases in these three varieties, quite often one could imagine one were looking at three divergent dialects of a language which might have been unified a millennium ago. The other pan-Celtic phrasebook (Knox 1997) solves this dilemma by simply omitting Manx and Cornish and concentrating on living languages. The approach to Cornish in Gunn's phrasebook is quite an effort to make for a language whose fluent speakers in all varieties do not number above a few hundred) but it does not do so for Breton, where the *KLT* form, characteristic of the three bishoprics of Cornouaille, Léon and Tréguier, is taken as standard, but where there is still a salient number of speakers of the more gallicised south-eastern variety *Gwenedeg* or Vannetais (to say nothing of the oft-forgotten *Goelo* in the north-east). Given that there are probably as many people with an active or passive command of Gewnedeg, which is only partially intelligible to speakers of KLT, as there are native speakers of Irish, Scottish Gaelic, Cornish and Manx put together, this is a surprising omission.

Such problems do not arise with processes of standardisation in Manx, where hardline purism and linguistic ethnic cleansing have been less active, and where the debates between people who wish to borrow fairly freely from English in order to fill lexical gaps, and those who wish to rely on coinages from Irish models, are less virulent than they have been in Cornwall. Here too the matter is much less pressing since far more of the traditional Manx vocabulary has been recorded. Here the form taken as the source for revival is that of 'Classical Manx' of the Bible translation and the bulk of original writings, that is, the nineteenth century, with some acknowledgment of the role of recordings of spoken Manx in our understanding of how the language was pronounced.

It should be mentioned that there is considerable diatopic variation with the other spoken Celtic languages. In the case of Welsh, for instance, there is a High-Low diglossia between a literary form of what is essentially Biblical Welsh on the one hand, and spoken north-western, north-eastern, south-western and south-eastern varieties on the other, though a koineised form of the spoken language is becoming commoner in print. As far as Scottish Gaelic is concerned, the chief dialectal distinction is that of the core versus the periphery. Most Gaelic-speaking areas use dialects which differ considerably from that of the island of Lewis in regard to morphosyntax, phonology (including the absence of a typical 'sing-song' intonation which marks off Lewis Gaelic-speakers to the amusement of others) and lexicon. Nevertheless, Lewis Gaelic is the variety with the single greatest number of speakers; it is essentially the form used in the modern version of the Bible, and also in BBC and Grampian TV broadcasting from Stornoway (which itself has been anglophone since the 1920s). Consequently, Lewis Gaelic is in an advantageous position over other varieties, and is taken as a de facto standard of sorts.

The fact or prospect of political independence, which I mentioned earlier in regard to Mannin, highlights the contributions which ideologies, both political and scholastic, have made to the debate. They have not been enlightening, although when reading *engagé* literature it may be hard to discern this. It is rare to come across an author who can state things as they are in an objective way. Maryon MacDonald wrote several works, including an article in a leading anthropological journal (MacDonald 1986) dealing with the rise of the Breton militant movement, its construction of Celtia and Celtic and Breton identity, and its implacably hostile attitude towards French (which in many cases was these militants' mother-tongue). She was pretty much boiled in academic oil for her heretical pains and for being politically incorrect *avant la lettre*, as the critiques of her article (Cohen et al., 1986) indicate. To the best of my knowledge, incidentally, none of her critics have or had any competence in a Celtic language – unlike MacDonald herself, who was a learner of Breton with parents who knew Irish and Welsh. Durkacz (1995) is also well-informed and free from polemic.

Edwards (1984), a keen observer of and participant in the Irish scene though himself born in Southampton, is similarly candid about the relations between Irish and English in Ireland; his remarks offended a lot of the *bien-pensants* but his claims were valid nonetheless. His work is important because it focuses upon the role of a beleaguered Celtic language in the one modern nation-state where such a language has been elevated to official status, despite the fact that at no time in the history of an independent Ireland has Irish been the native language of a majority of the population.

This is not the place to delve deeply into the multiple ironies of Irish history, a history often described in terms of dichotomies which never reflected the realities of cultural, political, religious and linguistic *bricolage*. The history of English assaults upon Irish in Ireland began with the Statutes of Kilkenny in 1366, about a century after the warring factions in the country had been united for the first time by the English Crown for greater ease of administration. This reversal came nine centuries after the Irish had begun what Ó Fiaich (1972: 72) might have called 'the Irish regime'. In the course of these they invaded Scotland and accessible parts of northern England, Wales and Cornwall, establishing a brief-lasting dynasty in south Wales, conquering most of what is now Scotland and in time ensuring the extirpation (by replacement with Goidelic) of Cumbric, Pictish Celtic and the mysterious Pictish, and many pockets of Norse, these last both from the north and from the Isle of Man. Both Celtic and non-Celtic languages in Britain were replaced by Goidelic, just as it had replaced Ivernic and whatever else might have been spoken in Ireland, and just as Celtic languages had eaten away at the territory of Raetic, Lusitanian, Iberian and other languages in Europe in the last millennium BC.

Events in the thirteenth and fourteenth centuries set the seal for some severe changes. It is pretty certain, as Edwards (1984: 281) points out, that Irish was on the slope to irreversible decline by the early seventeenth century, the era of the first Irish Bible and early printings in Irish (for Protestant consumption). But massive Protestant emigration to Ireland was by no means synonymous with a shift to English. Here, as elsewhere in Celtia (for example, in Cardiganshire and the Scottish Highlands at different times), numbers of immigrant people shifted to Celtic languages which they heard spoken all around them, while many planters, of Ayrshire stock, spoke Gaelic natively and often knew no English. The decisive factor in language shift in the monoglot heartlands of western Ireland was the Great Hunger of the 1840s, which brought untold misery to the undiversified agriculture of rural Ireland in the face of apathy from the British Government, and which almost devastated the Scottish Highlands too. After that, in practical terms everything was up for the Irish language, and it is remarkable that so much of a speech-community, and so much interest in the language, has survived.

That it did so is very largely thanks to those imperialist bugbears of Irish national ideology, the middle-class anglophone Protestants, including Marxists such as Douglas Hyde, who were instrumental in forming the Gaelic League in 1893. They did much to try to solve the problems of standardisation caused by dialectal fragmentation of Irish and the loss of its unified literary language since the seventeenth century. The crafting of a national ideology regarding the Irish language since the formation of the Gaelic League has been a fascinating exercise in the manipulation of facts. This is true also of the facts of Irish independence, which are somewhat different from those which are apprehended by, say, Irish-Americans in Boston. Put simply, without the efforts of mostly Irish-born Protestants of English stock (and at least during the time of the 1795 Rebellion, also those of Scottish descent: most of the men and women hanged for 'the wearing of the green' were Protestants), an independent Ireland would not now exist, while the Irish language would be extinct, with little interest in reviving it for any but symbolic purposes. Irish would have become what Manx is today. (The existence of an independent Irish state, free from the imperialist yoke, owes much to the efforts of half-English activists such as Michael Collins and Padraig Pearse, and to the Spanish-American Eamon de Valera.)

The quiet redefinition of Eire on monocultural ethnic lines, and the reinstatement of Irish as an key marker of Irish ethnicity and identity, have been largely accomplished by the Catholic Church in Ireland. It was this self-same body which had supported the use of English over Irish in schools, which favoured the founding of Maynooth College as a place where trainees could receive a seminarian education in *English* (principally in reaction because the Church of Ireland had resumed its use of Irish for missionising purposes among the Catholic poor) and whose secular patron Daniel O'Connell was so dismissive of his native language. The main contributions of the Catholic Church to the fostering of Irish came after independence. Their tenor can be seen in the pedagogically bizarre pronouncements of the Jesuit Professor T. Corcoran, (cited in Edwards 1984: 283-4). However, one should not forget the efforts of the zealously anti-British Christian Brothers, whose devotion to the Irish language resulted in textbooks and efforts to instil Irish into young minds with a pedagogy inspired by rum, the lash and sodomy. These succeeded in putting many off Irish, and much else besides, for life. At the same time the role of the Catholic Church as the one true constant upholder of Irish identity and as defender of Irish as an encapsulation of that identity, was consistently reinforced in the popular Irish press.

The corollary of this was that interest in Irish, which had once been quite strong among Northern Irish Protestants, was reduced considerably (Blaney 1993 gives a good account of Presbyterian interaction with Irish, including details of Presbyterian ministers in Ulster who speak Irish). All this has been exacerbated by the appropriation of Irish as a symbolic medium by republican terrorist groups, few of whose members or supporters seem actually to be fluent in the language, though Irish (and Lallans) seem to be enjoying revivals among Ulster Protestants at present. Between them the Catholic Church, (my own church, which betrayed its own congregants time and time again, and which stood so much for the British status quo and against the use of Irish for centuries), and the monolithic monocultural state ideology emanating from Dublin have almost managed to politicise Irish out of existence.

Meanwhile, the standardisation of Irish is still not complete. Despite the vagaries of the Irish spelling system, such a dictionary as Mac Mathúna and Ó Corráin (1995) provides no phonetic transcription to help a learner of Irish in pronouncing a word. Pronunciation has not been standardised; the three main varieties of Ulster, Connacht and Munster Irish remain, and would-be speakers have to learn one of these or else opt for what is sometimes called 'Dublin Irish' (*sic*: the language was extinct in Dublin City by the eighteenth century) which is that propagated by the school system, especially in Leinster, and which pleases nobody much, as comments reported in Hindley (1990) indicate. One hapless reviewer of this dictionary (Anon. 1998) may have thought that Cois Fhairrge was in Kerry when it is in Galway, but the suggestion that Cois Fhairrge pronunciation be adopted as a stop-gap is not a bad one, since this is what is used by Ó Siadhail (1986: 233–4), who points out that several spellings used therein are dialectal and not actually standardised.

On the whole, the results of compulsory Irish in Irish schools have not been particularly promising. Little reversal of language shift has taken place, and while the number of people who can converse in Irish has certainly grown, the number of people who wish to speak only Irish and who wish to bring up their children speaking Irish has not done so. This is largely because even in those schools where Irish was the medium of instruction, what was taught often bore little resemblance to what was actually spoken in the nearest Gaeltacht. A friend told me some years ago that at school after several years of Irish-language instruction he was sent to Dingle in Kerry and quickly found that he simply could not understand the Irish spoken natively in this Gaeltacht area nearest to his Tipperary home. School Irish and 'real Irish' were not the same.

But there are exceptions. The perpetuation of what is essentially School Irish, reinforced with contact with speakers of native Irish in the Gaeltacht, has been described for the Shaw's Road community in West Belfast in an illuminating study by Maguire (1991). This community bought up several properties in the same area in an attempt to found an Irish-language community, and Maguire carefully describes the history of this attempt, while profiling the type of Irish used by children who were born into this community and who were raised speaking Irish. This latter study is one of the most valuable parts of the book, and it shows the impact of Gaeltacht Irish, and also English, on their Irish *parole*.

Such influence is not unparalleled: I have been informed by recent observers of children who have learned their Welsh through immersion in Welsh-medium kindergartens and schools that their variety of Welsh exhibits more English loans, a reduction in the rules for use of the mutations and for the formation of different types of plurals. Indeed, I heard such Welsh in Cerrigydrudion, Gwynedd in 1988. The resulting Welsh is much simpler in structure than the spoken Welsh around them. However, this variety has managed to gain some prestige among the grandparents of these young speakers, simply because it is school-sanctioned Welsh, while their own Welsh dates from a time when the language was frowned upon in school (which is why they spoke to their children, the young speakers' parents, in English).

To Celtic nationalists imbued with linguistic purism this very claim is, of course, heretical. MacDonald (1986) cogently describes the way in which such revivalists railed against imagined English or French 'corruptions' in their Celtic languages. That *all* languages borrow features from others, especially from prestigious languages, that Breton would have no nasalised vowels and Welsh no words for 'fish', 'milk' or 'to rub' were it not for the influence of such languages of prestige as French, English and (often forgotten) Latin, are points one is not permitted to discuss in front of a language ideologue.

It is also easy to move a further step, to translate these puristic discourses into other spheres of existence and to ask "Who are the real Celts/Irish/Welsh?" and by extension, "Who *aren't* genuine Celts?". Henry Jenner did so (Jenner 1904), portraying English Midlanders as barely human, and he was not the last. Celtic nationalism, pan-Celticism and Fascism have too frequently been cosy bedfellows this century; too often claims by Celtic nationalists of a lack of agency have been used as pretexts for random bloodletting. Such xenophobia by many towards potential speakers of every background explains why the Celtic languages are still dying.

For it is a fact that speakers of what one might call 'The New Celtic languages', learned often early but as second languages by people whose parents spoke English, French or other languages, will play an ever bigger part in the future of Celtic languages. The future of *Gaeilge* lies with the despised School Irish of the 'jackeens', not with local native varieties. Most speakers of Irish and many of Breton are learners; all speakers of Cornish or Manx learned the language from other learners, and quite a few people now writing in Welsh or Gaelic (such as George Campbell Hay in the latter) learned them as second languages.

Celtic languages are spoken in areas which have not been monocultural for generations and which have never been so blessed with diversity. And unless there is any chance for immigrants – and this includes English- and French-speakers as much as Corfiotes in Gwynedd, Somalis in Butetown, Bambaras in Morlaix, Cantonese in Penwith, Urdu-speakers in Lewis and Bengali shopkeepers in Mayo – to be encouraged to learn and use these and to be accounted equal with other users of Celtic languages, there is no meaningful future for Celtic languages or for Celtia.

Acknowledgments

I would like to thank Ellis Bacon, Tom Cleary, Dick Gendall, Mils Hills, Laura Hills, Reg Hindley, Phil Kelly, Neil Kennedy, Sue Lewis, Russell Murray, Lornadh Nic Uilleim, Philip Payton, Ian Press, Glanville Price, Brian Stowell, Johann Unger and our honoree Donald Kenrick for their assistance in the preparation of this paper. None of them necessarily agrees with for the views expressed, which unless otherwise stated are entirely my own.

References

Anonymous, 1998 "Review of Mac Mathúna and Ó Corráin 1995" *Forum for Modern Language Studies* XXXIV, p.289.

Blaney, Joseph, 1993 *The Presbyterians and Irish*, Private, Belfast.

Broderick, George, 1984-6 *A Handbook of Late Spoken Manx*, 3 Vols. Niemeyer, Tubingen.

Cohen, Anthony P., Frankenberg, Ronald J., Grillo, Ralph D., San Roman, Teresa, Shokheid, Moshe, and Weingrod, Alex, 1986 "Responses to Maryon MacDonald" *Current Anthropology* 27: 341-4.

Durkacz, Victor Edward, 1995 *The Decline of the Celtic Languages*, John Donald, Edinburgh.

Edwards, John, 1984 "Irish and English in Ireland" in Peter Trudgill ed. *Language in the British Isles*, Cambridge University Press, Cambridge, 480-99.

Grant, Anthony, 1998 "Defending Kernewek Kemmyn" in Payton (ed.), 1998, pp. 194-9.

Gunn, Marion, 1993 *Da mihi manum* Everson Gunn Partners, Dublin.

Hindley, Reg., 1990 *The Death of the Irish Language: a Qualified Obituary* Routledge, London.

Jackson, Kenneth, 1955 *Contributions to the Study of Manx Phonology*, Nelson, Edinburgh.

Jenner, Henry, 1904 *Handbook of the Cornish Language* Nutt, London.

Jones, Mari C., 1998 "Death of a Language, Birth of an Identity: Brittany and the Bretons" *Language Problems and Language Planning* 22 (2): 129-42.

Knox, William, 1997 *The Pan-Celtic Phrasebook* Y Lolfa, Talybont.

MacDonald, Maryon, 1986 "Celtic Ethnic Kinship and the Problem of being English" *Current Anthropology* 27: 333-47.

Mac Mathúna, Séamus and Ailbhe Ó Corráin, 1995 *Collins Gem Irish Dictionary* Harper Collins, London.

Maguire, Gabrielle, 1991 *Our Own Language: an Irish Initiative* Multilingual Matters, Clevedon.

Ó Fiaich, Tomás' 1972 "The Great Controversy" in Seán Ó Tuama, ed. *The Gaelic League Idea*, Mercier, Cork, pp. 61-73.

Ó Murchú, Máirtin, 1985 *The Irish Language*, Government of Ireland. (Aspects of Ireland 10), Dublin.

O Siadhail, Mícheál, 1988 *Learning Irish*, Yale University Press, Yale.

Payton, Philip (ed.), 1998, *Cornish Studies – Six*, University of Exeter Press and Institute of Cornish Studies, Exeter.

Price, Glanville, 1984 *The Languages of Britain*, Edward Arnold, London.

Price, Glanville, 1998 "Modern Cornish in Context." in Payton (ed.), 1998, 187-93.

CHAPTER FIVE

ANTI-GYPSYISM RESEARCH:
THE CREATION OF A NEW FIELD OF STUDY

Herbert Heuss

"*Anti-gypsyism is not a new phenomenon,*" remarks Kenrick (1998b: 56). Any theoretical charting of its history, however, requires an analysis of how the strengths of Romani culture expose and provoke the pathologies of European culture; that is, a recognition that if we are ever going to transform 'swords into ploughshares', we are going to need smiths. The Roma are one of the very few linked constellations of ethnic groups who have gained definition as a people or Volk, without going on to build a nation-state. They might, in the sense that Christoph Türcke (1992: 137) speaks of a Jewish "culture of expectancy", be said to have a culture of 'wait and see', a culture which has given them the strength to survive centuries of migrations and persecution.

Our present-day society, enlightened as it is, has a technological capacity which carries with it a full set of options for self-destruction. The culture that maintains this capacity requires the imposition of industrial-strength discipline. A comprehensive governmental system, usually in the form of the nation-state, has to be built, and once in place its rules have to be enforced, again and again, in an exemplary fashion.

So, day by day, humanity works to strengthen the structures of its own repression, and fails to make use of the possibilities that our productive capacity offers us to reduce poverty, or to overcome hunger and disease. Our niggling awareness of this failure, whether conscious or subconscious, may be the reason why we ostracise those who are not complicit in the modern state, whether because they are marginalised or because they remain deliberately independent in their cultural and social organisation.

The 'Gypsy' life imagined by the majority of people is a constant reminder to them that their chosen lifestyle of profit maximisation is not the purpose of life as such, that things don't have to be that way. The 'Gypsies' are seen as persisting in a state of nature, some atavistic mixture of resignation, lethargy, sensitivity and mobility. To let children be brought up in such a way is such a transgression of the post-Enlightenment requirement for people to be educated above the state of nature, that both the Gypsy culture and those who bear it have to be anathematised.

And yet, at the same time, the 'Gypsies' also represent an idealised state of nature, the Arcadian shepherd's lifestyle of the Romantics. And finally, as a possible third way, the socialisation practices of the Sinti and Roma, with their 'wait and see' culture, may indicate 'new', (but actually old) escape routes from a work-oriented society which is slowly driving itself insane, routes that had dropped out of sight in our post-modern society. It is from the coming together of these three self-contradictory imaginations that anti-Gypsyism draws its explosive force. The complex structure of the image of the Gypsy as a threat to society is a key component within our general picture of the stranger as an enemy.

Anti-Gypsyism designates a construct which hypothetically assigns social phenomena (mostly of an undesirable nature) to the minority group who call themselves the Roma. A causal relationship is posited between these phenomena and their presumed cause – the "Gypsies". This presumptive causal relationship is so firmly anchored that it can neither be changed nor nullified by any empirical evidence. Such explanations derived from the long term social construction of reality then give rise to bigotry and prejudice of extreme intransigence.

In this paper, the term "Gypsy" is used either where it is a reference to sources or where the image of "Gypsies" fabricated by the majority and its institutions is meant. The term "Roma" is used to denote the actual members of the minority concerned.

In their seminal work on the persecution of Roma under the Nazis, Donald Kenrick and Grattan Puxon (1972) documented the long history of anti-Gypsy images and their function in the process of persecution. In the same way as anti-Semitism, anti-Gypsyism constitutes a template justifying the persecution of minorities, and thus explains the resemblances in the history of Roma and Jews (Kenrick 1986). This paper is an attempt to trace the function of these images and the functional transformations they have undergone.

We cannot address the concept of anti-Gypsyism without considering its most extreme form, the extermination of Roma under the Nazi regime, without putting Auschwitz at the centre of our contemplation. Dlugoborski's (1998) bibliography shows that there has in recent years been an increase in the number of works detailing the genocide practised on Europe's Roma, and the question of "How could this happen?" has been supplemented by the question of "Why?" The answer still eludes us. The explanation that the Roma were persecuted for racist reasons is not satisfactory because it is, so to speak, self-referring, or circular.

The explanation must be sought in terms of socio-historical theory which will show what function the persecution and extermination of the Roma minority played for the maintenance of Nazi domination (domination in the sense that Max Weber uses the word "Herrschaft"). It was not, after all, the case that Roma were numerous enough to be physically threatening. We cannot, of course, complete such a theoretical exercise within the confines of this paper, but we can use the existing literature to lay a foundation for identifying the important questions for future researches into anti-Gypsyism. This work started in 1998, the year which saw the formation in Germany of the 'Gesellschaft für Antiziganismusforschung' (Society for Anti-Gypsyism Research), which is systematically investigating the phenomenon of antipathy to Gypsies.

Power and the search for a solution to the 'Gypsy Problem'

There is a manifest continuity in anti-Gypsyist ideas, their images and their motives, which have appeared with perennial consistency ever since the Roma impinged on German and European history. Since at least the middle of the eighteenth century, one can follow the tracks of anti-Gypsyism from the Enlightenment to the Nazi genocide: the Enlightenment's wish to "improve" Gypsies was always aimed at causing the Gypsies as such to disappear. By contrast, the qualitative changes in hostility towards Roma have remained largely unnoticed.

The anti-Gypsyist images so often described were initially located on the level of individual prejudices. At the same time, however, since the Roma arrived in Germany, the number of ordinances, edicts and highly detailed proscriptions directed against Gypsies grew inexorably. These edicts were often ritually re-affirmed on certain occasions, like Imperial Diets. Into the twentieth century, new decrees regularly consist of reminders to implement preceding decrees. The function of these decrees would not appear primarily aimed at persecuting the Roma (although brutal persecution was a recurrent phenomenon), but at manifesting the regulatory powers of the state as such. It must not be forgotten in this context how complicated the legal system of those times was. There were several overlapping legal systems co-existing, with ecclesiastical law providing the only over-arching element; but legal power also resided in the lord of the manor, the feudal nobleman and, ultimately, the emperor. Inequality between free men and serfs, nobles and peasants was taken for granted. At the same time, the minorities, Jews and Roma alike, possessed their own jurisdiction, which was also confirmed to them by the authorities. The question of equality for Roma did not arise until the moment when the emergent nation state demanded equal treatment for all its citizens.

In Germany, the emperor's power was the initial issue: the edicts passed by the Imperial Diets against Gypsies were the first example of a new kind of law, one that applied everywhere in the Empire and to everyone. These edicts enabled the officials of the emperor to arrest a subject even on the land of his feudal lord. The purpose, however, of passing these edicts was possibly not so much actually to see them universally enforced, but rather to draft an initial formulation, a kind of blueprint of laws that could in principle be universally enforced. Fundamentally, the sovereign ruler began in the sixteenth century to assert the claim that he was, by virtue of the divine right vested in him, solely responsible for establishing law and order. The means for maintaining this law and order was (the) police: "Police" was a synonym of "Policy". "Political Economy" was originally termed "Police Economy". It meant meant that which preserved good order in the state. It was only the enlightened reformers of the eighteenth and nineteenth centuries who attempted to make legislation into an consistently enforceable instrument of governmental action. Previously society's economic and political functioning depended upon the incomplete enforcement of such laws. (The rich fought duels, raped servants, listened to Gypsy musicians and tolerated highway robbery unless they were themselves its victims). In the nineteenth century, however, the policy became that of enforcing existing laws equally, in their entirety, precisely so as to establish social order on a new level of rigour (c.f. Schlumbohn 1997).

Prior to this, records show that at the same period and within the same state cases of extreme persecution of Roma co-existed with situations where both the population and the authorities found themselves able to live peaceably with Roma. The question to be addressed is whether these extreme cases of Roma persecution, where the most draconian punishments were frequently imposed, going far beyond the existing laws, were an early example of the "Gypsy's" function as a surrogate victim, penalised in order to keep in line a population which itself remained largely impervious to discipline.

These atrocities should be seen as more than the outcome of specific local resentments. They were, however inconsistent, an early form of modern state action, taken by duly constituted authority, within its officials' sphere of jurisdiction. That is, the atrocities were presented by those committing them as "due process" not personal malice. While governmental action initially consisted of issuing ordinances (which legitimised the localised atrocities) these ordinances were not consistently enforced until the time of the Enlightenment. From the late eighteenth century onwards edicts and ordinances were not just issued, and then left for lay magistrates to enforce or not as they chose; the state now put in place the bureaucracy to apply its laws without restriction. All the state's actions were required to be based on laws, and concomitantly the laws were required to be applied without restriction. This was dependent on defining the population as citizens, that is as legal subjects. For this to work it had to apply even to those who were manifestly still being excluded from the new order, Jews and Roma and Sinte. They also had to become citizens in law, as were the rest of the population. Enlightenment thinkers believed the instrument for this integration was to be education, or, to be more precise, education for work as the precondition for being a "useful citizen". It will be shown that it is precisely the enlightened view that "Gypsies" can be re-constituted by education, and can if necessary be compulsorily moulded into citizens, that opens the door to well-meaning interventionism.

To the extent to which the Enlightenment was linked to a demand for all action to be founded on reason, inveterate prejudices had to be converted into at least acceptable cognitive forms. Traditional anti-Semitism had to be replaced by a version utilising rational forms of argument, which, however, could still carry out the functions of traditional anti-Semitism of providing stereotypes against which the majority could define itself. This does not, of course, mean that modern anti-Semitism was therefore amenable to rational proof or justification, but that it created for itself an internally consistent logical system. This logic meant it could be the basis of a world view which could explain everything for its adherents. Modern anti-Semitism, of the kind which emerged in the 1870s, no longer wanted Jews to be discriminated against, ostracized and persecuted; it simply wanted them to disappear. In the same way, anti-Roma policies were aimed at causing the Gypsies to disappear.

Disappearance did not at first mean the physical elimination of the Jews or the Roma and Sinte. The "improvement" of Jews and Roma alike aimed at their complete integration, or more precisely: assimilation. This process, it was thought, might well take several generations, but had to commence immediately (c.f. Grellmann 1787 and Dohm 1781). Until the years immediately prior to the First World War, this position, derived as it was from Enlightenment thinking, dominated much of the political scene. In the "Zeitschrift für Staats- und Gemeindeverwaltung im Grossherzogtum Hessen" (State and Municipal Administration Journal for the Grand Duchy of Hesse) for 1901/02, several articles appeared under the title "On Eliminating the Gypsy Nuisance" (Welcker 1901). In the tradition of classical German criminal law, they demanded that the existing laws should first be enforced: *"Wir glauben, nachgewiesen zu haben, dass die Polizei genügend Mittel hat, den Zigeuner unter das Gesetz zu beugen."* ("We believe we have demonstrated that the police have sufficient resources at their disposal to subject the Gypsies to the rigor of the law.") In this text only legal (and that meant rational) measures were conceivable, with no tendency towards racist ostracism and extermination. On the contrary, the centuries of expulsion and persecution, and their effects on the "Gypsies'" mindset are cited:

> *"Ein Volk wird durch Jahrhunderte auf Europa von Ort zu Ort gehetzt und den Tieren der Wildnis gleich behandelt. Es werden Gesetze geschmiedet, so grausam, dass selbst die Richter, die unter dem Banne der Carolina criminalis stehen, sie zu streng finden und nicht durchführen. Denn jedes Strafgesetz setzt eine strafbare Handlung voraus, dass aber die blosse Existenz eines Volkes eine strafbare Handlung sei, war für diese alten Richter etwas neues."*
> (Welcker 1902)

> "A people are hounded from place to place in Europe throughout the centuries, and treated like the beasts of the wilderness. Laws are devised so cruel that even the judges still mesmerised by the Carolina criminalis deem them too severe, and refrain from applying them. For every penal statute presupposes a criminal act, but for these venerable judges it was something new that the mere existence of a people constituted a criminal act."

The state security police in Germany had recently been separated from the municipal welfare police, and since 1870, the police had been exposed to competition from new branches of science: medicine, psychology, social welfare. They were under compelling pressure to modernise (primarily to enable them to combat the internal enemy of the Empire, the Social Democrats.) The liberal, classical tradition of the Enlightenment continued to operate but a new form of modernity took shape. In 1899, almost contemporaneously with the deliberations in Hesse on integrating the Roma, the Intelligence Service for the Security Police in Regard to the Gypsies was established in Bavaria which systematically collected all available data on the Roma and Sinte for the entire German Empire at a central location. This was a new development, since up to then the German provinces and mini-states had jealously guarded their police monopolies. The role of the 'Gypsy Police Department' in the modernisation of German police administration and in carrying out the genocide under the Third Reich has been repeatedly described (Kenrick and Puxon 1972, Fings and Sparing 1992, Heuss 1995). For the first time, total registration and surveillance of an entire category of the population was planned and implemented. The 'Gypsy Headquarters' possessed modern technical equipment. Telegraphy, photography, fingerprint systems, identity cards, the very latest technical innovations were for the first time comprehensively deployed against the Roma and Sinte, so as to subject a comparatively small number of people to what was intended to be total surveillance.

The technocrats' vocabulary did not differ in its essentials from that of the thinkers of the liberal Enlightenment: both spoke of a "Gypsy nuisance" which had to be "finally eliminated". This is often seen as evidence for a continuity of anti-Gypsyism extending from Grellmann (if not from Luther) to Auschwitz. And, indeed we cannot neglect investigation of the origins of anti-Gypsyism in our search for an explanation of the intended extermination of the Roma in Europe, and the actual murder of hundreds of thousands. Anti-Gypsyism alone, however, as we argued above, is as inadequate as racism as an explanation for the Nazi murders. Both concepts are to a certain extent self-referring or circular. (They explain oppression merely by positing a tendency to oppress). They are unsatisfactory as long as they fail to describe the specific nature of the tendencies which constitute the social phenomena designated by these terms. The similar vocabulary must not obscure the fact that concrete social and political conditions determine the direction of developments.

One example of anti-Gypsyism motivated by law and order considerations is that of Wilhelm Leuschner, who in 1929, as Hessian Minister of the Interior, submitted to the provincial parliament a "Law for Combating the Sinister Activities of Gypsies". Wilhelm Leuschner was a resistance fighter against Hitler, and was executed on 29 September 1944. Earlier, as a representative of the prohibited trade unions in the Third Reich, he had been repeatedly incarcerated in concentration camps. Nonetheless, Wilhelm Leuschner supported the 'Gypsy Act' in the provincial parliament: the aim of the act, he said, was *"die Zigeunerplage (als) dauernde Gefährdung der öffentlichen Sicherheit und Ordnung (einer) einheitlichen Bekämpfung" zuzuführen, (da) trotz energischen Vorgehens eine Ausrottung des Übels bisher nicht möglich war."*(Hesse Parl, Records, 1931, Nos.274,452) (to provide "co-ordinated countermeasures against the Gypsy nuisance, (which is) a permanent menace to public safety and order, (since) in spite of energetic endeavours it has hitherto proved impossible to extirpate this evil.")

Today, Hesse's most prestigious medal is named after Wilhelm Leuschner. His views show how the the policy of integrating the "Gypsies" was a powerful means of education in citizenship. This law and order policy, which regularly sought to subdue and secure the "Gypsies", was not directed primarily at the Roma, but at the members of the majority, for whom the "Gypsies" were a demonstration of what they could expect if they refused to submit to the constraints of modern society. The integrative power of the "Gypsy" image is exemplified by the fact that this image was made into a link between political enemies, namely the Social Democrats and the conservative/reactionary forces of the Weimar Republic. This function, acting as a connecting link between divergent forces, rendered the figure of the "Gypsy" indispensable in the repertoire of governmental law and order policies.

For the Social Democrats in Germany, in particular, every form of idleness was regarded as theft. For them, every human being's existence was founded on work. A just society was to emerge by putting the Social Democrats in charge of the state, and thus having labour instead of capital governing the body politic. The Social Democrats' policy was aimed at taking charge of the state and they believed that an involvement in or even a take-over of the apparatus of power could be achieved all the more easily the more unequivocally the state deployed force against the non-workers.

The enlightenment and the ideal of work

Besides demonstrating the efficacy of new forms of regulation for 'combating Gypsies', we can from the very beginning discern a dimension which hitherto has been largely ignored by researchers (c.f. Brückner 1998). This was the idea that, if we are to give due respect to the ideal of free work in its modern-day form, it must be presented as the norm through the social ostracism of the "Gypsy". Through the concept of work, which played a special role in the formation of the German nation state, not only was the majority's definition repeatedly re-affirmed, but also (the reverse side of the coin), the ostracism of Jews and Roma was systematised.

In Old High German, the word for "work" means something like: tribulation, hardship, affliction, adversity (Storfer 1935 : 30). For free-born Germans, not working was taken for granted; work was reserved for slaves and serfs. It was only with the Reformation that the concept of work began to be revalued in Germany and linked to a rejection of ecclesiastical or aristocratic idleness and to an anathematisation of poverty. As Conze (1972: 164, our translation) remarks, "When Christian poverty, living from the alms of others, was repudiated, and the beggar regarded as a disreputable phenomenon deserving of elimination, this led to the thought that work was both punishment and discipline/education, and could therefore be enforced by the authorities. This explains the spread of workhouses and penitentiaries, which had been proliferating since the sixteenth century from their origins in the Calvinist nations, particularly Holland."

As the eighteenth century drew to a close, the Enlightenment gave rise to a call for "free work". In Germany, this demand was linked to calls for liberating the peasants (from being tied to the land), for economic freedom, freedom of movement, freedom of competition, and (of course) with calls for emancipation of the Jews. From the start, emancipation was linked to the demand that Jews should then turn to productive work like the rest of the population. This demand was raised both by the pro-Jewish party and by opponents of emancipation, and from the very beginnings of modern anti-Semitism it formed part of its discourse.

For Adolf Stoecker, (cited in Oomen and Schmid, 1978) equality meant that Jews would have to participate equally in productive work: *"Für mich gipfelt die Judenfrage in der Frage, ob die Juden, welche unter uns leben, lernen werden, sich an der gesamten deutschen Arbeit, auch an der harten, sauren Arbeit des Handwerks, der Fabrik, des Landbaues zu beteiligen. Weiter sollen wir nichts von ihnen verlangen."* ("For me, the Jewish question culminates in the question of whether the Jews living amongst us learn to participate in the totality of German work, in the hard, arduous work of the craft trades, the factory, the farmland. We should not demand from them any more than this.") Wilhelm Marr, (also cited in Oomen and Schmid, 1978) to whom the term 'anti-Semitism' in its modern form is first attributed, did not see religion as the cause of hatred for the Jews: *"Die generelle Feindschaft gegen die Juden hatte andere Gründe. Erstens die Scheu vor wirklicher Arbeit."* ("The general antipathy to the Jews had other reasons: first among them their distaste for genuine work.")

Christian Wilhelm Dohm (1781: 100), the author of the first publication to urge equal rights for the Jews, also believed that work, or industriousness, was a fundamental value in society. In order to achieve true betterment, he wanted Jews to become craftsmen and farmers: *"In der That ist das Leben des geschickten Handwerkers vielleicht der reinste Genuss, der sich in unserer bürgerlichen Gesellschaft finden mag ... Die starke Arbeit macht ihn gesund, und die Gleichförmigkeit derselben bringt eine gewisse stille Ruhe in seinen Geist."* ("In actuality, the life of a skilled craftsman is perhaps the purest form of gratification one can find in our civil society ... The heavy work renders him healthy and its uniformity instils a certain calm peace in his spirit.").

Dohm asserts (1781: 34) *"Verdorbenheit der Juden eine nothwendige Folge der drückenden Verfassung..., in der sie sich seit vielen Jahrhunderten befinden."* ("The Jews' debasement is a necessary consequence of the oppressive condition ... in which they have subsisted for many centuries." As a means for overcoming this "debased disposition", Dohm recommended work, which after all, he points out, would do the Jews' constitutions good as well. As an example of enlightened policy-making, Dohm (1781: 87ff) cited the settlement of Roma in Banat under the government of Josef II:

> *"Die Zigeuner sind unstreitig eine sehr verwilderte Nation. Die unmenschliche Politik, mit der man sie in fast allen Ländern zu Verbannten erklärt, ihr Leben sogar jedem Muthwilligen Preiss gegeben, hat sie von allem ehrlichen Gebrauch entwöhnt, und gezwungen, als natürliche Feinde der bürgerlichen Gesellschaften, von dem Raube und Beeinträchtigungen derselben zu leben. Erst unter der letzten österreichischen Regierung hat man angefangen, im Banat Temeswar, wo*

sie am häufigsten sich aufhalten, ihnen Wohnungen anzuweisen, sie zu Ackerbau und anderen Beschäftigungen anzuhalten. Die Erfahrung lehrt, dass es äusserst schwer sey, sie an diesen festen Aufenthalt und bleibende Beschäftigung nachhaltig zu gewöhnen, und dass sie dem bequemern und ruhigern Leben das unsichere und beschwerliche Umherstreichen vorziehen. Aber die Kinder der itzigen, zum Theil im Schoosse der bürgerlichen Gesellschaft geboren, werden gewiss schon besser in dieselbe einpassen. Sollten aber auch erst die Nachkommen der itzigen Zigeuner nach mehr als einem Jahrhundert ghlücklichere Menschen und gute Bürger werden; so wird doch dieses unstreitig die Regierung nicht abhalten, ihre weisen Bemühungen fortzusetzen."

"The Gypsies are incontestably a very rude and feral nation. The inhumane policy under which in almost all countries they have been declared outlaw, their lives even rendered forfeit to the whim of any passer-by, has estranged them from all reputable courses, and compelled them to live as natural enemies of civil societies, which they rob and injure. Only under the last Austrian government has a start been made, in Banat Temeswar, where they most frequently subsist, in allotting them dwellings, in exhorting them to pursue farming and other occupations. Experience has taught that it is extremely difficult to habituate them lastingly to this fixed abode and continuous employment, and that they prefer the uncertain and arduous existence of a nomad to the more comfortable and tranquil life. But the children of the present-day generation, some of them born in the lap of civil society, will certainly be more conformable to it. Should, however, a century or more pass before the descendants of the present-day Gypsies become happier persons and good citizens, this will beyond question not deter the government from continuing its sagacious endeavours."

Thus from the beginnings of the Enlightenment the Roma were objects of governmental emancipation policies, without themselves actively seeking emancipation, at least in Germany. 1783 saw the publication of Grellmann's work *The Gypsies*. This book was a success with the public, and has since been regarded as the beginning of serious academic study of the Roma's history. Grellmann, who was for some time a member of Lichtenberg's household in Göttingen, urged (like Dohm for the Jews) education for the 'Gypsies':

"Jeder Mensch hat Anlagen und Kräfte: der Zigeuner aber eben nicht im geringsten Masse. Weiss er nun nicht gehörig damit umzugehen, so lehre es ihn der Staat, und halte ihn so lange im Gängelband, bis die Absicht erreicht ist. Liegt auch gleich beim ersten Geschlecht die Wurzel des Verderbens zu tief, als dass sie bald anfangs auszurotten wäre, so wird sich doch eine fortgesetzte Mühe beym zweyten oder dritten Geschlecht belohnen. Und nun denke man sich den Zigeuner, wenn er aufgehört hat, Zigeuner zu seyn; denke sich ihn mit seiner Fruchtbarkeit und seinen zahlreichen Nachkommen, die alle zu brauchbaren Bürgern umgeschaffen sind; und man wird fühlen, wie wenig wirthschaftlich es war, ihn als Schlacke wegzuwerfen." (Grellmann 1787: 183)

"Every person has dispositions and talents: and the Gypsy certainly no less than others. If he is too ignorant to utilise them properly, then the state shall teach him, and shall keep him in leading reins until the purpose has been achieved. If in the first generation the roots of debasement are too deep to be extirpated immediately, then continued efforts will be rewarded in the second or third generation. And now let us imagine the Gypsy when he has ceased to be a Gypsy, imagine him with all his fertility and his numerous progeny, all of them transformed into serviceable citizens, and we will perceive how uneconomic it was to cast him aside as dross."

Above all, however, Grellmann sees a dichotomy between work and idleness, which appears to be a fundamental principle for Western civilisation: the creation of work as a social and cultural category, whose enforcement required centuries of lengthy efforts, and which today measures a person's value by his contribution to productive work. Grellmann (1787: 80) singles out the "Gypsies'" idleness as the quintessential disposition of this group:

"Hier entdeckt sich zugleich der Grund, warum Armuth und Dürftigkeit ein so gemeines Loos dieser Menschen ist. Er liegt in ihrer Faulheit, und übermässigen Neigung zur Gemächlichkeit. Sucht man Menschen, die im Schweisse ihres Angesichts ihr Brod essen, so wird man sie überall leichter, als unter dem Volke der Zigeuner finden. Jede Arbeit ist ihr Feind, wenn sie mühsam ist, und viele Anstrengung erfordert."

"Here also is revealed the reason why poverty and indigence is the common lot of these folk. It lies in their indolence and their excessive predisposition to otiosity. If one seeks people earning their bread in the sweat of their brows, nowhere will they be more difficult to find than among the Gypsies. Work of all kind is their enemy, if it is arduous and requires copious effort."

Nor does Grellmann (1787: 162) forget to condemn once again idleness as such, distinguishing it from the rest and leisure that are approved values in Christian tradition: *"Aber diese an sich liebenswürdige Zufriedenheit, ist bey dem Zigeuner so wenig, als bey dem Irokesen, Tugend, und entspringt aus dem Übermaasse seines Leichtsinns."* ("But this inherently laudable satisfaction is no more a virtue among the Gypsies than among the Iroquois, and springs from their intolerable lightness of spirit.")

For Grellmann, work constitutes both the purpose of life as ordained by God, and the individual's justification for existence, and it is precisely this assumption that work is both the purpose of and the justification for living, that is fundamentally challenged by the Roma by their continuing to exist. Thus the continued social existence of the Roma signifies the failure not only of the Enlightenment, but of the Enlightenment thinkers themselves.

Grellmann, in common with the other Enlightenment thinkers who supported emancipation for the Jews, thought that the "betterment of the Gypsies ", like the "civic betterment of the Jews", should always be enforced by the state. They shared the argument that the withholding of equal rights had been a significant reason for that "debasement" of the Jews and the "Gypsies" and that every "betterment" would be seen in relation to this "debasement". Grellmann (1787: 70) repeatedly cites the state of nature in which the "Gypsies" are alleged to live: *"Dass der grösste Theil der Zigeuner noch ganz unbearbeitet in den Händen der rohen Natur liege, oder wenigstens kaum auf der ersten*

Stufe zur Menschwerdung stehe ..." ("The greater part of the Gypsies still lies entirely unformed in the hands of raw Nature, or at least has hardly reached the first step on the ladder to true humanity..."). Gradually, over generations, however, this "raw Nature" can be overcome. This historical/pedagogic approach is likewise encountered in the contemporary discussion on "bettering" the Jews. Coupled to the probation of the emancipees, however, is an injunction to abandon their Jewishness or their identity as Roma. The aim of this development was never the emancipation of the minority, but the erasure of its social existence. Jews were required no longer to be Jews, Gypsies were required to cease being Gypsies, both were required to become useful citizens of the state. The emancipation causes the emancipees to disappear.

Thus "to cease being a Gypsy" has very early on been conceived and enunciated. In Grellmann's case, of course, this cessation does not mean the end of the Roma's physical existence.

Grellmann's position was repeatedly reproduced by various authors. In 1842, von Heister (1842: 26) reiterated Grellmann's position that in all deliberations *"zunächst erwogen werden, dass der Zigeuner keinen grösseren Feind kennt als die Arbeit, wenn diese irgend dauernd und anstrengend seine Kräfte in Anspruch nimmt ..."* ("it must first be considered that the Gypsy knows no greater enemy than work, if this continuously and arduously taxes his strength ...")

The demand for freedom to work meant nothing less than the complete dissolution of the existing economic and social order. The separation of productive and unproductive work revolutionised the traditional values: the feudal ruling classes were now seen as no less unproductive than beggars and play-actors. Praise of work goes hand in hand with the Enlightenment: work was no longer to be a torment and a burden but a means of enjoyment. Work was lauded as the source of all true pleasure, as if it was impossible to live without work, when habituation had enabled its pleasurability to be discovered. For Karl Marx, later on, work was seen to evolve from a necessity into life's cardinal need, at the moment when the 'realm of freedom' arrived. Work became an educational imperative; children at school were required to learn how to work, it was here that a predisposition to work was to be cultivated. This simultaneously entailed the demand that no one should now be permitted to be a useless member of society. It became the citizen's duty to render himself of use to the state through assiduous labour, and conversely, it was the state's task to implement economic rationality, which was unable to tolerate the unemployed or beggars (Conze 1972: 154 ff).

Very different sections of society thus found common ground in this idealisation of work, despite (or even perhaps because of) the radical changes in the nature of work as more modern industrial forms of work were enforced. For the liberal forces, work and freedom were at first inseparably linked but the state was soon to set limits to the freedom of liberal capitalism. Protection of work was part of Bismarck's policy. The conservative middle class was able to claim work for its own, and demanded from the state not only protection for both the workers and the unemployed, but also an imposed obligation to work. The early socialists based their demand for equality and general, equal prosperity on the safeguarding of this affluence by an obligation to work within the community. Finally, the Social Democrats in Germany wanted to replace the state of capital with a state of work. Their aim was not power in society but rule over society, by taking over the apparatus of state control. The internal logic of this policy meant that participation in governmental power could be attained all the more easily when the non-workers, here embodied and exemplified by the "Gypsies", could be countered by the state's use of force. At the same time, the Social Democrat leadership could publicly proclaim that it supported the principle of state enforcement. Here we find a reason for the remarkable commitment of Social Democrats to enforcing "Gypsy legislation".

The enforcement of work was always regarded as a political/pedagogic task, ultimately to be handled by the state. It was only under National Socialism that the concept of work was radically redefined, by being anchored in the racist context of Nazi policies. Hitler himself developed his anti-Semitism from the concept of work. While work was performed by Aryans for idealistic reasons, work performed by Jews was solely selfish in nature; accordingly, Aryans' work was 'culture creation', while Jewish work was 'parasitism'. *"Ariertum bedeutet sittliche Auffassung der Arbeit und dadurch ... Sozialismus, Gemeinsinn, Gemeinnutz vor Eigennutz – Judentum bedeutet egoistische Auffassung der Arbeit und dadurch Mammonismus und Materialismus, das konträre Gegenteil des Sozialismus."* (Hitler, 1968) ("Aryanism signifies a moral conception of work and thus ... socialism, a sense of community, the common good over self-interest; while Jewishness signifies a selfish conception of work, and therefore mammonism and materialism, the diametric opposite of socialism.") In line with the evolution and radicalisation of the Nazis' persecution policies, Jews were here, like Roma, no longer ostracised as individuals, but as a group, as an entire minority. The task of research on anti-Gypsyism is to trace and if possible to understand this development, which solely on the grounds of their ethnic affiliation first ostracised the members of the Jewish and Roma minorities and deprived them of their rights, before then deporting and exterminating them.

Towards a methodology for anti-Gypsyism research

Anti-Gypsyism research must not be primarily read as an attempt to explain existing patterns of violence. Their causes lie beyond both the Roma themselves and the image of "Gypsies" created by the majority. Anti-Gypsyism research must not posit the existing structures of prejudice as the primary cause for the persecution of Roma, or else they will retrospectively rationalise the irrationality of the historical forms of these antipathies. This also means that a historical continuity of anti-Gypsyist stereotypes cannot be unconditionally postulated. That the image of "Gypsies" remained the same over the course of centuries does not necessarily mean that the function of this image did not change. The image of the "Gypsy" had a different function under feudalism from under the Weimar Republic, and a different one there from in the Federal Republic of Germany.

The Bavarian Gypsy Act of 1926 is often cited as an example of how the Wilhelmine Empire's policies were intensified and radicalised. Under this law, Roma could simply be sent to a workhouse, or even sentenced to a term in prison. But until now no case has been found in the Bavarian archives of any Roma sentenced under this law. Committal to workhouses was already possible under existing legislation. The project of passing a 'Gypsies Act', was pursued with considerable energy over the course of years. But even when finally achieved, it did not at first have any practical consequences. The crucial new element in this law was the introduction of a new category, that of race, in the legislation of the German provinces. The ministerial resolution for implementing the law includes the words: *"Der Begriff 'Zigeuner' ist allgemein bekannt und bedarf keiner näheren Erläuterung. Die Rassenkunde gibt darüber Aufschluss, wer als Zigeuner anzusehen ist."* ("The term 'Gypsy' is generally known and requires no further explanation. Racial studies provide information on who is to be regarded as a Gypsy.") It would be superficial to interpret this merely as a manifestation of racially motivated anti-Gypsyism, anticipating the Third Reich. The aim of enforcing the Gypsy laws in Germany was not primarily to provide a legal breakthrough for some form of anti-Gypsyism. The primary consideration was not to combat imaginary "sinister Gypsy activities", but rather to implement a change in the function of the police. It was now possible for the police not only to prosecute offenders, following the commission of a criminal offence, but also to take independent preventive action. *"Nicht mehr die Verfolgung begangener Straftaten, sondern die planmässige Bekämpfung des Verbrechertums ohne Beziehung zu einer bestimmten Straftat ist das hauptsächliche Arbeitsgebiet der Polizei."* (Reich, 1926: 834 ff). ("The main work of the police is no longer the investigation of offences committed, but the systematic combating of criminality without reference to a particular criminal offence.")

A functional analysis of the laws passed against Roma in the Weimar Republic has to begin with precisely this transformation in the development of the overall legal framework. In Germany, the incipient modernisation of the police had long been pioneered by its operation towards Roma and Sinte. The centralised, nationwide records maintained since 1899, were followed by the introduction of identity cards as predecessors of the internal passports introduced in the Third Reich, and the registration of all Roma fingerprints without reference to any criminal offence. This modernisation process made use of all the newest technology and aimed to overcome problems presented by the provincial boundaries inside the German Empire. It was, however, fundamentally constrained by the German federal constitution, which made it difficult to centralise data. This obstacle of internal borders was overcome for the first time by the institution of comprehensive surveillance of the Roma. The constitution and the criminal law of the Weimar Republic guaranteed that everyone was presumed innocent until proved guilty. With the introduction of the 'race' category in the Bavarian Gypsy Act, which was then adopted in provincial legislation elsewhere, there was for the first time an option for prosecuting, and even imprisoning, people solely on the grounds of their ethnic affiliation without any connection to a specific criminal offence.

For as long as the Weimar Republic existed, and basic rights were guaranteed under the constitution, Roma were discriminated against and ostracised, but their existence as such was not put in question. When the Nazis came to power, however, the situation changed once again, fundamentally and radically. While in the Weimar Republic a biological paradigm shift to a racially based form of legislation emerged with the Bavarian Gypsy Act, the Third Reich went much further to make racial studies the direct basis of governmental practice. The state made new laws not merely mentioning race, but setting up institutions where 'racial scientists' researched genealogies, took tissue samples and made decisions about the fate of individuals and groups. Racism was no longer just an idea but was organised to put policy into practice. This change meant that the traditional inconsistent and intermittent ostracism became total. At the moment when the Nazis made the race concept the foundation of the state, even the physical existence of the Roma was fundamentally put into question.

Meticulous investigation of the interaction between the race-science and National Socialist institutions, as exemplified by the persecution and extermination of the Roma, may show how and why this minority, which played no role in National Socialism's political vision, became a focus of the regime's extermination policies. In this context, it is within the institutional framework of the human sciences themselves that we see the development of the inhuman objectives which were both expected and acted on by the National Socialist regime. The Racial Hygiene Research Institute at the Reich Health Department, which played a crucial role in preparing and legitimising, as well as planning and implementing the persecution and extermination of the Roma, used its racial hygiene (ethnic cleansing?) theories as a basis for advising the Third Reich's legislators and its administrative agencies. Although the image of the Gypsies, the antipathies towards them, remained the same, the context had altered radically.

It will be one of the tasks of anti-Gypsyism research to reconstruct these changes in context, each of them entailing a functional transformation in anti-Gypsyism. A comparison with anti-Semitism will have to play a major role in this context, not so much for the obvious resemblances as for the differences involved. Anti-Semitism, for instance, had since the Enlightenment no longer been firmly rooted in German society (i.e. in unlegislated segregation), and in the Wilhelmine Empire was not even firmly embedded in the state's legal system. In the same way it is difficult to point to popular, socially rooted manifestations of anti-Gypsyism, as opposed to an anti-Gypsyism which was anchored directly in the institutions of the state itself. The Roma themselves had almost never put forward any demands of their own for emancipation, any more than the German state had ever seriously endeavoured to bring this about. Thus there was no popular spontaneous socially organised anti-Gypsyism either reacting to new laws.

However, in the context of the "Gypsy" issue, disparate forces found no difficulty in concurring, even forces which in the context of anti-Semitism appeared to belong to opposing camps (c.f. Volkov 1990). While 'emancipation' and 'anti-Semitism' are terms symbolising two different political camps, the example of the "Gypsies" illustrates that enlightened liberals and conservative anti-modernists both utilised anti-Gypsyism, and indeed it constituted a bridge between these camps. The demand for ostracism, for expulsion of the "Gypsies", was one which every social group could support, particularly those who were otherwise in favour of emancipation. The anathematisation of anti-Semitism among progressive and liberal circles, in particular, could be sidestepped by an anti-Gypsyism which presented equally as scientifically based racial studies and as a social-cleansing response to the "social question". Anti-Semitism as a world view ultimately created a mass basis for National Socialism, and was recurrently employed to re-affirm the loyalty of the masses to their Führer, whereas anti-Gypsyism can be understood as a directly practical instrument for integrating divergent forces within the national community, and also in the unmediated sense that anti-Gypsyism repeatedly recommended and legitimised action taken by the National Socialist regime. Anti-Semitism supplied the simplistic, overarching explicatory model that everything was the Jews' fault; anti-Gypsyism simultaneously created and sharpened the cutting edge of the system of social ostracism based on racist criteria.

The almost invisible social organisation of anti-Gypsyism does not mean that it has been less effective thereby. On the contrary: the way in which antipathies against "Gypsies" have repeatedly been revived by the state as a matter of course without ever needing a specific reason is evidence for the cross-class efficiency of anti-Gypsyism. Finally, the work of building the scientific basis for anti-Gypsyism provided the radicalising arguments which shaped the modernissation process of both the state and society as a whole. These arguments were ultimately to transform the social question into a race question, to which the practical policy answer was the extinction of all persons not members of the national community.

References

Brückner, W., 1998 *"Arbeit macht frei". Herkunft und Hintergrund der KZ-Devise,*. Otto-von-Freisingen-Vorlesungen der Katholischen Universität Eichstätt, heruasgegeben von der Geschichts- und Gesellschaftswissenschaftlichen Fakultät der Katholischen Universität Eichstätt, vol. 13, Leske und Budrich Verlag, Opladen.

Conze, W., 1972 "Arbeit" in Conze, W., Bruno, O., and Koselleck R., eds. *Geschichtliche Grundbegriffe. Historisches Lexikon zur politisch-sozialen Sprache in Deutschland*. Volume 1 A-D, Klett, Stuttgart.

Dlugoborski, W., Ed., 1998 *Sinti und Roma im KL Auschwitz-Birkenau 1943-44 vor dem Hintergrund ihrer Verfolgung unter der Naziherrschaft*, Verlag Staatliches Museum Auschwitz-Birkenau, Oswiecim.

Dohm, Christian Wilhelm, 1781: *Über die bürgerliche Verbesserung der Juden, Fr. Nicolai,* Berlin und Stettin.

Fings, Carola und Frank Sparing, 1992 : *"z.Zt. Zigeunerlager". Die Verfolgung der Düsseldorfer Sinti und Roma im Nationalsozialismus* Volksblatt-Verlag, Köln.

Grellmann, H.M.G., 1787 (2nd ed.) *Historischer Versuch über die Zigeuner betreffend Lebensart und Verfassung Sitten und Schicksale dieses Volkes in Europa, nebst ihrem Ursprung,* Dieterich, Göttingen.

Heister, Carl von 1842 *Ethnographische und geschichtliche Notizen über die Zigeuner,* Gräfe und Unzer, Königsberg.

Hesse Parliamentary Records 1927/31. Fourth Parliament. Parliament Office Publications No. 1-998, Darmstadt 1931, Issues No. 274 and 452.

Heuss, Herbert, 1995 "Darmstadt. Auschwitz. Die Verfolgung der Sinti in Darmstadt" in Strauss, A. ed. *Hornhaut auf der Seele* Publications of the Hesse Verband deutscher Sinti und Roma, No,1, Darmstadt.

Hitler, Adolf,: 1968 *"Warum wir Antisemiten sind,"* reprinted in: Vierteljahreshefte für Zeitgeschichte No.16.

Löwenthal, L. and Hager, F., 1992: *"Gespräche" in: Hager, F. ed.: Geschichte denken. Ein Notizbuch für Leo Löwenthal,* Reclam Verlag, Leipzig.

Marr, W., 1978 "Gegen religiosen Antisemitismus – Antisemitismus als Kampf ums Dasein." cited in Oomen and Schmid 1978. (First published 1879: in Der Sieg des Judenthums über das Germanenthum. Vom nicht confessionellen Standpunkt aus betrachtet, Costenobel, Bern.)

Oomen, H-H. and Schmid, H-D., eds., 1978 Vorurteile gegen Minderheiten, Philipp Reclan jun., Stuttgart.

Reich, H., 1926 "Das bayerische Zigeuner- und Arbeitsscheuengesetz", Juristische Rundschau 2.

Schlumbohn, J., 1997 "Gesetze, die nicht durchgeführt wurden – ein Strukturmerkmal des frühneuzeitlichen Staates?" Geschichte und Gesellschaft. Zeitschrift für Historische Sozialwissenschaft, Anno. 23, No. 4

Stoecker, A., 1978 "Die Juden als Fremdkörper im Staate", cited in Oomen and Schmid. (First published 1880 as Das moderne Judenthum in Deutschland, besonders in Berlin: Zwei Reden in der christlich-sozialen Arbeiterpartei, Weigandt und Grieben, Berlin.)

Storfer, A. J., 1935, Wörter und ihre Schicksale, Atlantis, Berlin and Zürich.

Türcke, C. 1992 "Abwarten", in: Hager F.ed. Geschichte denken. Ein Notizbuch für Leo Löwenthal, Reclam Verlag, Leipzig.

Welcker, Adolph, 1901-2 "Zur Beseitigung der Zigeunerplage" Zeitschrift für Staats- und Gemeinde-Verwaltung im Grossherzogtum Hessen. Anno. 26th, No. 18, 25 December and 15 January.

Welcker, Adolph, 1902 "Die Zigeunerplage" Darmstädter Zeitung No.60, Supplement, 5 February.

Volkov, S., 1990 Jüdisches Leben und Antisemitismus im 19. und 20. Jahrhundert: 10 Essays, C. H. Beck, Munich.

German Sinto leader Romani Rose (left) with another delegate at the Third World Romani Congress in Göttingen, West Germany 1981. *Photograph by David Altheer*

CHAPTER SIX

"MY NAME IN THE THIRD REICH WAS z:5742"

THE POLITICAL ART OF THE AUSTRIAN ROM KARL STOJKA

Susan Tebbutt

"Once the Gypsies were the stars in the skies over Europe, and although isolated, they lit up the night with the common light which emanated from them" (Stojka 1994: 8).

Against invisibility: Stojka's autobiographical work

Karl Stojka, born in 1931 near Vienna, is the first Romani artist to record his experiences of the Holocaust in both writing and art and to be internationally acclaimed, with exhibitions in Europe, America and Asia. His family had been in Austria for 300 years and his ethnic affiliation is a key element in his writing and art. One of the key reasons for recording his life in words and pictures is to counteract the all-too-prevalent 'invisibility' of the Roma and Sinte (Europe's largest single ethnic minority group, but its least understood and most persecuted one) and to "light up the night". It is ironic that the words spoken by Hitler when he opened the House of German Art in Munich in 1937 are so relevant to Stojka's work: "We believe that especially today, when in so many spheres the highest individual achievements are being manifested, in art also the highest value of personality will once again assert itself" (Welch 1993: 174).

In his autobiography *Auf der ganzen Welt zu Hause* (*At home in the whole world* 1994), Stojka writes of the registration, persecution and deportation of the Romani people. He also writes of his life in the post-war period and his travels round the world, including time selling carpets in the USA. It was only after he returned to Vienna in 1973 that he was encouraged to turn his artistic talent to depicting the events which continued to haunt him day and night, namely the inhumanity, the barbarism and the excessive evil of the Nazi period. Painting was at once a type of therapy, a legacy for his fellow Roma and Sinte, and a way of creating a deeper understanding among non-Roma and Sinte of the suffering of the Romani people. Before exploring the images, techniques and significance of Stojka's highly political art it is necessary to appreciate its socio-historical and cultural context.

Persecution of the Roma and Sinte

From their first recorded arrival in Germany in the fifteenth century, the Roma and Sinte had been subjected to a persecution which become exacerbated at the turn of the nineteenth century. In 1936 the Racial Hygiene Population Biology Research Unit was set up in Berlin under the auspices of the Reich Federal Security Office and it was from here that Robert Ritter, Eva Justin and colleagues set out to interview, measure, classify and register Roma and Sinte in their camps (Kenrick 1972, 1996a, 1999a). The scapegoating, marginalisation and exclusion ended in the genocide of around half a million European Roma and Sinte.

Representing the Holocaust

Is it possible to represent the Holocaust in literature or art? From the autobiographical writing produced during or immediately after the war preserved in the form of diaries, scribbled writing on scraps of paper, or sketches miraculously preserved and smuggled to the outside world, to work produced years or even decades after the demise of the Nazi regime, there is no one appropriate form of Holocaust representation. Whilst some critics might feel that the most telling testimonies are those created "from within the whirlwind", Young (1988: 25) points out that this simplistic approach has limitations, because although "the exigencies of time and memory may weigh heavily on the factuality of a given report, they are in other ways no less mediational than the linguistic, cultural, and religious patterns of mind and expression that frame a writer's narrative moment, during or after the Holocaust".

In her seminal study of Holocaust literature and art Ezrahi (1980:4) argues that the representation of the Holocaust is in essence "an oscillation and a struggle between continuity and discontinuity with the cultural as well as with the historical past", but it is not possible to apply her model directly to the case of the Romani Holocaust. Much attention has been paid in the 1990s to the representation of black people, to images of Jews over the ages (Nochlin and Garb 1995) and to constructions of whiteness and the moral vocabulary of black and white (Dyer 1997), but the Roma and Sinte fall just outside each of the three categories. Often reproached for their 'swarthy skin', compared to the Jews in their position in society (Wippermann 1997), they remain a much neglected minority group. The Romani cultural past is elusive, and since Romani is primarily an oral language, there are not the same number of written works as there are works by Jews or members of other persecuted groups, and it is only in the last quarter of the twentieth century that the Romani genocide has begun to be represented in literature, with the autobiographical writing of Alfred Lessing, Ceija and Karl Stojka and Philomena Franz presenting insider ethnographic reports of the Romani Holocaust (c.f. Tebbutt 1998:133-43).

If the number of *writers* dealing with the Romani Holocaust is tiny, the number of *artists* is even smaller. Over the centuries images of Roma and Sinte in art, variously colourful, amusing or thought-provoking, had primarily been created by non-Roma and Sinte, and tended towards the stereotypical. Successive artists, from Georges de la Tour to Van Gogh, had painted Gypsies against a rural backdrop, demonising or romanticising their presence, but rarely giving prominence to an individual Romani person. It was only towards the middle of the twentieth century that painters such as Dame Laura Knight, Otto Mueller or Otto Pankok actually focused on individual Romani personalities, yet even Pankok, who lived with Gypsies for many years and whose work was banned by Hitler as degenerate, does not tackle the topic of the Holocaust directly (although his Passion cycle, with its religious connotations, hints at the suffering of the Romani people in a more generalised way). Most importantly, the outsider gaze does not and cannot convey the passions felt by the insider, the sufferer, the victim.

Whereas there have been many works of art created by Jews which reflect impressions of the Nazi regime from an insider perspective, Stojka is the first Romani artist to portray the Romani experience of the Holocaust. Ezrahi (1980) highlights the manipulation of language within the representation of the Holocaust universe and this is of direct relevance to the ways in which Stojka reconfigures familiar visual images.

Images of a life: Karl Stojka's art

'Autobiography' literally means writing or drawing one's own life and in his art Stojka is complementing his autobiographical writing. Clark, in his study of propaganda and art in the twentieth century, claims that "art can become propaganda through its function and site, its framing within public and private spaces and its relationship with a network of other kinds of objects and actions" (1997:13), and continues: "artists who have opposed the ruling values of their time have often tried to use art specifically to counteract or subvert the messages of the mass media" (1997: 14). Propaganda or protest art can be of the right-wing or left-wing variety, and Stojka's art has a strong political message, aiming as it does to subvert the more dominant right-wing images of the Third Reich, reclaiming the art of propaganda in order to disseminate the history of the persecution of the Roma and Sinte to a wider audience.

In *Gas* (1998) and *Ein Kind in Birkenau* (*A Child in Birkenau,* 1995), the major exhibition catalogues containing a selection of Stojka's prolific work, the only paintings which do not deal directly with the Holocaust are the representations of neo-Nazi right-wing attacks on foreigners in Germany in the 1990s, and here too the continuity of the creative impulse is clear, namely to expose the perniciousness of racist ideology. The great majority of Stojka's Holocaust paintings depict scenes, which he himself had experienced first-hand but just occasionally he thematises events which had shocked or moved him greatly. Far from detracting from the authenticity of the autobiographical account, this registering of outside events is in line with normal practice in autobiographies. Geographically Stojka's *oeuvre* covers events as far afield as Struthof in occupied Alsace, Dachau in Germany, Lackenbach and Mauthausen in Austria, and Litzmannstadt, Lodz, Auschwitz and Majdanek in Poland.

Stojka's style is resonant of Expressionism, with its bold primary colours, strong sense of graphic design, and emphasis on the emotions, but also has echoes of the political poster. Just as a number, Z:5742, was tattoed indelibly on his arm, so his paintings bear the imprint of his suffering, with the number defiantly painted beside his signature. A further layer is added to many of the paintings in the form of a verbal message, usually painted in capital letters, indicating the place or theme of the painting. In addition to the words on the paintings themselves Stojka gives a sentence or two of commentary on each painting in the catalogues.

There has been no attempt to date to classify Stojka's paintings but I feel they fall naturally into four groups: first the scenes from his own childhood, second the representation of the Nazi obsession with racist ideology, third the exposure of the concentration camp universe and, fourth, his images and counter-images of traps and survival.

Childhood and family 'snapshots'

In order to appreciate the contrast between Stojka's early years and his later suffering it is helpful to look first at the penultimate image in the catalogue *Gas*. *We loved freedom more than everything else* is an idyllic picture of a Gypsy van in the middle of the countryside. A broad, bright blue river divides the painting diagonally from just above the bottom left corner to just below the top right corner. Below the river there are wild flowers and grass, above the river in the top centre there is a Gypsy van with figures happily relaxing near it. The palette of warm yellowy greens creates a restful, serene atmosphere, in sharp contrast to the harsh black lines and bold primary colours of the other works, which portray persecution, inhumanity and intolerance.

Freedom and family harmony were short-lived for Stojka, who learnt of the death of his father when the ashes and bones were returned unceremoniously to the family. The portrayal of the suicide of his father on the electric fence in Mauthausen concentration camp speaks volumes. The chilling image of the blue-striped, uniformed body spread-eagled diagonally, head down, the barbed wire at the top of the painting bent out of line by the weight of the body, is clearly a work of the imagination, but captures powerfully the feeling of bitterness and despair at the loss of a father.

Just before his twelfth birthday he and other members of his family were arrested, and one work shows the arrest of a Jewish boy. "He, too, was arrested in school – a few months later they came and took me away from school, right to prison – why us? We were only human beings, him a Jew, me a Rom, a Gypsy. We were both children of 10, 11 years, but Hitler was afraid of us and so we had to be put in a concentration camp" (Stojka 1998).

In his autobiography he writes: "Z: 5742 became my number. I still bear it on my arm to this day. Z for Zigeuner [Gypsy]. Two dots for full Gypsy, one dot was half-Gypsy and no dot stood for mixed race" (Stojka 1994:38). The bitter title of the self-portrait which opens the *Gas* catalogue exemplifies Stojka's interweaving of reality and political comment. *My name in the Third Reich was Z5742* is a provocation, a challenge to the viewer. Stojka depicts himself as a young vulnerable boy, sitting barefoot, his head downcast, his face tipped slightly to one side, mouth and eyes thoughtful and melancholy. His knees are tucked up under his chin, his arms round his ankles, is one of a human being huddled together, pulling himself into the minimum possible space trying to protect himself from the world around him. The wooded boards provide no comfort; the setting is one of isolation. The positioning of the boy in the centre of the portrait is such that the lines of the boards behind him draw the eye to the face and its expression of sadness, and from there vertically down to the number so indelibly scratched into the lower arm. The reality, that in the Nazi regime with its bureaucratic, racist inhuman system of classification Karl Stojka was given a number which was tattooed on his arm, is merged with the sense of loss of human dignity which this entailed. Clearly, he was still known by his name to his friends and family, but Stojka is making a political point, that he had been reduced to a number to all intents and purposes.

Further images of the innocence of youth are to be found in the poignant portrait of the artist and his three brothers and sisters. Behind five horizontal parallel rows of barbed wire the four children gaze straight at the viewer. In the tradition of the group photograph, all have folded their arms in the same way, left arm over right, but here this serves to expose the tattooed numbers. On closer inspection the barbed wire turns out to be lines of interlinked swastikas symbolising the power of the Nazi regime which forms a boundary between those persecuted by the regime and those considered fit to be allowed their freedom, with the children trapped behind the propaganda, the power which the swastika represents. Rows of barbed wire in the form of swastikas are also to be seen in a painting of the shooting by the SS of a woman who asked for water for her child, in an image of Nordhausen and one of Auschwitz-Birkenau. Stojka's commentary on the painting of himself and his siblings: *We were nothing but numbers*, may be seen as counter-discourse, in that each child in the painting is clearly more than just a number, differentiated as they are in terms of facial expression and colour of clothing.

The painting of the murder of his brother Ossi at the age of six and a half is striking. Draped across a black swastika and solid red background is Ossi's emaciated body, his mouth gaping wide open. In the bottom right of the painting the words "Der Schrei" ("The scream") pick up on Edvard Munch's famous work of that name.

Taken as a group, the images of his childhood and family bear witness to the horrific infringements of human rights and the attempted reduction of individuals, even children, to mere statistics. This dehumanisation process did not merely affect his own family, but is shown on a wider scale in the series of paintings depicting aspects of the implementation of Nazi racist policies in the Third Reich.

The Nazi obsession with racist ideology

The registering and assessing of the Gypsy became an obsession with the Nazis, and Stojka shows how the Wankostätte in Vienna became the first collective camp for Gypsies in Austria. His painting *Eva Justin and Dr. Ritter doing their work* portrays his grandmother, the object of pseudo-scientific research, sitting meekly while Justin, the woman in control, is using the other woman for her own career purposes, measuring her face with a long tape measure. The portrait is one of a power relationship, yet paradoxically Stojka reverses the power in pictorial terms, since it is the grandmother, dressed in a long scarlet dress, who has colour and who is the real focus of interest, whilst the sketchy outlines of Eva Justin reduce her to one of the grey mass of Nazis researchers.

"Just like the other major group of outsiders in Europe, the Jews, we were always on the run from destruction, whether it was in the form of assimilation or violence" (Stojka 1994:7). The Race Laws passed in Nuremberg applied not only to Jews but also to Roma and Sinte, and in a number of paintings Stojka illustrates the ways in which the National Socialist party rendered many areas of everyday life taboo for certain minority groups. The Jews had to wear a yellow Star of David, the Roma and Sinte a triangle with a Z. Both were forbidden from travelling by public transport, owning bicycles or going to cafés or swimming pools. One painting depicts a type of tug-of-war between a Nazi officer on the left of the painting and three Jewish women on the right. On the left stands the officer wrenching the bicycle by the front wheel from one of the women, and the bicycle is balanced precariously on its back wheel. Above the bicycle in the centre of the picture there dangles a flag with a swastika on it which is almost as large as the bicycle wheel itself. The physical struggle symbolises the removal of mobility and freedom from the Jews.

How can the implementation of racist policy be depicted? One painting of a shop window shows two jackbooted Nazi officers with swastika armbands looking at a sign which reads: "Hitler Nazi Defend yourselves! Don't buy from humans". On the left a woman with a Star of David sewn onto her coat is just walking into the picture. The subtle reworking of the Nazi slogan serves to interrogate the Nazi racist propaganda to be seen everywhere. Similarly, the boarded up shop-front of bookshop-owner Hermann Tuchner with the words "IS IN DACHAU" daubed across it in large letters, and below that a yellow Star of David and the word "JEW" convey the interrogation of prevalent ideology with a minimum of words and brush-strokes. Stojka is not reflecting the everyday reality but presenting with hindsight a critical reinterpretation of the prevalent images.

It is in the distillation of the senselessness of labelling and categorising people that

Stojka's critique of the Nazi policies is particularly effective. One painting consists entirely of eighteen different, brightly coloured, triangular labels, with numbers and categories (such as emigrant, Gypsy, homosexual or political prisoner) set against a background of vertical stripes reminiscent of prisoner's uniforms, which fade from strong pine green and dark green stripes at the top of the painting into a paler denimy blue and black at the bottom of the painting. Whilst the viewer can see merely categories and numbers, in short, the world as perceived by Nazi guards and researchers, behind these labels there remain people, and it is the very brightness of these labels and their collectively visually appealing patterns and rhythms which points in turn back to the individuality of the wearers.

People with half faces makes a similar point. Only half of each prisoner with his coloured label is visible, the line of blue-striped people stretching diagonally from front left to back right, each slightly smaller than the one in front, giving the illusion that the line stretches on beyond the edge of the picture to infinity. Stojka is demonstrating that although the clothes and belongings may have been taken away and the person fitted into a striped camp overall, with the appropriate badge attached to the clothing, it was not possible to eliminate the whole of a person, even though to all outward appearances the person had become subsumed into the regime, the universe of the concentration camp. The artist is challenging the viewer to look beyond his image to the real human beings in their entirety.

Whilst the artist recognises how invidious the categorisation of the uncategorisable is, the Nazi regime continued to categorise people into Aryan and non-Aryan, desirable and undesirable, and deport people to the concentration camps. In the following section I would like to look at Stojka's uncompromising exposure of the concentration camp universe.

The exposure of the concentration camp universe

Whereas many representations of the Holocaust stop short of the catacyclsmic, Stojka shows a wide range of images of the concentration camp universe, from the bedraggled creatures arriving at the camps, still wearing their own clothing, to the spartan accommodation and aspects of the daily routine, right through to the gassing and disposal of bodies.

Stojka's commentary on his portrayal of the sleeping accommodation reads: "We were put into wooden barracks. There were wooden beds, one on top of each other, 3 levels high. They were called 'Buxen' each of them measuring 2 by 2 meters. We had the one on the very top. We were 7 people. In some of these "Buxen" there were 10 to 15 people" (Stojka 1998). This interior scene has none of the quiet, subdued harmony of the Dutch or Flemish genre interior, but is characterised by chaos, pain, and a lack of space, hygiene and privacy. Many of the faces are at an angle, looking into the mid-distance or at the ground, evading the look of the viewer. In the infirmary too the accommodation was primitive, and one painting of the rows of wooden planks which served as beds for the sick is entitled *The infirmary was the antechamber to the crematorium*. Not all the sick even reached the infirmary. Another painting simply bears the title *The children died of hunger and diseases*.

Mass deprivation and degradation characterise the concentration camp universe. In his autobiography Stojka writes: "At 6.30 am we had to turn out for roll-call. Then there were 60,000 to 80,000 prisoners in the yard for roll-call, standing in blocks, and each block comprised about 1,000 to 1,500 people" (Stojka 1994:50). The painting *Mauthausen 1941 – somewhere there is my father* shows a mass of people gathered in a square, red flags with swastikas emblazoned on them waving in the breeze. The Nazis may see only the mass but Stojka reminds the viewer of the presence of the individual, in this case his father. The people portrayed here are not waiting voluntarily but are obliged to turn out in rain, snow, wind or hail and wait, often for hours, to be registered. This is a far cry from the scenes of jubilation and celebration of the Nazi cause which characterised shots of Hitler's mass rallies in Leni Riefenstahl's award-winning film, *The Triumph of the Will* (1935). It is important to remember that the scenes in Riefenstahl's films were cut and edited from miles of footage and equally provide a construction rather than a representation of reality, as is shown by the analyses by Welch (1993) and Zeman (1973) of the systematic and calculated uses of propaganda in all walks of life in the Nazi period.

In contrast to the concentration camp motto, "Work liberates", above the entrance gate, work for the inmates was, like the infirmary, frequently the antechamber to death. Stojka's moving depiction of the almost skeletal faces of men hard at work building the road from Buchenwald to Weimar has nothing of the liberating force of work about it.

How can death itself be portrayed? In *Only because she asked for water for her child, the SS shot her dead* the SS officer, a death-like figure entirely depicted in black and white, a badge on his belt proclaiming in large letters "Gott mit uns" ("God with us") even has black gaps between his teeth which give his face a skeletal air. The only splash of colour is the red border of his swastika armband. His right arm is raised, pointing his gun at a woman holding her child in her arms. Here, as in *They didn't cry for long*, a stark image of a guard with his gun pointed straight at a woman and child, death is about to occur. The viewer can imagine what would happen next and it is this projection of what is not visible which, it could be argued, makes these images even more compelling than those in which death has already occurred, such as the image of Buchenwald: "It was in Buchenwald where several prisoners ran away. Only two were caught, the others were shot while attempting to escape. Also these two were finally slain", which shows two men hanging lifeless from the posts to which their bodies have been tied.

The death of individuals is difficult enough to capture in a single image. The representation of mass extermination has seldom been attempted. One of Stojka's paintings has the caption: "The extinction machinery of Hitler's Germans killing all those Gypsies and Jews worked according to a precisely calculated system", yet the picture which it accompanies hardly has the air of precision or exactitude. People are being unloaded from trucks, a guard stands on duty with a gun in a watch tower and masses of people wait to be 'processed' at the camp. Here, and in the work *They had to go into the gas chamber* the viewer is reminded of the loss of individuality, pride, strength and dignity, and of how human beings were reduced to little more than living skeletons.

Paintings such as *They had to go into the gas chamber* and *After having gassed them, they were roasted and burned* show vulnerable naked adults and children about to enter the 'bath and disinfection' area and be gassed. The moment of death is imminent. The painting *That's how they deceived the people*, portraying the night of 2 August 1944 when almost 3,000 Sinti and Roma were murdered, shows three large 'shower heads' looming over a tightly packed mass of naked people. In all these works the images of the naked body are far removed from those encouraged in art during the Hitler regime (c.f. Taylor and van der Will 1990: 14-52).

Stojka deliberately exposes the indignity with which even the dead are treated. He shows men shovelling bodies into the ovens as piles of corpses lie thrown together on the floor awaiting cremation. In another painting he shows the corpses' hair being cut off and their golden teeth wrenched out. The simple shape of the crematorium chimney with smoke reappears in many of the paintings and evokes the barbaric murder of thousands. Stojka's commentary on one painting: "They killed everything. The wind whistled a soft song of death through the empty wooden barracks. There was death everywhere. Hitler's Nazis killed a whole people. But some were stronger than Hitler" (Stojka 1998) foreshadows some of the images of hope to be discussed later.

Implicit criticism of the role of the Church is evident in the painting of Auschwitz entitled *God and the church were watching*, which juxtaposes the black shape of the smoking crematorium chimney and an explosive outburst of golden light. *He was a victim too* portrays Jesus wearing a yellow Star of David, suspended from two posts on the barbed wire perimeter fence of the concentration camp, only visible behind some two dozen horizontal rows of barbed wire. The painting both traces anti-Semitism back to the crucifixion, and underlines the parallels between anti-Semitism and anti-Gypsyism.

A way out of the trap?

In his autobiography Stojka writes: "The crematorium was only 300 metres away from our barracks. Day and night you saw the fires. There was an atrocious stink. The main street in the camp was in front of our barracks. We called it the one-way street to hell" (Stojka 1994: 40). This is shown visually in *One-way street Auschwitz*, a very graphic work using only three main colours, black, beige and rust, with a truck full of Stars of David with the word "Auschwitz" painted on its side moving from right to left, in the mid-distance a sign with an arrow saying "one way". Numerous stars appear to be tumbling out of the truck onto the road, perhaps indicating that one or two might not end up in Auschwitz. A further abstract representation of anti-Semitism is to be seen in *Trapped in the swastika*. Against a blood-red background a black swastika, its edges spiky with barbed wire, fills the entire painting. At the intersection of the bars of the swastika lies a yellow Star of David with the word "Jude" (Jew). Stojka's art is concerned with freeing the Jew from the trap, giving power back to persecuted minorities.

Stojka is the first Romani artist to highlight the fate of Roma and Sinte in the Holocaust. Although the desolate image of two bare trees, an empty Gypsy caravan, and the words *We Sinti are in the gas chamber in Auschwitz* subverts traditional images of the romantic, idyllic, nomadic Romani life, the painting is also an act of defiance, since not all the Roma and Sinte did perish.

The tension between the written words and reality is also evident in *There was no way out*, a strong graphic image of the main gate at Auschwitz. The diagonal lines draw the viewer in to the only part of the painting which does not consist of thick, hard, black lines against an almost luminous pale background, into a small area in which the thick lines enclose what appear at first glimpse to be pieces of barbed wire, but which on closer scrutiny turn out to be in the shape of Stojka's own number, 5742. Although all the visual evidence appears to point to the inevitability of death, for Stojka himself there was a way out. The motif of the trap is employed to similar effect in another work. *I was trapped by the light* is a graphic representation of a circle of thirteen black watchtowers with their yellow spotlights trained on the centre of the circle. In this centre is the 'I' of the painting, represented not by a person but by a black triangle containing the letter Z, and beside it the number 5742. He may have been trapped by the light but did finally manage to survive.

Of all the re-framing of Nazi propaganda, symbols and terminology, the most powerful is *Mein Kampf Z5742 I have survived*. In the top third of the painting Stojka takes the title of Hitler's seminal work *Mein Kampf* (*My struggle*), which he writes in white letters against a black background in his own bold uneven capitals rather than the Gothic script normally associated with the words. In the middle section there is a red triangle with a white Z and to its right the numbers 5742 in black against a red and white background, and in the bottom section are the triumphant words "I have survived", again in white letters against a black background. Here he both mourns those who lost their lives, but at the same time celebrates the victory of the survivors, including himself, over fascism and racist ideology.

Conclusion

Stojka's autobiographical art is both extremely personal and highly political. He aims to point out how ludicrous and inhumane the Nazi racist policies were and to highlight the persecution of Roma and Sinte, focusing particularly on many degrading aspects of the concentration camp system culminating in genocide.

He is not the ethnographer who comes in and watches an ethnic group as an outsider, but an insider who is distanced from his experiences not by ethnicity but by time. That time has enabled him to create distance between himself and the perpetrators of the genocide of many members of his own family and thousands of his race. He constructs his paintings to provoke the viewer to adopt a critical standpoint towards the works.

The incorporation of written text into the pictures gives the works something of the air of the protest poster, or propaganda document. At times the words may underline the message, but they may also be used against the grain to subvert the visual image with a type of *Verfremdungseffekt* (alienation effect) created at the intersection of the verbal and visual discourse. He provides a critical reframing of the visual symbols which came to represent whole categories of people in the National Socialist period. He skilfully interweaves the faces, the buildings, the swastikas, his own concentration camp number, and images such as that of the crematorium chimney, with a powerful element of transgression, going beyond the normal limits of representation, to create a vibrant yet disturbing new landscape, whose broad brush-strokes, bright colours and strong visual contrasts have an immediate emotional impact on the viewer.

Karl Stojka is the first Romani artist to provide a political testimony to his past. His protest art aims to render his ethnic group visible, whilst raising awareness of and sensitivity to the parallels between anti-Semitism and anti-Gypsyism. In producing an impressive number of highly original, and intensely dramatic and moving works which do not shy aware from portraying the cataclysmic, he has not only succeeded in his goal of contributing to our knowledge of the Romani Holocaust, but has enriched Romani, Austrian and indeed world culture.

References

Clark, Toby, 1997 *Art and propaganda in the twentieth century: the political image in the age of mass culture*, Weidenfeld and Nicholson, London.

Dyer, Richard, 1997 *White*, Routledge, London and New York.

Ezrahi, Sidra DeKoven, 1980 *By words alone: The Holocaust in Literature*, University of Chicago Press, Chicago.

Nochlin, Linda and Tamar Garb, 1995 *The Jew in the text: modernity and the construction of identity*, Thames and Hudson, London.

Stojka, Karl and Reinhard Pohanka, 1994 *Auf der ganzen Welt zu Hause: Das Leben und Wandern des Zigeuners Karl Stojka*, Picus, Vienna.

Stojka, Karl, 1995 *Ein Kind in Birkenau*, Karl Stojka (Eigendruck), Vienna. Note: in this and the 1998 catalogue there are neither page numbers, official titles nor information on the paintings' dimensions. In this paper I refer to the paintings by the one or two-line commentaries Stojka provides, which are given in German and English in *Gas* (1998). The English translations are used throughout. Translations from *Ein Kind in Birkenau* are my own.

Stojka, Karl, 1998, 2nd edn. *Gas*, Karl Stojka (Eigendruck), Vienna.

Taylor, Brandon and Wilfried van der Will, 1990 *The Nazification of art*, Winchester Press, Winchester.
Tebbutt, Susan, ed.1998 *Sinti and Roma: Gypsies in German-speaking society and literature*, Berghahn, New York and Oxford.
Welch, David, 1993 *The Third Reich: politics and propaganda*, Routledge, London and New York.
Wippermann, Wolfgang, 1997 *'Wie die Zigeuner': Antisemitismus und Antiziganismus im Vergleich*, Elefanten Press, Berlin.
Young, James E., 1988, *Writing and rewriting the Holocaust*, Indiana University Press, Indianapolis.
Zeman, Z. A. B., 1973 (2nd edn, 1st publ. 1964) *Nazi propaganda*, Oxford University Press, Oxford

CHAPTER SEVEN

MYTH AS PROCESS

Elena Marushiakova and Vesselin Popov

"We used to have a great king, a Rom. He was our prince. He was our king. The Gypsies used to live all together at that time in one place, in one beautiful country. The name of that country was Sind. There was much happiness, much joy there. The name of our chief was Mar Amengo Dep. He had two brothers. The name of one was Romano, the name of the other was Singan. That was good, but then there was a big war there. The Moslems caused the war. They made ashes and dust of the Gypsy country. All the Gypsies fled together from their own land. They began to wander as poor men in other countries, in other lands. At that time the three brothers took their followers and moved off, they marched along many roads. Some went to Arabia, some went to Byzantium, some went to Armenia." (Kenrick and Puxon 1972: 13)

THIS LEGEND, which has appeared many times in various publications, was recorded in the town of Shumen, Bulgaria in the 1960s by Donald Kenrick as told by a local Rom, Ali Tchaushev. It provides a good illustration of the complex way in which Romani folklore works in the Balkans, both in its nature, or structure, and in its processes of transmission and reproduction. This folkore is not a dead or stagnant heritage, merely revered and reproduced as a symbol of ethno-cultural tradition, but a living dynamic system in constant development, with various functions, including that of recording the history of the community as in the legend cited above.

History and the traditions which we label 'folklore' have a special place in the life of Balkan nations, where the processes of ethno-national development began later than Western Europe, in the nineteenth century, and are still active now. History is not so much a science as part of the national mythology. Each nation in the Balkans has its own historical mythology dating from ancient times (most often from the cradle of world civilisation) which reveals its glorious historical past. It is constantly resurrected and projected in different guises in modern times, especially in crisis situations. In the Balkans nations live more closed lives – closed within the patterns and inferiority complexes of their historical past rather than open to the problems of the present and the perspective of the future. Folklore traditions are important to the Balkan nations because they are an integral part of "historical neo-mythology", which often makes use of their substance and arguments to explain contemporary problems.

'Gypsies' in the Balkans are no exception to this general rule; they do not live in a world of their own. Their complex historical destiny has always been an indelible part of the surrounding macrosociety. The legends about their origins are a well-developed and diverse genre because the question of the origin of any people is one of the primary epistemological issues underlying the identity of a group, and one that must be tackled within the corpus of, and at the level of folkore. Unlike other Balkan nations the Roma do not have their own official institutions for science and education which explains why the answers to this question have remained on this level for centuries.

Gypsy folklore, however, is not a completely closed, self-sufficient and self-developing system. It is strongly influenced by the 'official' culture of the macrosociety where Roma live and by the general cultural and historical context of the Balkans. In particular, Gypsy legends about their origins express the extremely complicated relations between folklore and 'official' culture, which can either make use of typically archaic folklore plots, forms and approaches, joining them together with the respected and established religious images or 'prove' them by the 'achievements' of modern 'scientific' knowledge.

Probably the most archaic are the roots of the legends attributing the origin of 'Gypsies' to their descent from a brother and a sister. In some variants the names of the brother and sister are Tchin and Genia, (Marushiakova and Popov 1994: 19–21), which is a naive etymology of the Turkish word *Tchingene*, meaning 'Gypsies'. Somewhat related is the legend about a boy and a girl saved respectively by St George and St Vassil (or *Bango Vassil*, i.e. Vassil the lame one) when all Roma were threatened with annihilation. This explains why these are the saints most revered by the Roma today (Marushiakova and Popov 1994: 103). Even these legends seek to prove their truth with evidence from 'outside' outside the Romani community, in accordance with the spirit of the religious tradition of the macrosociety, whether Christian or a Muslim (or, as is often the case, a combination of both). That is why the Biblical images of Abraham, King Namrut, Archangels Michael and Gabriel, St George and St Vassil appear in these legends.

A frequent phenomenon in many legends is the relation between the origin and scattering of the Gypsies around the world with their mythical leaders and the 'lost kingdom' theme located in ancient Biblical Egypt. Popular among Balkan Roma is the cycle of legends about the Gypsy 'king Pharaoh' [Phirion, Phiraun, Pheravin, etc.] (Djordjevic 1933: 122–3; Marushiakova and Popov 1994: 22–31, 49–50). Most variants of these legends were recorded in the first half of our century but quite a few of them are still popular today. They tell about the kingdom of the Gypsies in Egypt, retell the story of Moses (or Misai), describe the popular Biblical theme about the parting of the sea, the escape of the Jews and the drowning of the soldiers of the Egyptian king. Sometimes these legends mention St Vassil, who saved the Gypsies with the help of some geese. This explains the celebration of Vasiliovden (Vasilitsa, i.e. the day of Vassil – the Romani New Year) with roast geese honouring the saviour goose. (Djordjevic 1933: 126–7; Marushiakova and Popov 1994: 49–50).

The 'Egyptian' cycle of legends has complex relations with the development of the social and political thinking of the Gypsies. The belief that 'Gypsies' came from Egypt originated in the Balkans in about the thirteenth or fourteenth centuries when various Byzantine sources referred to 'Tsigani' and 'Egyptians', either separately or as if they were the same people (Marushiakova and Popov 2000). When they first came to Western Europe Roma also presented themselves as newcomers from 'Little Egypt'. This belief continued to be reported among the Roma until the time of the Ottoman Empire, when Johan Kampelen noted in one of his descriptions of the Gypsies in the region of Nish in 1740 that they were proud of their Egyptian roots (Ionov, 1983: 128–9).

The nineteenth century saw a new stage in the development of Romani historical awareness on the Balkans. As well as the type of folkloric epistemology which sought to ground itself in biblical authority, attempts were made to prove the Egyptian origin of Gypsies scientifically and thus lead on to a discussion of the problems hindering their social emancipation. In 1866 Petko Ratchev Slaveikov, a famous Bulgarian poet and publicist, wrote an article, "The Gypsies", for the *Gaida* newspaper in Istanbul (Marushiakova and Popov 1995: 36–45). The article claimed the Gypsies originated in ancient Egypt and that they had brought the achievements of civilisation and scientific knowledge to ancient Greece and that their language had influenced the Greek language (including the claim that the name of Athens was derived from 'atsingani'). This was far removed from the prevailing scientific understanding of the origin of Gypsies; this claim can be best understood as part of the intricate social struggle for an independent Bulgarian church, separate from the dominance of the Greek Patriarchy.

Nonetheless, this obscure article provoked an interesting and perhaps paradoxical 'feedback', which had a continuing influence on representatives of the Gypsy community. The following year, 1867, *Macedonia*, a newly established newspaper edited by P. R. Slaveikov, published a 'Letter to the Editor' signed by 'An Egyptian' from the town of Prilep in Macedonia (Marushiakova and Popov 1995: 36–45). Building on the thesis, developed by the newspaper editor, about the origin of the Gypsies, the author cited the Bible to claim that Gypsies had the right to have their own place in the Christian church. In the context of disputes between the autonomous and would-be autonomous patriarchates of the church in the Balkans (which continue to the present day) the implication was that each nation (including the Gypsies) should establish its own church.

The idea that each nation should have its own church (in the same way that it is supposed to have its own language and even its own alphabet) is seen in the Balkans as proving a nation's right to exist as independent and equal to others. If we consider this we can understand the point of legends about the Gypsies whose church was made of bacon (or cheese) which they ate (Djordjevic 1933: 29–30; Block 1936: 180) or another cycle of legends about the Gypsies having their own alphabet which was eaten by a donkey (Tong 1989: 169; Marushiakova and Popov 1994: 53–54).

These legends are popular among both the Roma and the surrounding population. They help explain the low social status of the Roma (a public image which has hardly changed today). Sometimes there still is a mingling of separate themes such as legends about the Jews hiding the Gypsy alphabet in a pyramid in the grave of 'King Pharaoh' in Egypt (Marushiakova and Popov 1995: 26–7; Studii Romani 1998).

In the example of the 'Letter to the Editor' from 'An Egyptian' (written by a 'Gypsy', Ilia Naumtchev, who became a clergyman in the Bulgarian Orthodox Church), the concept of the Egyptian origin of Gypsies transcended the level of folklore and reached the realm of community historical awareness (and more specifically the awareness of its leaders). It became an argument in support of the movement for the emancipation of the Romani community as early as the nineteenth-century. This is not the only example. At the beginning of the last century, during the struggle of Bulgarian Gypsies against the ban on voting imposed on many of the nomadic and settled Muslim Roma in 1901 (Marushiakova and Popov 1997: 29–30), this belief was widely accepted as we can see from the documents of the First Congress of the Gypsies in 1905, whose signatories defined themselves as representatives of the "Coptic population" (Vecherna poshta 1905). The self-identification of the Gypsies as Copts has ancient roots. In many documents of the Ottoman Empire between the fifteenth and the eighteenth centuries they were referred to as "Kýpts" (Marushiakova and Popov 2000).

The first Gypsy organisation in Bulgaria, established in 1919 (or according to other sources in 1921 or 1931) also bore the name 'Egypt' (Marushiakova and Popov 1997: 30). In time, however, under the influence of the surrounding population, the concept of their Indian origin (which we discuss later) gradually spread among the Roma, and the concept of ancient Egyptian origin remained in the level of folklore. In some instances there has been an interesting combination with contemporary geographical knowledge, for example "my grandfather came to Sofia from Egypt, passing through Spain and France" (Studii Romani 1997).

The Egyptian theory, however, was far from disappearing from the Balkans. On the contrary, it underwent a powerful revival in the countries of former Yugoslavia and Albania, where it was transformed to a new and qualitatively higher level. We have in mind the so-called 'Egyptians' in Macedonia and Kosovo and the 'Yevgi' in Albania who had been perceived for centuries by the surrounding populations as Gypsies. Their existance in recent years as independent communities different from the rest of the Romani community was explained in a rather naive manner, as mainly being the result of the social and political influences of the state and the surrounding population within former Yugoslavia and the new countries which were established later (ERRC 1998: 34–8; Willems 1997: 1–3). To understand these processes, we have to consider the manner in which various Gypsy communities in the Balkans have often had to exercise a choice of preferred ethnic identity.

Trends towards the religious and ethnic assimilation of the Gypsies by the predominant communities have always existed in the Balkans. These processes, either voluntary or under pressure, have existed since the time of the Ottoman Empire and more recently in the ethno-national Christian Orthodox countries. At the same time, from as early as the last century, there was a tendency for Gypsy communities to claim a different identity, neither Romani, nor the same as that of the surrounding society. This was partly a reaction against the pressure of assimilation, but also an attempt to avoid the widespread negative attitudes shown towards the Gypsies in the Balkans. Whilst all Balkan nations are historical enemies they are still of equal standing as communities whilst the Gypsies have always been an exception: they are a community of the lowest order, incompatible with the others. That is why when Gypsies seek a new preferred identity, their search is always directed towards another minority, which has a higher social status than the Romani one, such as the Turks and Vlachs (i.e. Romanians) in Bulgaria and Greece, the Albanians and the Turks and Vlachs in former Yugoslavia.

The adamant refusal of other minorities to accept the Gypsies has quite often led to a third way, the creation of a new identity as the ultimate means of achieving a higher social status as a people. This can be observed among the Albanian-speaking Egyptchani/Yevgi. It seems that in their communities these processes have acquired a routine and new dimensions in the overall context of the dissolution of Yugoslavia and the establishment of new states and nations. This began in the 1970s with the first attempts to have a separate entry for Egyptchani (Egyptians) in the population censuses in Yugoslavia. The long struggle ended with success in the population census in 1991. The establishment of the Egyptchani association in 1990 in Ohrid, Macedonia, the Democratic Movement Party in 1991 in Struga, Macedonia, the formation of independent associations of the Egyptchani in Macedonia, Serbia and Kosovo after the dissolution of Yugoslavia in 1992; the establishment of similar associations in Albania (the first one was founded in Korcha in 1992); the formation of the Balkan Union of the Egyptians in 1998 in Ohrid: all these are stages in the formation of a new community. This has been accompanied by the presentation of the appropriate folklore, accompanied by 'scientific' explanation. The first book published by the Association of the Egyptians was dedicated to their myths and legends (Risteski 1991) and the second to their ethno-genesis (Zemon 1996), i.e. again we have a repetition of the familiar Balkan patterns of putting their own folklore first and emphasising the extreme importance of their early history. It is of little importance to the community how far these theses about the origin of the 'Egyptians' can be justified scientifically since each nation in the Balkans has its own school of history and positions on the key issues which almost never coincide with those of their neighbours. This 'scientific' quest for the ethno-genesis of the 'Egyptians' in Macedonia does not, however, emerge in a vacuum – to a great extent it corresponds to the legends of the 'Agupti' living in the Rhodope mountains of Bulgaria, recorded in the 1950s, where their origin was attributed to Egyptian slaves brought to the Balkans by Roman soldiers (Primovski 1955: 248).

Similar quests for a 'third road', for new variants of identity, can be observed in other Gypsy communities who prefer not to be known as Gypsies. Since they are not accepted as 'Turks' by the surrounding Bulgarian population or by Bulgarian Turks some of them prefer to call themselves simply 'millet' (i.e. people) or 'Muslims'. They then look for explanations for their own origin. Examples such as this can be observed at all stages of development, sometimes in an increasingly obvious way, for example, 'Usta Millet' in the region of the town of Dobritch, are now beginning to create their 'own history' according to which they are the descendants of an unknown tribe of blacksmiths from Afghanistan, who were the most famous gunsmiths at the time of the Ottoman Empire (Studii Romani 1999).

Another variation of this type of identity quest can be seen among some Xoraxane Roma (Turkish Roma) from the Ludogorie region who claim they are descendants of people of Arab origin, from the Koreysha clan who lived in Bulgaria in 1200–1300 AD. Proof can be seen in the Muslim tombstones from all over the region (in Russe, Razgrad, Silistra, Dulovo, Isperih, Kubrat) dating from the reign of King Kaloyan around 1205 AD (Donald Kenrick, personal communication). This is a repetition of a persistent historical myth of Arab origin which is also common among Bulgarian Muslims (the so called Pomaks), and is based on a mistaken reading (whether deliberate or otherwise) of the years on Muslim tombstones which, of course, are dated according to the Islamic calendar, but are interpreted according to the Christian one.

The 'Turkish Gypsies' (Muslims) also sometimes combine their claim of an Arab origin with the 'Indian thesis' in a kind of compromise. According to one legend recorded in the region of the town of Sliven the Roma come from India but they are 'hasýl Arabs' (i.e. true Arabs). Their names are Arabic and since there is no great difference between the Indian and the Arab languages, it is easy to understand the words in Indian movies. This story is 'confirmed' through a familiar traditional formula – according to the informant this has been read in a secret book kept in the attic of his school, and that was why he was punished by the school principal.

The Rumanian-speaking Rudari in Bulgaria have introduced a similar variant, so far mostly at the level of folklore. They are beginning to present themselves as 'true Vlachs', or 'the oldest Rumanians'. One of their popular legends derives Rudari origin from their ancient kingdom in the Balkans. Following its destruction some of them crossed the Danube and laid the foundations of the Rumanian people, while their true direct ancestors, the Rudari of today, remained in Bulgarian lands. In some instances their explanations already have begun to follow the trail of quasi-historical knowledge, leaning on naive historical research, (Ionov 1998) which asserts the unity of Rudari with present day Rumanians; gradually this reasoning is acquired by the Rudari themselves, assisted by the efforts of the autodidact authors.

Very important for the development of Romani historical thinking is the penetration of the 'Indian thesis' about their origin. This process is determined by the advance of modern scientific knowledge in the Balkans and more particularly the concept of ancient India as the ancient Romani motherland. The Balkan nations became familiar with these scientific theses for the first time in the second half of the nineteenth century. They gradually entered the public mind in the first half of the twentieth century, and eventually reached the Roma and are now reflected in their legends. One such legend is the one about their chief Berko who fought in India and then brought his army to new lands and founded the modern town of Berkovitsa in north-western Bulgaria, near the chestnut forests which provided them with a living (Marushiakova and Popov, 1994: 17–18). Thus they introduced new historical evidence into the formal structure of an old legend with an anecdotal content, based on naive etymology. This newly created legend quickly acquired the form of quasi-historical knowledge and was reflected in the new Romani press from the second half of the 1940s, for example: "Our minority has lived in Bulgaria since the seventh century, where our forefathers settled led by the leader of Gypsies all over the world – Berko – a very dangerous adversary of the then Indian Emperor – Abdurrahman" (Romano Essi 1948).

The popularisation of the 'Indian connection' was very much influenced by the two waves of Indian movies shown in Bulgaria which enjoyed huge success among the Bulgarian Roma in the 1950's and 1970's. In these movies the Roma found a linguistic proximity to their ancient homeland. Active processes of searching for new knowledge about their historical destiny developed in the Romani communities. A typical example in this respect is Ali Tchaushev, Donald Kenrick's informant, who told him the legend cited in the beginning of the article.

Ali Tchaushev was born in the town of Shumen. In the 1950's and 1960's he was socially active in the system of the Fatherland Front (a popular organisation dominated by the Bulgarian Communist party) and established a number of Romani cultural and educational associations in Shumen and the surrounding region. He was deeply interested in Romani history and especially in the ancient Romani homeland, India. He made contacts with the Indian embassy and Indian students studying in Bulgaria. The Indian writer Chaman Lal mentioned him when he described his visit to Bulgaria in the beginning of the 1960's: "A Muslim Gypsy travelled 500 miles to meet with me in Sofia" (Lal 1969: 13).

The legend told by Ali Tchaushev becomes quite easy to understand in this context (Kenrick 1985: 75). He was very familiar with different sources of modern historical research on the origin and early migrations of the Roma, which he translated into the ethno-cultural language of the Roma in Bulgaria in the guise of a folk myth of origin, using the typical folklore means of asserting its truth value: I have heard this from my old grandfather" (Marushiakova and Popov 1994: 63–5).

Another factor which made a considerable contribution to the development of Romani historical thinking on the Balkans was the development of the international Romani movement and the work of some of its activists in the Balkan countries, such as Grattan Puxon in former Yugoslavia and Donald Kenrick himself in Bulgaria. The establishing first World Romani Congress in 1971 in London, leading to the formation of the International Romani Union and the second Congress in Geneva in 1978 and subsequent congresses in Göttingen (1981) and Warsaw (1990), and the first World Festival of Romani Culture in Chandigarh in 1976 all broadened the world view of the Romani representatives and acquainted them with the developments of modern science. The impetus towards building a Romani historical school within the framework of the academic traditions of the Balkan nations began to acquire a coherent momentum of its own, based on and directed towards close ties with the Indian homeland. It is reflected most vividly in the academic writings of Rajko Djuric, president of the Romani Union. (Djuric 1983, Djuric et al. 1996)

The influence of contemporary historiography on the historical thinking of Balkan Roma was especially active after the changes in Eastern Europe in 1989. For Bulgaria in particular this included the end of bans on proclaiming Romani identity, and an end to restrictions on the access to information which had been imposed by the former regime. These processes can sometimes be a transition from science to modernised folklore forms. A typical example of this is how Roma perceive the work of Donald Kenrick and more specifically his book *From India to the Mediterranean* published in Bulgaria (1996a, Bulgarian tr. 1998). Young Romani poets inspired by this book composed poetic myths and legends based on its historical themes, which are currently in the process of being illustrated by Romani artists with the purpose of distributing them in the Romani environment in the form of cartoons. In view of the processes which have developed until now, when we were planning this paper, we thought it would not be too far-fetched to say that in a few years or decades the coming academic generation will discover Romani legends 'in the field' in Bulgaria, such as legends about the Persian king Bahram Ghur or other historical personalities. (But, as is often the case, reality exceeded our expectations. Only six months later, during our expedition in Dobrudja in the autumn of 1999, we made a recording in the town of Dobritch of this legend told in Romanes. After he told us the legend, the informant reluctantly admitted having read it in Donald Kenrick's book. It is obvious that he will present it as a very old legend upon other occasions.)

Thus, the processes of change in the historical thinking of the Romani community are not limited to the works of a few authors but are often disseminated through

Donald Kenrick showing his book *Gypsies: From India to the Mediterranean* to English Gypsy leader, Tom Lee.

the mechanism of folklore. The concept of an Indian origin is generally predominant now among most Roma on the Balkans, but it is still explained by the classical means of folklore and legends, and still uses traditional mechanisms to prove their truth (for example emphasising the presence of specific forefathers): "All Gypsies were in India. And a river came ... the Tsigan [Gypsy] river ... and it dragged all the Gypsies and scattered them everywhere ... This I have remembered from my grandfather ... He had also been there ... His grandfather had lived in India." (Marushiakova and Popov 1995: 29) In other instances the legend has a pseudo-historical explanation: "... this was written in an old book ... published during the time of Todor Zhivkov, it was studied in schools back then" (Studii Romani 1997).

The Indian thread however, is not the only one in the modern development of Romani historical thinking. Their double status – a specific ethnic community and at the same time a minority in the different ethno-national states on the Balkans, determines their place in the context of the respective national histories. Typical examples are the widely popular narratives relating the settlement of Roma in Bulgarian lands with the establishment and early stages of development of the Bulgarian state.

This is one of the few instances when we can confidently make hypotheses about the initial basis of a cycle of Romani legends. We have in mind a book written in the end of last century by the Bulgarian author Peter Odjakov. Very naively it 'proved' that the Gypsies settled in Bulgarian lands together with the proto-Bulgarians led by king Asparukh, who laid the foundations of the Bulgarian state in the year 681 AD (Odjakov 1885: 8–11). This idea reached the Roma through the secondary channels of the macrosociety and immediately found a place in their folklore. There it began to develop along its own ways, following its own laws, reaching not merely completed folklore forms (such as the legend about the Gypsy chief Berko which pinpoints the time of his arrival in Bulgaria as the seventh century.) There were also numerous publications in the Gypsy press in the end of the 1940s confirming this thesis. Eventually this led to changes in the community identity of some Gypsy groups. In some places in Bulgaria today we can find Gypsy groups which the surrounding population often ironically calls "Bulgarians of King Asparukh". Moreover, sometimes such Gypsies may come to perceive this concept as a group self-appellation and look for related scientific proofs of their origin. During the so called 'process of revival' in the second half of the 1980s, when Bulgarian scientists were 'proving' the Bulgarian origin of the Bulgarian Turkish population, the Ethnographic Institute with Museum of the Bulgarian Academy of Sciences received a letter from a group of Gypsies demanding that "science speak out" and explain their origin. The letter told about how they had come to Bulgarian lands together with the proto-Bulgarians of King Asparukh as blacksmiths servicing his army.

Legends exist also which associate the presence of blacksmith Gypsies with the Bulgarian Khan Krum. In some publications and conversations with his Romani informants in the 1930s, Dr Naiden Sheytanov popularised the hypothesis about Gypsy settlement in Bulgarian lands during the first half of ninth century (when Khan Krum was the ruler of Bulgaria), which had previously been suggested by other authors as well. Among the Roma this legend quickly grew into the popular contemporary story of the Gypsy blacksmiths who plated with silver the skull of the Byzantine emperor Nikiphorus I Gennik, who perished in combat in 811, and made it into a special cup from which Khan Krum would drink during feasts, according to Bulgarian patriotic legends (Studii Romani 1997).

This line of thought which links the origin and early history of the Roma with important moments in Bulgarian history, is reflected in another thesis popular among the Roma on the folklore level. According to it they are heirs of a mythical kingdom destroyed by the armies of Alexander the Great during his conquests in the Middle East. The Roma who settled for good in Bulgarian lands, became the four main castes, together with Thraceans, Slavs and Proto-Bulgarians. After the adoption of Christianity in 865 the Bulgarian nation emerged from these four castes (Studii Romani 1998).

Similar is the development of the ideology of the political party Democratic Movement, Rodolyubie, registered in 1998. According to its leader this is the party of the Rudara and the word Rudara does not derive from the word 'ruda' (ore) but from the word 'rod' (family or clan in Bulgarian) because "we are descendants of the first old Bulgarian clans who settled in these lands together with Khan Asparukh at the time when the Bulgarian state was founded."

At present, the new stage in development of the Romani community leads to new forms of socially constructed quasi-historical knowledge which become part of established Balkan traditions. At the same time the modern forms of scientific knowledge are combined with the old and modernised folklore legends. Typical in this respect are the works of Romani writers which present a complex and comprehensive picture of the ethnogenesis of Bulgarian Roma – some of them, the so called Turkish Gypsies (i.e. Muslims) are descendants from slaves brought to the Balkans from Egypt by Julius Caesar; others are descendants of the Indian mercenaries of Emperor Trajan, who settled in Bulgarian lands. In the new lands these two population groups mixed with the descendants of the ancient Thraceans and Illirians and thus the new community was born: the Roma (the name derives from Romei i.e. Romans). Gradually some of them settled beyond the Danube and laid the beginning of the Rumanian people, yet others settled in Western Europe (Marushiakova and Popov 1995: 46–8).

Yet in other instances quasi-historical knowledge may be directed far back into the past, towards the roots of human civilisation. An example is the wish to derive the origin of Gypsies from Ancient Mesopotamia and prove their kinship with the ancient Sumerians (Studii Romani 1996). A variant of this search for origins is the quick popularisation among the Roma of the concept of Gypsies as descendants from Mohendzho Daro, which appeared in other East European countries (Studii Romani 1998).

Some specific literary forms have found their place in the general framework of the modern emancipation processes of the Romani community. We can define them most generally as historical neo-mythology. These are the attempts to lay bridges to modern science or at least to use its formal features. A typical example is the poetry of the so-called author's legends by the Roma poetess, Sally Ibrahim. In her work she presents a new genre – historical neo-mythology – on the border between folklore and fictional creativity. Sally Ibrahim's texts (*Descendants of Atlantis*, and *The Roma Myth – a Truth*) actively use the 'achievements' of modern 'unorthodox' para-science. Through para-scientific phraseology the poems describe the extraordinary historical destiny of the Roma – their homeland is Atlantis, they are the messengers of God, missionaries of a higher civilisation, the disseminators of human culture around the world, their language is mankind's proto-language (a number of naive etymological examples are cited to prove this point) and others (Marushiakova and Popov 1994: 65–8).

Similar are the speculations of the popular singer Anita Christie, which have appeared in the media quite a few times. According to her, the Gypsies come from the mythic town of Shamballa (popular in Bulgaria from the works of famous Russian painter and philosopher Nikolai Rërich) situated between India and China. In a cosmic Shamballa corresponding to the Shamballa on Earth, the Gypsies were "Buddhi-Manusha" (meaning people who are incarnations of Buddha); they were masters of the great cosmic knowledge, which they had scattered among people around the world and it had been taken away from them but they would get it back (Studii Romani 1998). Similar stories can be heard from other representatives of the Romani intelligentsia (Studii Romani 1998). They link the popular ideas of Eastern religious philosophy with the theme of the Gypsies as a chosen people.

We should not be bothered by the fact that these concepts and writings belong to individual authors and are disseminated by individual members of the Romani community. Each folklore text belongs to a certain author upon its birth and it becomes a collective piece of work by way of its perception and function in a certain social environment. The fact that similar ideas thrive in everyday Romani life is proved by the statements, heard during field research, that Gypsies are neither Christians nor Muslims, they are actually Buddhists (Studii Romani 1998). Usually informants cannot supply evidence about this fact, but this is an easy to overcome obstacle – publications by Romani authors looking for evidence have appeared in many editions (Kyutchukov 1994: 18–19).

The idea of the Roma as a Chosen people can be found in other levels today, moving away from folklore. For example, the coming of Islamic preachers among the Roma, (however restricted it may be because of the existing prejudice towards them), has led to the pilgrimage of Roma to Mecca. One of them, who came back from pilgrimage, told in detail about the dream he had there, how Allah gave him a mysterious book, written in the Romani language and containing the truth about Islam (Studii Romani 1996). A variant of the idea of the Gypsies as a chosen people can be found in many hymns in the now popular among the Roma new Evangelical churches, which contain expressions such as "we are God's favourite children", "God loves us, the Gypsies" and others (Marushiakova and Popov 1995: 102–8; Studii Romani 1997). As we can see from this overview, Roma on the Balkans are living through processes of active change in community awareness. These changes, reflected in different historical ideas, function on different levels and acquire different eclectic forms (ranging from the traditional or very modernised folklore through quasi-historical knowledge to modern 'unorthodox' para-science). The eclectic nature of these dynamic processes was heralded by the fact that this is a regular stage of development of the historical thinking of each nation. The Roma have a lot to make up for and this is the reason for the rapid development of this type of thinking.

The processes in the Romani community never cease but at present, under the new social and political conditions, they develop particularly rapidly and to a certain extent with many contradictions. We have to emphasise the place these processes have in the framework of an ever-growing Roma nationalism. And we also have to consider the fact that they are influenced by a number of external factors coming from the macrosociety, not least among which is the scientific work of specialists whose writings, and the ideas and concepts they express, often penetrate quickly into the Romani environment. Again, this brings to the forefront the issue of the moral responsibility of scientists towards the target of their study.

References

Block, M., 1936 *Zigeuner und ihre Seele. Dargestellt auf Grund eigener Reisen und Forschungen*, Bibliographisches Institut, Leipzig (translated into English by Kuczynski B. and Taylor D., 1838, *Gypsies, their life and customs*, Methuen, London).

Djordjević, T., 1933 *Naš narodni žhivot* [Our Folk Life] kn. 7, (Vol.7); privately published, Belgrade.

Djurić, R., 1983 *Seobe Roma: Krugovi pakla i venac srece*, [Circle of Hell and Wreath of Luck], Biblioteka Publicistika, Belgrade.

Djuric, R., Becken J., and Bengsch A.B., 1996 *Ohne Heim ohne Grab*, Aufbau Verlag, Berlin.

Dujzings, G., 1997 "The Making of Egyptians in Kosovo and Macedonia" in Govers C and Vermeulen H (eds.), *The politics of ethnic consciousness*, London, Macmillan, pp.194–222.

E.R.R.C. (European Roma Rights Center), 1998 *A pleasant fiction: the human rights situation of Roma in Macedonia*, ERRC Country Reports Series No 7, Budapest.

Ionov, M. (ed.) 1986 *Nemski i avstriiski patepisi za Balkanite* [German and Austrian Traveller-books on Balkans] Nauka i izkustvo, Sofia

Ionov, V., 1998 *Vlashkiat etnos: Prevratnosti i razvoi prez vekovete* [The Vlach people: changes and development during the centuries], Lovech, Sofia.

Kyutchukov, H., 1994 "It's difficult to estimate Gypsies", *Patrin*, No. 2, pp. 18–19.

Lal, C., 1969 *Gypsies, forgotten children of India*, Government of India Ministry of Information and Broadcasting Publications Division, New Delhi.

Marushiakova, A.E., and Popov, V. (eds.), 1994 *Studii Romani* Club 90, Sofia.

Marushiakova, A.E., and Popov, V. (eds.), 1995 *Studii Romani* Club 90, Sofia.

Marushiakova, A.E., and Popov, V. (eds.), 1997 *Roma (Gypsies) in Bulgaria* Peter Lang Verlag, Frankfurt am Main.

Marushiakova, A.E., and Popov V., 2000 *The Gypsies in Ottoman Empire*, University of Hertfordshire Press, Hatfield.

Odjakov, P., 1885 *Obichaino nasledstveno pravo*, [Traditional Hereditary Law], Russe, Sofia.

Primovski, A.T., 1955 "Kovachite Agupti v grad Madan", [The Agupts Smiths in Madan], *Izvestia na Etnografskia Institut s muzei*, kn.II., BAN, Sofia, pp. 217–61.

Risteski, S.T., 1991 *Narodni Prikazni, predania i obichai kai Egyptchanite/ Egjucite vo Makedonia*, [Folk Tales, legends and customs of Egyptians in Macedonia], Association of the Egyptians, Ohrid.

Romano Essi, (newspaper) 1948 No. 9, 14.01; (anonymous).

Studii Romani 1996, 1997, 1998 – Archive of the Minority Studies Society, Studii Romani, Sofia.

Tong, D., 1989 *Gypsy folktales*, Harcourt Brace Jovanovic, San Diego.

Vecherna poshta, (newspaper) 1905, ann. VI, No. 1565, 22.12; (anonymous).

Willems, W., 1997 *In Search of the true Gypsy. from enlightenment to final solution*. Frank Cass, London.

Zemon, R. (ed.), 1996 *Zbornik na trudovi za etnogenezata na Egypchanite vo Makedonia*, [Collection of works on ethnogenesis of the Egyptians in Macedonia], Logos-T, Skopje.

CHAPTER EIGHT

THE ROMANI MOVEMENT:
REBIRTH AND THE FIRST WORLD ROMANI CONGRESS IN RETROSPECT

Grattan Puxon

THE TURN OF the millennium is witnessing a rapid growth of Romani political activity. The shocking increase in anti-Gypsy violence and racial intolerance, evident throughout Europe, has begun to politicise and unite a new generation to a degree not seen before.

Although the roots of the Romani national movement can be traced back into the nineteenth century, its rise dates largely from the years after the Second World War. Fascist-led repression destroyed almost every vestige of would-be self-determination.

One of the rare exceptions was the Pan-Hellenic Association of Roma, which kept up a shadowy existence in Athens. In the post-1945 era, however, cold war conditions prevented any organisational link with Roma in neighbouring Yugoslavia and Bulgaria, let alone Albania, so much so that Abdi Faik's *Phralipe* (Brotherhood), founded in 1948 in Skopje, remained out of touch with its large Greek counterpart for twenty-five years.

My involvement began on the very periphery, at the other end of Europe, at a time when few groups were active. In 1960, I received my call-up papers for the British army and to avoid induction ran away to the Republic of Ireland where I was soon drawn into the milieu of the Irish Travellers.

Our initial attempt to organise came in 1962 when Itinerant Action manifested itself as a string of banner-bearing horse-drawn carts parading outside Dublin City Hall. That winter, already forced to move on from Bow Lane by a municipal bailiff, I drove my wagon up to Ballyfermot to join Travellers occupying factory land at the Ring Road.

Travellers' spokesman Joe Donohue believed his plea at a recent public session of the Irish Government's Commission on Itinerancy had rendered this ground a safe haven, and lots more were pulling on daily. By Christmas, a big makeshift hut stood at the centre of the camp – St. Christopher's, a unique *Minceir* school. (*Minceir* is the name used for themselves in *Gammon*, the Irish Travellers' own language.)

But lessons had been going barely two weeks before *gardai* and workmen appeared in the pre-dawn of a Sunday morning to shift us. Resistance through a sit-in inside the school ended only after a promise was given to allow everyone a month on another piece of ground.

We lined up the wagons on the Ring Road and the ponies clattered off towards Walkinstown. Behind, the school and a cluster of abandoned shacks burned fiercely in the breeze.

Over the following year a series of eviction battles were fought around the outskirts of Dublin, each escalating in numbers and intensity. For a while, the Travellers' campaign attracted the support of Sinn Fein and to facilitate an occupation of the Landsdowne Park, an IRA 'flying column' on bicycles rode ahead of our wagons to demolish concrete bollards blocking the gate. But these allies would not participate in non-violent sit-downs, preferring a stand-up picket line, leaving Travellers to get punched and kicked by the eviction squads. Anxiety increased when armed Special Branch officers turned up to keep an eye on the IRA.

The involvement of extreme Republicans led later to my arrest under the Special Powers Act. Charges, including possession of explosives, were not dropped until the following year. Fortunately, I obtained bail and was able to join in the final takeover of land at Palmerstown.

The squatters' settlement here, which became known as Cherry Orchard after the nearby hospital, sprawled over twenty-six acres and drew Travellers from all over Ireland. A resurrected St Christopher's served both as school and meeting house for the camp committee (Puxon and Puxon 1967).

The stand at Cherry Orchard lasted two years. Entrenched behind ditches and barricades the Travellers could not be moved. Former Minister for Health Dr Noel Brown visited the encampment and asked questions in the *Dail*. British MPs Norman Dodds, champion of English Gypsies, and Barbara Castle, together with Bertrand Russell and Canon John Collins of CND, called for a just solution of Ireland's so-called itinerant problem.

A French television crew shot scenes of newly arriving barrel-tops and Tinkers begging on O'Connell Bridge, in the centre of Dublin. The report was seen in Paris by Ionel Rotaru, a Romanian-born writer known as Vaida Voevod, then heading a Romani group called Communauté Mondiale Gitane. Formed in 1959, it had a nucleus of followers among French Kalderash and Yugoslav Roma living in the bidonvilles of the capital. At the time, the CMG was in the throes of a crisis of its own. Vaida had been travelling extensively in eastern Europe and Turkey, spreading word of Romanestan, a future Romani state which he hoped could be created with the help of Nazi war crimes reparations. Irritated by this publicity during a period of *rapprochement* between France and West Germany, the French Interior Ministry declared the CMG illegal, on the basis that Rotaru was a non-citizen (Liégeois 1976).

Vaida had to quit France and came briefly to London, as the guest of sociologist Richard Hauser, whose Centre for Group Studies was beginning to take an interest in

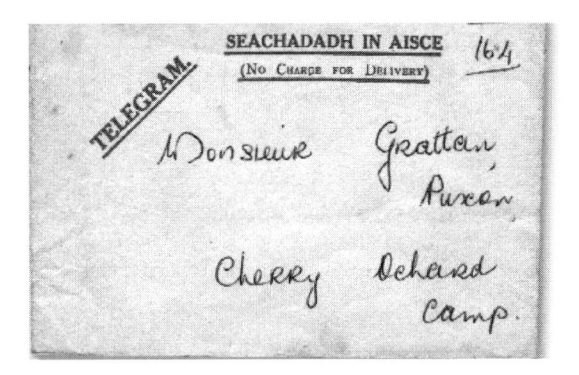

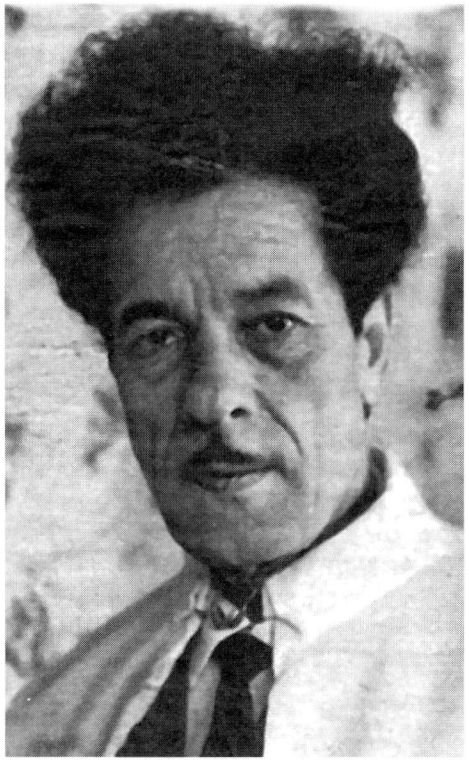

Ional Rotaru, known as Vaida Voevod, and the telegram he sent to Cherry Orchard camp which led to the recruitment of Grattan Puxon into the CMG.

the Romani cause. Hauser arranged a press conference, then Vaida headed on to Ireland, where he pitched up at the shortest notice at the gate of Cherry Orchard.

A bonfire blazing high in the Voevod's honour lit our faces as we talked, in a mixture of Serbian, Romanes and French, long into the night. The next morning, unaware in my youthful enthusiasm of what I might getting into, I agreed not just to join the CMG but become instantly a member of the Directing Committee of the newly outlawed organisation. It seemed of no consequence to Vaida that I was not a Rom.

When Vaida Voevod removed permanently to Vienna his chief lieutenant Jacques Dauvergne, assuming the nom de guerre, Vanko Rouda, succeeded in registering a new association, the Comité International Tzigane (CIT). Although his brother Jean, as Leulea Rouda, helped with the documentation of individual war crime indemnification cases, the more contentious issue of block reparations and the idea of Romanestan receded into the background. However, twelve years later, while I was living in Serbia, I met some of Vaida's original adherents. He is still remembered, if more dimly now, even among the elderly of Kosovo Mitrovica.

The CIT, like its predecessor, though claiming to speak for 'le peuple Tzigane', lacked the credentials and the resources to pursue issues outside France, except intermittently. Vanko Rouda, though often abroad, came later to concern himself mostly with the problems of the Manouches and emigré Yugoslav Roma. We had been corresponding for many months when late in 1965 Rouda, then twenty-nine, visited Ireland to take part in my abortive attempt to set up the Irish Travellers Community. The venue was Ballinasloe Town Hall. Lawrence Ward, last of the bare-fist pugilists to carry the title King of the Tinkers, brought in a following from the annual horse fair which, with the contingent from Dublin, constituted the convention. All went well until candles and water were produced for a culminating ceremony in which Vanko was to become a godparent of two of Lawrence's grandchildren. At sight of the *Kirivo*-making paraphernalia, Father Fehilly, the recently appointed Chaplain to Itinerants, warned the Wards that if they participated in the Romani ritual they would be breaking Catholic baptismal vows. The harmony in the hall turned to consternation and the meeting ended in disarray.

Nevertheless, Lawrence Ward soon after trekked the 120 miles to Cherry Orchard, the Wards' eight barrel-tops arriving on the eve of a showdown. The camp mustered, lining up this time armed with sticks, bars and bottles to face 150 *gardai* and three coachloads of day-hired unemployed, assembled outside the fever hospital. As I parlayed with the senior officer the opposing lines leered. It seemed inevitable some blood would be shed. I told the officer, "We don't want violence but if you come in here you'll be provoking a fight. A lot of people are going to get hurt on both sides."

He strode back across the road, swagger stick tucked under his arm. Heads bobbed together in consultation; minutes passed. All of a sudden, he gave an order and ranks turned. The guards began to tramp away. The day-men, visibly relieved, followed in their wake, the odd milk bottle and stone rattling down upon the tarmac behind them.

The Travellers had won. Cherry Orchard was saved. Most would move in time to Labre Park, a big municipal site built nearby. It would have kitchen-hut *tigeens* (a kind of basic housing devised for Travellers) and its own junior National School. Meanwhile St Christopher's closed. The children were bussed instead to a convent in the city. Like the Grey Geese of old, the chiefs of 'The Irish Travellers Community' departed, Donohue and Johnny Connors to England, Ward to his native Loughrea, where his people too got their *tigeens*.

A new Dublin Itinerant Settlement Committee, headed by Father Fehilly, included no Travellers. None sat either on the later National Advisory Committee. Those who had created power out of a barrel-top had now to go cap-in-hand to the priest's door. Charity, albeit on a scale unseen, before, was still the Tinker's portion. They would remain politically impoverished for a decade to come.

For me it was the end of Ireland and I left on a boat for Liverpool. In some vital respects I had failed, defeated by the outdated paternalism of the Catholic church. Yet the next day, coming down the motorway towards London, I was all too keen to try again. For better or for worse, I knew I had committed myself to this cause and was in it for the long haul.

At the invitation of Brian Richardson, of the Sevenoaks Gypsy Liaison Group, I came to Bromley and pulled into a lane beside his house at Knockholt. Through Brian, I met a lot of Travellers then on the roadsides in north Kent. Many had been in Darenth Woods or lost long-standing yards like Corke's Meadow, closed by compulsory purchase order. Exposed to new harassment they were desperate for a respite. That autumn a crowd led by Solly Brown moved their trailers onto vacant lots around the remains of the old 'prefabs', (pre-fabricated dwellings set up after World War Two) at St Mary's Cray near Bromley.

Born in Corke's Meadow, Solly had been at the final Darenth Woods eviction, when Norman Dodds had joined the last hold-outs. Later on he had stayed at Dodds' temporarily licensed site at Cobham (c.f. Dodds 1966). After much shifting about, he and others had succeeded in obtaining a ground from Bromley Council at Star Lane. Most went down into Kent fruit picking in the summer only to learn on their return that the Star Lane site was about to be closed. Although they had retained their rent books, they were refused re-admission. Determined to test their rights in court, they occupied the ground but instead of taking legal proceedings, Bromley tried four times to evict them by force. In the last attempt, policemen punched and kicked those offering sit-down resistance. A pregnant woman was flung into the mud. To stop assault, Solly and his brother Fred blocked the gate with car-bodies and short lengths of railway line were set in concrete along the fence, an ultimate defence inspired and executed by a local showman, Dennis Marriner.

The stand-off at Star Lane continued through the winter. Meanwhile, Donald Kenrick, then a newcomer to the campaign, had alerted us to a fresh confrontation taking place in East London. Joe Eastwood and others had pulled onto a large bombsite at Mary Street, Canning Town, known locally as 'The Debris'. Before I could get down there, Joe had already shifted to a smaller patch of bombsite at the end of a street behind Rathbone Market. We had several talks about Newham Council and their employment of security men with dogs. I went to have a look at these dogs, which happened to be housed in kennels close by. I found a Newham security guard feeding four German Shepherds. On the spur of the moment, I said I was preparing a report for the Home Office. When I got back to the trailers, a new arrival, John Brazil, was manhandling a little kitchen-hut off his lorry. As it slid to the ground, he turned to me with a grin and said, "D'you want this for a site office?" Next time I saw it the hut had a sign on the door 'Gypsy Council Office'. Johnny's comment was, "To fight the council we need a council of our own."

The Gypsy Council hut, located not more than a few miles from the present permanent Gypsy Council office at Aveley, played a similar role to the school huts at the Dublin Ring Road and Cherry Orchard, as a rallying point for resistance. Newham

Press cutting of the foundation meeting of the Gypsy Council (10 December 1966)
Note the "Travellers Community Meeting" notice on the wall. At the table are Grattan Puxon, Anton Santiago, Vanko Rouda and a young lawyer taking notes

Council tried once more, bringing in a JCB bulldozer – but no dogs now. The digger was brought to a halt by a draw-bar sit-down led by Joe's wife, Mary, with her newest grandchild perched on her lap.

Gypsies in metropolitan Essex and Kent had been badly hit by the war-time blitz which had produced the bombsites and the littered wastelands of 'The Debris'. Together with other Londoners, they had fled East London to share squatter settlements from Abbey Wood to the Erith Marshes but while the other homeless were eventually re-housed, Gypsies received no help in the post-war reconstruction. Now they were ready to help themselves.

For the purpose of consolidating the campaign, I booked a small hall at the rear of the Bull's Head in St Paul's Cray. Painted on the pub wall were the words 'No Gipsies' (Puxon 1968). I told the licensee it was needed for a Human Rights Day meeting. When forty Gypsies arrived that Sunday afternoon, 11 December 1966, he tried to turn us away but I had his receipt. Believing in the link with the CIT, I had invited Vanko Rouda. With him into the Bull's Head came his brother, Leulea, Algerian-born Anton Santiago and a singer called Cholai. Kenrick, in a role he was to undertake at many international gatherings, acted as their interpreter.

The name of the new association on the little green cards handed out during the course of this foundation meeting was Travellers Community, mimicking that of Vaida's Communauté Mondiale Gitane. And so it was reported in the Kentish Times. However, it was Johnny Brazil's Gypsy Council that struck the better chord, and under this title the organisation soon became known among Travellers throughout Britain.

The Gypsy Council campaign of resistance to forced move-ons now spread rapidly from the London area to the Midlands and the North. Outstanding leadership there was provided by Irish Travellers, notably Johnny Connors, and Tommy O'Doherty, founder in 1959 of the Society of Travelling People. Many ugly confrontations occurred and there were injuries and arrests but the circus of perpetual chivvying slowed down. Towns long hostile to Travellers found themselves with a minor Gypsy revolt on their hands and began to negotiate. Harold Wilson's Labour Government took to consulting with the Gypsy Council. Whitehall appeared to condone its militant tactics. What civil servants could never accomplish through policy circulars, Gypsies were quickly achieving by refusing to be shifted.

The next year, out of a need to help children on roadsides and temporary stopping places, the Council ran its first Romano Drom caravan schools. The pilot project took place on a disused Battle of Britain airfield at Hornchurch, East London (Acton 1974). In charge was Thomas Acton, then a student at Oxford, who had already been involved in a stand made by families led by Arthur Bowers amid derelict prefabs at Slade Park.

Parallel with the activities of the Gypsy Council in the UK, Kari Huttunen set up the Finnish Gypsy Association and its magazine Zirickli (Huttunen 1971, 1972). The Secretariado Gitano established branches in almost every main town in Spain. At the same time French Roma, still lacking any official recognition founded the new Association des Gitans et Tziganes de France, with Resistance hero Archange Stenegri its president. Even more dramatic were the developments in Czechoslovakia, where in the spring of 1968 a group in Bratislava addressed a bold demand to the National Assembly. They wrote, "We Roma, though living in a social democratic state, find our position grave and cruel." They rejected the measures taken over the past decade regarding the 'Gypsy Question'. Instead they wanted recognition of the 300,000 Roma in Czechoslovakia as a national minority. Specifically they sought permission to found a union, with voluntary membership, and legislation that would enable Roma to elect their own representatives to central and local government.

Two prominent Roma among the signatories were Anton Facuna, an architect and member of the regional planning commission, and Dr Jan Cibula, the house doctor for a construction enterprise employing many Roma. A few weeks later I went to

Bratislava to discuss with them a link up with the emerging international movement. We talked for hours of their hopes under the government of Alexander Dubchek. Facuna told me that he had wanted Roma to take a real part in the communist revolution since joining the wartime partisans. Both he and Cibula had been warned that their Romani nationalist views could lead to arrest. But now they headed a preparatory committee planning the first Romani national congress, and sought to elect Roma to the new Slovak National Council and create a chair of Romani Studies at Bratislava University.

Despite the official policy of dispersal, Facuna had earlier enabled several large colonies to consolidate themselves near the city. As we drove to see them, he told me how he had obtained improved roads, lighting, drainage and mains supplies for the villages. Numbers of families were building themselves new houses with the help of loans. In one village a group of blacksmiths had formed a co-operative producing high-quality wroughtiron work. A selection had been included in the Czechoslovak pavilion at Expo '67 in Montreal.

That summer they waited anxiously for an official response to their demands. Instead, just weeks after my visit, the Russian tanks rolled in and the thaw was over. Almost as the columns reached Prague, a radio broadcast was made in Romanes appealing to Roma to stand by the legitimate government (Puxon 1969). In mid-November, however, Facuna received a reply. Nationality status was denied but Roma could go ahead with their congress and establish a union. Shortly afterwards his daughter Vera wrote to me: "A great event. Today the Union was accepted into the National Front."

Facuna at once pressed for the suppression of all previous laws and decrees that in contravention of the constitution trespassed upon the rights of Roma. The Slovak Union Romano Jekhetaniben was followed by the foundation in Brno of an association for Roma in Czech lands. It was headed by Miroslav Holomek, cousin of Thomas Holomek who was to lead the Czech Romani delegation to the first World Romani Congress. The two unions published magazines and created affiliated labour brigades which gained regular contracts and better rates of pay for their members. Two hundred local amateur song and dance ensembles and thirty Romani football clubs came into being. During the first three years membership of the two unions rose to over 20,000. Not until after the World Romani Congress in 1971 did the new Czechoslovak government begin to see this activity as a threat to the state and begin to talk again about the 'Gypsy problem'. In 1973 the Communist Party, through the National Front, compelled the Romani Unions to dissolve (Puxon 1987).

Late in 1968 a request came for evidence to be given to the Council of Europe's Commission on Social and Health Questions. Gypsies on the road in England were suffering a cruel winter, made worse by the half-hearted attitude of the government. The Caravan Sites Act had been passed, with support from all parties. For the first time legislation was on the statute book that favoured the Gypsy minority. Yet the vital Part II

The first CIT delegation to the Council of Europe in Strasbourg in 1969, holding the earlier version of the Romani flag, blue and green diagonal.
Left to right: Jimmy Hanrahan (Ireland), Leulea Rouda, General Secretary of the CIT, Manfred Wood, President of the Gypsy Council, Tommy O'Doherty, Maisa Rouda (wife of Vanko Rouda), Nuknu (wife of Jimmy Hanrahan), Charles Douglas (Scotland), Mehmet Sakijevic (Yugoslavia), Grattan Puxon, then Secretary of the Gypsy Council.

of the Act had been suspended because its immediate implementation "would place an additional economic burden" on local authorities at a time when money was scarce. Consequently, instead of building the urgently needed caravan parks, councils launched another pogrom to rid themselves of Gypsies.

The severest harassment was taking place on in the Birmingham area. In Staffordshire that October one of the biggest police operations in the county's history had been mounted to evict families at Brownhills. A boy of six lost an eye and a hand in an explosion during the first attempt. Detonators had been cast onto a camp fire "by persons unknown". At George Street in Walsall three children were burned to death during a caravan fire, which never would have happened had the corporation not towed the trailer onto a busy street. In the south of England three petrol bombs were lobbed at a lone caravan in Kent. A woman and child were badly burned.

To collect first-hand evidence for the Council of Europe, Vanko Rouda came to the Midlands, with Charlois Reinhardt and Jacques Gaslian. As a result of their intervention at Walsall, a brief truce was arranged over Christmas. Soon after, seen off by a

Minceir bagpipe-player at Manchester, Gypsy Council members were heading for Strasbourg with 200 pages of documents and a reel of television film. The delegation was led by Gypsy Council president Manfri Wood, who had been injured at the battle of Brownhills, and included two Irish Travellers, James Hanrahan and Tommy O'Doherty.

A preliminary meeting in Paris was unhappily marred. Rouda collapsed with a heart attack and we waited anxious hours for news from the hospital. He could not, of course, accompany us on the road to Alsace. Leulea Rouda and I had to take charge. The issue had been raised in the assembly by the Swedish MP Daniel Wiklund. None of us had yet met him. Driving over the frozen streets to the Council of Europe headquarters, we felt a little like the lion on the way to the Wizard of Oz. The buildings, however, were unimposing, even slightly dilapidated. The flags of the member states flapped at their masts. The CIT delegation was filmed holding the blue and green Romani flag outside the main entrance.

We were met by the quietly spoken Swiss secretary of the Social Commission, Marc Sands. With the help of his assistant, Johannes de Jonge from Holland, and a tape-recorder, he would spend all morning taking our evidence. In the afternoon a group of parliamentarians on the commission assembled to view the film material. They were visibly shaken by the scenes of brutality in which British police and security men set about women and children in a Midlands encampment. *The Times* reporter, Pat Healy noted in her despatch (*The Times*, 19, January 1969) that Mr Sands wanted to see for himself the situation in France, Britain and elsewhere.

The following spring, Sands and De Jonge had a look at some of the trouble spots in East London Boroughs. At Beckton Road, Newham, families were lodged behind barricades of old car bodies, daubed with slogans 'Gypsies Unite and Fight' and 'We Shall Not Be Moved'. The women told Mr Sands they had no water supply or sanitation. The next day the Home Office allowed Johnny Connors to travel under escort from Winson Green Prison, Birmingham, to meet Wiklund. What Johnny told him, I do not know but when in September Wiklund presented his report (Wiklund 1969), there was a sharp protest from the Irish representatives. The *Irish Times* (1 October) reported that Timothy O'Connor, TD had said that a pamphlet I had written (Puxon and Puxon, 1967) was "a pack of falsehoods". Ireland, he maintained, was making real efforts on behalf of Gypsies and no discrimination existed in the Republic.

The next month his colleague, Patrick Donegan, later to become Eire Minister for Defence, acted in a way that appeared to prove otherwise. On a Sunday night Donegan, with one of his farm-hands, approached a lay-by at Monasterboice, on the main Dublin to Belfast Road, where Travellers were encamped. They opened fire with shotguns. He admitted subsequently that he meant to frighten them away and was fined £20 for intimidation. Among those camped in the lay-by were James Hanrahan, his wife Nuknu and son Patrick, CIT delegates to the Council of Europe the previous January.

Despite the Irish outburst, Wiklund's Report and recommendations were adopted with minor amendments. It said that discrimination practised against Gypsies in member states was "incompatible with ideals underlying the European Convention on Human Rights and the UN Declaration on Human Rights". Each country was urged to take the necessary steps to stop discrimination, either in legislation or in administrative practice. The report stated that throughout Europe as a whole, the majority of Roma led a settled life. The most acute difficulties arose for some 300,000 Travelling Gypsies in west and northern Europe. The assembly agreed that for them properly serviced caravan sites should be built near towns and villages. Local authorities ought to allocate houses to those seeking permanent residence, especially where the climate made caravans unsuitable. To overcome educational handicaps, special classes should be arranged that would link up satisfactorily with local secondary schools.

Further, the report stressed the necessity to consult Roma themselves. In the past, any attempt at political organisation by Gypsies had met resistance because it cut across national frontiers. Only recently had it become possible for them to set up "a successful form of international co-operation" through the CIT, with headquarters in Paris.

In the concluding paragraph, Wiklund wrote: "In recent years, Gypsy organisations in Europe have tried to promote the cultural and political development of Gypsies: the Council of Europe should now in my view accept the challenge of helping them to seek social justice and a respected place in modern European society." As an initial step, he recommended that member states should create national bodies composed of government and Gypsy representatives, to prepare plans for improving their position. By inference this was a criticism of all the countries where 'gaje experts' rather than Roma were habitually consulted.

After the publication of the Strasbourg report, the CIT took up the matter of education with UNESCO. We were anxious that the world body should be briefed pending possible adoption of a programme to help Romani children. In April 1970 Vanko and Leulea Rouda and myself held discussions with UNESCO departmental heads explaining the linguistic barriers between Romani children and the curricula of state schools. Following the model of educational work by the CIT, including the Romano Drom Caravan Schools in Britain, we suggested that UNESCO might assist in the development of literacy material designed for Roma, and in the training of Romani teachers.

At the same time the movement made its peace with the Catholic church. Derek Tipler went to the Vatican in January 1969 and talked with the head of Caritas. The dialogue led a year later to the issue of a report *A migrant minority oppressed: The Gypsies*, which was endorsed by the Pontifical Commission for Justice and Peace. It endorsed the Council of Europe recommendations and recognised that Roma were now organised in associations like the CIT and the Secretariado Gitano in Spain and remarked that similar developments were noticeable in eastern Europe.

The first congress

The notion of holding a big congress had been a major topic for a decade. Whenever I was in Paris, the subject of the would-be congress was aired – and then shelved again. With Vaida Voevod gone, the congress had replaced Romanestan at the top of the agenda. Early in 1966 Vanko Rouda wrote that the long-awaited congress would take place that summer. He talked of obtaining the Palais de l'UNESCO as a venue. I was asked to bring a delegation from Ireland. We had just been to lobby at Stormont, the Northern Ireland parliament. Isaac Lovell and Arthur Gentle, Romanichals from Lurgan, and others from Dublin were ready to come. But no congress materialised.

Even if such a gathering could be organised, no one knew whether Roma from communist east Europe would be permitted to attend and without them the event could have little impact. However, recent liberalisation within the eastern bloc seemed now to put a truly international gathering within the realms of possibility. By 1969 newly formed Romani organisations in both Czechoslovakia and Yugoslavia had held their own limited national congresses. I therefore advocated that we take a gamble. In the name of the CIT, I would take responsibility for arranging a 'preparatory conference' in London in 1971. Should sufficient representation be mustered, the assembly would be able to declare itself the First World Romani Congress. If not, it could pave the way for a fuller affair, possibly in Belgrade.

As I recall, the Gypsy Council, of which I was then secretary, showed initial coolness to the proposal but the argument that the congress would bring the spotlight of international attention on the situation in Britain eventually prevailed.

The primary practical task was to secure a suitable location. Brian Raywid, who had given up travelling to take a job as cook at a private school, offered help. The school, Cannock House, was a Georgian mansion seventeen miles from the centre of London. The headmaster, Mr. Baker, a member of the charitable Toc H, agreed after assurances to let us book the premises.

Shortly before, I moved down to Cannock House to take charge. The school stood in quiet grounds away from the main road. The library off the entrance hall would be utilised for general sessions. Delegates would sleep in the numerous dormitories on the upper floors.

Anti-Gypsy feeling in the village was running high. Residents were upset by an encampment of Gypsies on a local roadside. A protest meeting had packed the Memorial Hall and a committee had been set up pledged "to get rid of them once and for all". A local doctor called on shopkeepers to refuse service to the Gypsies. He wanted their caravans impounded by the police (*Orpington Times*, 9 March, 1971). Mr Baker cautioned me, for his sake and our own, to keep the location secret as long as possible.

Invitations said the purpose was to achieve "more effective co-ordination" within the movement. Slobodan Berberski sent a lengthy paper from Belgrade and said that he would head a Yugoslav contingent. Yugoslav-born Roma resident in France also

Donald Kenrick (far right) interpreting at the First World Romani Congress in London, 1971. *Behind the table from left to right, Vanko Rouda, Slobodan Berberski, Jan Cibula, Grattan Puxon.*

accepted. Notable among them was Jarko Jovanovic, a new member of the CIT and a former member of the Belgrade Radio Orchestra. A balalaika player in Paris nightclubs, he promised to bring his four sons to perform at the Gypsy festival on Hampstead Heath that would close the congress. From Barcelona the Secretariado Gitano signalled an affirmative. The West European and Scandinavian associations faced no passport difficulties. The Bulgarian embassy wrote requesting information, but in the event, the Communist party did not approve a delegation, although Demeter Golemanov had visited London the previous year. Finally, with four days to go, a telegram announced participation by the Czech Romani Union. The congress could count on representatives from countries with close on three million Roma.

The delegates were far from equal, however, in their status, reflecting the uneven development of the movement. Romania, for instance, was represented by a single musician who played a cymbalon at the festival. Vilho Koivisto came from the Finnish Evangelical Gypsy Mission, while Finland's Romani association remained absent through lack of funds. Macedonia sent Fajk Abdi, son of a blacksmith, now a member of parliament elected by the Romani township of Šuto Orizari.

Among those who came were Roma from the Arlija, Djambasa, Kalderasha and Lovara groups, as well as Sinte, Manush, Kale, Romanichals and Minceir. When at last I stood at the lectern before the assembly, I was aware that rarely had Roma from such widely different backgrounds been brought together. Spokesmen and observers from seventeen countries surrounded the coupled tables. To my right sat East Londoner Tom Lee, vice-president of the Gypsy Council. Near him, Dr Thomas Holomek, military advocate, led the Czech group. Juan de Dios Ramirez Heredia from Catalonia faced Kosovo-born Bedzhet Cuna.

Welcoming them on behalf of the Gypsy Council, I said: "In size we are not an important community in Britain but the Gypsy Council has been conscious since its foundation that we're part of a much bigger family. Affiliated from the outset to the World Romani movement, our links with the communities on the continent have been seen as a vital life-line. Your presence today brings an end to former isolation. Seeing Roma from so many countries is an assurance that we are not a minority but part of a nation ready to assert our separate identity and way of life" (Puxon 1971).

It was decided the work of the Congress should be divided between five commissions, including the Education Commission, the Cultural Commission and the War Crimes and Reparations Commission. The Nazi holocaust, despite the intervening quarter-century, still conjured doleful memories. Heavy emotion was engendered when Berberski, as president-elect, bid the assembly observe two minutes' silence "for the half-million of our people destroyed by fascism." Jarko wept openly. Next to me Leulea removed his glasses to wipe his eyes.

Joined by Donald Kenrick I had made a start on documenting the war period. We were assisted by the Wiener Library and later the Columbus Centre at Sussex University, which eventually published our research with Heinemann (Kenrick and Puxon, 1972). It proved that hundreds of thousands of Gypsies had been done to death in a policy of racial extermination. Yet the West German courts had all but closed the door on personal claims by maintaining the fiction that state security and not racial reasons had dictated the war-time measures. Relatively few of the victims remained alive and nobody suggested that their cases should not be pursued to the uttermost. Holomek felt particularly strongly that those who had suffered from medical experiments should receive help. He was confident the East German Communist Party would support their claims. A block settlement became one objective. The congress resolved any such funds should go to UNESCO to be spent on the education of the present and future generations of Romani children.

The work of the Education Commission had its roots in projects like the Romano Drom schools in Britain. The Gypsy Council had purchased a few caravans and more were donated, notably by Frank Sinatra and John Lennon and Yoko Ono. The presence of a caravan school on occasion inhibited local councils from moving families on and some children were helped to enter local schools. But volunteers giving basic instruction at roadsides and muddy encampments could really do little more than draw attention to the negligence of education authorities and the Department of Education itself.

The caravan schools soon found themselves overstretched. Professional help had to be sought. Unfortunately, the new intake did not always hold the same views as the Gypsy Council. The emphasis on self-help was replaced in some places by an insensitive zeal to uproot Gypsy children from their traditional communal life and thrust them ill-prepared into the maw of the state education system.

George Marriott, Gypsy Council treasurer, with Traveller children in front of the school caravan donated by John Lennon and Yoko Ono.
George Marriott, son of an Irish Traveller, was disabled while a British P.O.W. in World War II and fought a long fight for Gypsy caravan sites in Bedfordshire where this photograph was taken in 1972.

The National Gypsy Education Council, created in 1970, was chaired by Lady Plowden. As chair of the of the Commission which produced the 1967 Plowden Report, she had helped to spotlight the neglect of Gypsy children. But during her chairmanship, Gypsies remained an insignificant minority on the executive, as the link with the militant Gypsy Council was minimised. Even publications in the English Romani dialect were proscribed.

In 1973, after three years and much conflict, Lady Plowden formed a breakaway organisation and resigned from the National Gypsy Education Council, after first taking legal steps to freeze its assets. At the congress in 1971, however, she still paid lip service to the need to respect Romani culture. It came as an unexpected irony, therefore, when views similar to those of Lady Plowden were echoed by some east European Roma. Ladislav Demeter voiced their feelings when he said that travelling was undesirable. He told the congress that the settlement of nomadic families was a pre-requisite to the successful education of their children. "School attendance," he said, "should be made compulsory not only in theory but also in practice."

This statement brought on a brief but heated clash. Thomas Acton said that though only an observer, he was moved to express the attitude of parents who followed the travelling life. A decade ago they had been hostile or indifferent to formal education. School was an alien place where nomadic Gypsy children, if they gained admission at all, were subject to rebuke and derision. The Romano Drom schools had not just gained acceptance but were much in demand as a half-way house. Their job was to break down barriers on both sides and they therefore had a necessary role. The chair of the Education Commission, Antonin Daniel, said that before the war he had been one of the first Roma in Oslavany to attend secondary school and had later qualified as a teacher. But despite all the advances that had taken place, Roma remained backward in education. Only recently had it been acknowledged that many children entered school knowing little Czech or Slovak. As a result a few schools were being allowed to experiment with the use of Romanes in primary classes. It was obvious that Roma must be assisted to catch up, Daniel ended: "They too will then be able to contribute to the progress of society as a whole. I do not mean by this that Roma will disappear. I am in favour of integration, but not assimilation."

Clashes occurred also within the Cultural Commission, chaired by Dr Jan Cibula, who was now in exile from Czechoslovakia. Nonplussed by Cibula's presence, Thomas Holomek emphasised in a hesitant opening speech that the Czech Romani Union had full recognition and his attendance the approval of the Czechoslovak Communist Party. He claimed no discrimination existed like that in western Europe in the Czech provinces or Slovakia. Cibula, then living in exile in Switzerland, challenged him during a break in a bitter argument. He decried the fact that the more radical Slovak Romani Union he had founded with Anton Facuna, which represented two-thirds of the Roma in Czechoslovakia, had been prevented from sending a delegation. Antonin Daniel exerted himself to reconcile them. Holomek unbent a little and they came back arms linked.

Away from the Congress the hardships of English Gypsies went on unabated. Even as it deliberated, police and council workmen were evicting families encamped a few miles away at Rosehill, Sutton. In the assault Roy Wells, later London chairman of the Gypsy Council, was knocked down by a bulldozer and removed to hospital. From a camp by the North Circular Road Jeff Chandler criticised the meeting for "talking a lot of hot air" which did nothing to stop harassment. He was an old campaigner who spoke at Hyde Park Corner and had been with me in Ireland at some of the roughest confrontations. In the short term I felt he was justified. While they remained cloistered at Cannock House, the delegates were out of touch with realities just up the road. The *Evening News* (8 April, 1971) carried two pictures of the opening under the mocking headline "Sorry, Sir, the hedgehog is off." The reporter complained, "You might have thought it was a bankers' convention."

At that juncture I was too tired to care that the press had knocked us, and went to bed. Meanwhile, Melanie Spitta, a Sinti from West Germany, paid a call on roadside families at Badgers Mount. Having a television set hooked up to car batteries, they had seen a report on the Congress. They came around to Cannock House in time for a general assembly. On the platform Berberski, Rouda and Cibula looked out over the unexpected crowd. Behind them as a backdrop stretched a huge and as yet unfamiliar Romani flag, now embellished in red, by resolution of the congress, with the ashok chakra of India.

The Badgers Mount delegation made it plain they wanted to ask some questions. Len Cooper called up, "For whose benefit is all this going on? We don't know nothing about it."

Faik Abdi, on his feet to read the report of the Social Commission, lowered his notes. "We want to work together. We've come here from many countries to help one another". At his side, Donald Kenrick translated. He added "Nothing will be achieved unless you all join in."

"But what can we do, brother?" Cooper insisted.

"Listen, *phrala*," Faik retorted. "If I was a fisherman I could catch fish and give them to you. But tomorrow you'd be hungry again. Better if I can teach you how to catch fish yourselves."

"I can catch fish, pal," shouted Fred Brown, brother of the Orpington agitator Solly, when the speech had been interpreted.

I got up to put in a word. "Alright," I began, "here's something this Congress has done. You've heard of Gypsies going to parliament. Norman Dodds saw to that. But have you heard of British MPs coming to a Romani parliament? That's what's happened here yesterday."

The business went on in a better atmosphere. They sat patiently through Mateo Maximoff's report from the Language Commission and while a representative from the Indian High Commission, Weer Rajendra Rishi, pledged his support. In the evening Maximoff, a Pentecostal pastor and novelist, showed slides of Romani evangelical conventions and of the annual Gypsy pilgrimage to Saintes Maries-de-la-Mer. Raya Udovikova, who had started her career at the Moscow Romani Theatre, led some impromptu dancing and singing in the dining room. It was late when the English Gypsy motors drove away.

They were back again early next morning.

It had been arranged that the whole party should visit the Midlands to see what English Gypsies had to complain about. Len Cooper sat on the rear seat of the coach with his supporters, well satisfied. On the way Jarko Jovanovic rehearsed us for the new national anthem *Dzhelem, Dzhelem*, of which he did not write the final version (Acton, Hurley and Denaro, 1971 pp.14-15) until the journey home. As we passed through Birmingham, I pointed out some of the old battlefields, still ringed by trenches and the debris of abandoned encampments. Our destination was Slackey Lane on the outskirts of Walsall. Here a hundred families had come together on a stretch of wasteland to make a last stand against the most notorious of the Midland towns. It was an ugly spot. At the bottom of the lane was a refuse tip inhabited tenaciously by some of the Prices in

Weer Rajendra Rishi (right), editor of Roma and the main diplomatic link between the World Romani Congress and the Indian government, with Canadian Romani leader Ron Lee, and Thomas Acton. *Photograph by Belinda Acton.*

barrel-top wagons. The children were unavoidably dirty and some had painful sores. Further up Irish Travellers congregated among car bodies and tarmac tippings. We gathered in this forlorn landscape and burned a tent in memory of the child martyrs of George Street. Ladislav Demeter held a small Romani flag aloft and we sang the anthem. When the coach moved off, it was followed by a procession of trucks and vans. The local committee had prepared a reception in St. Patrick's Church Hall. The tables were loaded with plates of sandwiches and cakes. Joyce Webb, the heroine of numerous skirmishes, now stood over a tea urn.

It was a long road back to Orpington and we were already behind schedule. I therefore urged that we abandon the tea and make for the police station. The protest placards were picked up and an excited crowd arrived outside the new headquarters of the West Midlands Constabulary.

People filled the entrance lobby before the movement could be quelled. A delegation was invited to meet the senior officer in a smaller room. Appropriately Thomas Holomek acted as spokesman. He introduced himself to Chief Inspector Nealen as head of the Czech Romani contingent and a military advocate with the rank of colonel. Kenrick was at his side to interpret:

"When we learned in London about the deaths of three children, we decided at once to come here ourselves. We protest at the way you, and those under you have

Tent burning ceremony at Walsall, near Birmingham, during the First World Romani Congress.
From left to right (front row): Dr Jan Cibula, Jarko Jovanovic, Grattan Puxon. Behind: Bedzhet Cuna, flag holder Ladislav Demeter, Vasnko Rouda and Juan de Dios Ramirez Heredia.

continuously and mercilessly hounded Gypsy people in your district, culminating in these deaths. I personally cannot understand how British law can permit this to happen. We have been told by a member of the British parliament that the law requires each town and district to provide a proper caravan site for our people. Yet here today we have seen families living among rubbish, without water or any services. The children are not even going to school. You apparently follow a policy of doing everything to drive these families out of the district, even breaking the law yourselves to achieve this. We demand in future that the police stay within the law in their dealings with Roma; and treat them as equal citizens. As for these children's deaths, we urge an inquiry to find those responsible."

The Chief Inspector made a cautious reply. The deaths had been the subject of a coroner's court. A verdict of accidental death had been recorded. Police powers existed to remove vehicles, though he did not know precisely what the circumstances had been on that occasion. He undertook to make a full report to the Chief Constable.

In retrospect the London Congress can be seen to have provided both meeting and departure point. If it lacked the trappings of the grand occasion, which the Palais de l'UNESCO might have bestowed, nobody can deny its credibility. The assembly of those sixty delegates in Cannock House lent authoritative expression to the collective aspirations of the Romani people. Moreover, they vested a mandate in a permanent secretariat and international committee, which has since been renewed and enlarged by successive congresses. But because it was the first, those present had had the unique opportunity and privilege of adopting the Romani flag, re-uniting Roma symbolically with India as the ancient homeland and designating 8 April, the closing date, as Romani national day.

References

Acton, T.A., 1974 *Gypsy politics and social change*, Routledge and Kegan Paul, London.
Acton, T.A., Hurley, B., and Denaro R., 1971 *The Romano Drom song book*, Romanestan Publications, Oxford.
Dodds, N., 1966 *Gypsies, Didikois and Other Travellers*, Johnson, London.
Huttunen, K., 1971 "The Gypsy population and measures taken by the Finnish Government" Duplicated Report brought to the First World Romani Congress by V. Koivisto.
Huttunen, K., 1972 *Raportti suomen mustalaisista*, K.J. Gummerus Osakeyhtiön, Jyväskylässä, Finland.
Liégeois, J-P., 1976 *Mutation Tsigane La Révolution Bohémienne*, Editions Complexe, Brussels.
Puxon, G. and Puxon, V., 1967 *The Victims – Itinerants in Ireland*, Aisti Eireannacha, Dublin.
Puxon, G., 1968 *On the road*, National Council for Civil Liberties, London.
Puxon, G., 1969 "Gypsies and the Czech Crisis" *Journal of the Gypsy Lore Society*, Series III, Vol. XLVIII (1–2) pp. 57–9.
Puxon, G., 1971 "The First World Romani Congress" *Race Today*, June.
Puxon, G., 1987 (4th.ed.) *Roma Europe's Gypsies*, Minority Rights Group (Report No. 14), London.
Wiklund, D., 1969 *Report on the Situation of the Gypsies in Europe*, (Document 2629), Council of Europe, Strasbourg.

CHAPTER NINE

GYPSIES AND PLANNING POLICY

Diana Allen

AMONG ENGLISH GYPSIES Donald Kenrick is probably best now known as a friend and helper of those who struggle against the immense obstacles they encounter in obtaining planning permission to live on their own land. I first met him at the Festival on Hampstead Heath following the First World Romani Congress in 1971, when he was already well known as one of the leading supporters of the growing Gypsy movement for recognition of their rights as an ethnic minority group. I had recently become interested in the Gypsy situation, after reading the report of the 1965 government survey of *Gypsies and Other Travellers* (MHLG 1967).

I had decided to investigate the local position, as there were always Gypsies encamped by the roadside in and around the borders of Hertfordshire, Buckinghamshire and Bedfordshire where I live. Whenever I saw a caravan, I would introduce myself and ask if I could do anything to help, and almost invariably there was some problem which I could help to sort out. I soon realised the extent to which the poorer rural Gypsies, in these agricultural areas north of London, with no fixed address and limited communication with our world because of illiteracy, were still almost totally excluded from it. For most purposes they simply did not exist officially and had no means of calling on the help and support in the community which we take for granted. A local Gypsy Support Group was set up and between us, we tackled problems as they arose. These included the refusal of local doctors to take Gypsies on their list and the refusal of schools to take Gypsies as pupils. We involved social workers and health visitors and set up a system enabling Gypsies to claim benefits from the DHSS to which they were entitled and many other rights.

I became particularly interested in the many legal problems that arose. Local Gypsies were easy prey to police officers hoping to build up a record of successful prosecutions. Most of these were for motoring offences and the cure involved weaning the Gypsies from the idea that you could buy a car and drive it to pull your trailer in the same way that you could buy a horse and use it to tow your wagon. They discovered gradually from experience that it was necessary to obey certain rules which involved

"The idea that you could buy a car.... in the same way that you could buy a horse" – horse-trading at Stow Fair.

acquiring documents but many of them had little idea of how to obtain these documents and certainly no idea of why they were required. Some were insured without knowing that the insurance was invalid because they had never held a driving licence. Others held expired insurance because there was no way that they could receive the normal reminder at the date of renewal. Some had been refused driving licences because they had no address, unless a sympathetic householder provided them with one. I remember assisting one young Gypsy to apply for a driving licence and when I eventually took it to him from my address and handed it over, I left him standing by his trailer gazing in astonishment and disbelief.

Few of them had full licences and it was generally accepted among them that Gypsies could not pass a driving test because they could not read. Next time a test had been arranged I suggested that the young man involved when asked to read a number plate, should ask for a pencil and paper and write it down, and he passed his test. For a time after that, Gypsies from miles around applied for driving tests at Berkhamsted because "that is a place where Gypsies are allowed to pass driving tests". Others failed their test because of a defect in their vehicle and it became the regular practice for members of the support group to lend their own cars for the test to be taken.

When they were charged with various offences, Gypsies were regularly not represented in Court because they assumed that solicitors, as members of the establishment, would be hostile rather than helpful. They were frequently pressurised by the police to plead guilty to offences they had not committed, on the grounds that if they pleaded not guilty the case would be adjourned and they would be remanded in custody "for a long time". Over the years, however, it was possible to integrate them into the system so that they were properly represented, obtained legal aid and could obtain bail, which had always previously been refused them on the grounds of the police statement that they were of no fixed abode and would not attend court. Members of the support group began to offer themselves as surety and when bail was granted and the Gypsies turned up, as they invariably did, it soon began to be granted on the same basis as for other defendants.

The more serious and more complex side of Gypsies' dealings with the law involved their accommodation when travelling, or rather the lack of it. It soon became obvious to me that this was at the heart of what people referred to as "the Gypsy problem" which contrary to general opinion was a problem for the Gypsies and not because of them. Most of the local Gypsies had been brought up to a tradition of depending for much of their livelihood on farm work starting with the sugar beet hoeing in March and going right through to the potato picking in October or November. For the rest of the year they depended on calling from house to house, either offering services such as knife grinding, chair caning or repairing pans and broken plates with rivets, or selling articles such as clothes pegs, pots and pans, artificial flowers, and baskets. Sometimes women offered fortune telling. During the winter, they could generally arrange to stay in one place in a farmer's field or on some traditional stopping place on common land, so that the children could attend school.

For various reasons many elements of this way of life had died on them. Most of them had taken to scrap dealing which at that time was profitable. They had become motorised and exchanged their horse-drawn wagons for trailer caravans. They were obliged to travel all the year round and to stop almost entirely on roadside verges, where they became more visible and in most peoples' eyes, an untidy eyesore instead of a picturesque part of the countryside. The promise of stopping places or sites for everybody promised in the 1968 Caravan Sites Act had not been fulfilled although some permanent sites had been built, no effort whatsoever was being made to provide any legal accommodation for those Gypsies who were continuing to travel (Kenrick et al. 1999d: 89). Wherever they stopped there was an immediate outcry from local residents, who rang the police and local councils, insisting that the Gypsies should be moved immediately. Unfortunately, there were legal powers available that could be used against them, although it was not generally necessary for the police or council officials to do more than threaten them as the Gypsies moved without waiting for the inevitable court summons. To these Gypsies the threat of court proceedings appeared as a threat of imprisonment and they would move without further argument, only to be similarly treated in their next stopping place. Many people were putting pressure on local authorities to provide the sites which, from April 1970, it was their statutory duty to build, but it became obvious to me at an early stage that they would never provide enough sites unless the courts forced them to. Much of my work as a solicitor at that time involved defending Gypsies from every form of eviction and working for full implementation of the Caravan Sites Act.

However, I also became aware of another legal injustice which was being imposed on Gypsies and that is through the planning laws. Todd and Clark (1991: 12) in a Department of the Environment Report estimated the initial refusal rate for Gypsies applying for permission to live on their own land, or set up a small private site for themselves and their families at 90 per cent, while over the country as a whole 80 per cent of planning applications were being granted, although they also noted that Gypsies had a higher than average success rate at appeal (Todd and Clark 1991: 13). More detailed research (Williams 1999: 32,33) has since shown a Gypsy success rate at appeal of over 40 per cent during the 1980s but the Todd and Clark figure of 10 per cent success in initial applications has continued to be widely cited (Kenrick et al. 1999d: 139, Hawes and Perez 1996: 52) to encourage the implementation of the policy adopted (but neglected) by the government after the Cripps Report of 1977 in favour of Gypsies setting up their own sites with the assistance of local authorities.

Throughout the years there had always been some Gypsies in Britain deciding to settle in houses but the preferred method if they did not want to travel all the year round was to buy land and continue their traditional life in their caravans, travelling when they wished to, and returning for the winter. Planning laws introduced after the Second World War to control the sprawl of residential development meant, however, that this was no longer legally possible without a planning application involving the filling in of forms and the preparation of plans, which was beyond the scope of most Gypsies without outside help. To begin with most of them were unaware of the new requirements and continued as before, to buy land and settle on it and so were subject to enforcement proceedings by the local planning authority and had to move, often losing the savings which they had invested in the land in the first place. Sometimes subsequent non-Gypsy owners of the land from which the Gypsies had been driven were then given planning permission to build a house. Some local authorities took enforcement action against Gypsies settled on their own land when if they had known about it the Gypsies could have applied for a Certificate of Lawful Use.

Gradually the Gypsy community became aware that the appeal procedure offered them a remedy when threatened with eviction from their own land but they needed to have outside help. The first case in which I was involved was in 1974. I knew nothing about planning at that time but the consultant in our firm was a Town Planner and I prepared the case under his instruction and he presented at the Enquiry and we won. The land involved was a small plot cut off from the farm to which it belonged by a new motorway. It was still classified as agricultural, although there was no possible way in which it could be used agriculturally. It was, in fact, being used as an unofficial rubbish tip. I began to see that what Gypsies were now up against, if they wished to settle on their own land, was the misuse by local authorities of planning regulations to satisfy local voters who complained when Gypsies stopped anywhere near them. Although the classifications of land as agricultural, Green Belt, Outstanding Natural Beauty, and so on preserved genuine countryside from urban sprawl, ribbon development and exploitation by developers, they could also be applied to land which could be put to a better use without any harm to the countryside.

The next case which came to my firm was completely different in that it involved enforcement action against a number of Gypsies on land where the local authority had decided to make a permanent site. Following an election, the councillors of a different political party had reversed the decision and decided to evict them. Again I prepared the case, learning a lot about planning policy while doing so. My colleague was due to take over for the Enquiry. The day before it, he rang me to say he would be unable to come and that I would have to do it. I struggled through with help from a kindly Inspector and a sympathetic barrister briefed as an observer by a landowner and, again, we won.

Since the Cripps Report of 1977 and later the Wibberley Report of 1986 the Government has consistently urged local authorities to help Gypsies wherever possible both to acquire land and to set up their own sites but this advice has been almost totally ignored. Local authorities operate planning policies which allow them wide discretion in the granting of planning permission in accordance with increasingly complex and often conflicting policy guide lines (c.f. Wilson, 1998). Final decisions are made by council committees, consisting of councillors who are dependent for their position on election by voters. Politics, therefore, plays a large part in the decisions as do also personal prejudices of individual members of planning committees. Planning officials who deal with applications in the first place, and make recommendations to the committees who decide on them, also have their prejudices, which are not as a rule, in favour of Gypsies. They also depend for their jobs on the councillors who employ them and therefore, on the whole, will make recommendations which are likely to be acceptable to them. The majority of voters will object to any planning application which in any way affects their own property, such as being next door to it. Most of them will object on much wider grounds to Gypsies being given planning permission anywhere within their neighbourhood. Many will complain to their local councillor, who depends on their votes. These are the hurdles which have to be surmounted by Gypsies before they have any chance of living on their own land.

Planning Circulars, quite unrealistically, suggest that Gypsies should seek advice from local councils before they buy land in the hope of living on it. This, of course, is a non-starter and the Gypsies know it. Any planning official who finds out that a Gypsy is intending to apply for planning permission will immediately tell him that there is not the slightest chance of his obtaining it. A Gypsy intending to put his life savings into buying land in the hope of living on it may ask the advice of a sympathetic planner or solicitor. He must be told that 90 per cent of planning applications are refused by local authorities, and that an appeal against refusal of planning permission is a long and expensive procedure, and that the percentage of appeals which are won has never risen above 50 per cent and at the time of writing, is considerably lower (Williams 1999: 32,33). The Gypsy who takes a chance, therefore, is facing the prospect of probably being left at the end with nowhere to live, no money and a piece of land which is unsaleable, yet so desperate are they for the security that the Government advises them to seek, but does not help them to obtain, that there are still many who will continue to take the risk.

In my experience there are a number of ways in which a planning case can start. A Gypsy recommended by a friend or relation will make an appointment. The opening sentence will be "I've bought a piece of land and I want you to transfer the deeds." On enquiry you find that the so-called purchase has been similar to buying a horse. Money has been exchanged, a promise has been made and, in the Gypsy's view, the purchase is complete. It has to be explained that as there is nothing in writing, that the land is still the property of the vendor. Then it transpires that the client intends to live on the land permanently. It is explained to him that he is unlikely to obtain planning permission and it then transpires that he has moved onto the land, installed water, electricity and drainage, put up a fence, possibly sent his children to school and has nowhere to go if he moves off, which he certainly does not intend to do. After the purchase has been dealt with, the planning situation is explained including the financial implications of the near-certain refusal of planning permission and the subsequent appeal.

Another scenario is that the land had been properly conveyed but that the vendor had suggested that to save money he and the purchaser should use the same solicitor. As a further saving, no searches had been carried out. Some clients would say that they had no idea that once they bought land that they could not do what they wanted with it. Others said that as there was a derelict caravan on the land "it already had a licence". Others sought advice because they had bought and moved onto land and had "had these papers served on them" which in most cases they could not read and which proved to be Enforcement Notices requiring an immediate appeal.

In one case, land had been advertised at auction as having planning permission for a residential caravan. It was not until after the purchase was completed that the purchaser discovered that this was, in fact, only planning permission in connection with the livery stables which had previously been run there. The one scenario that *never* occurred was that of a sympathetic planning official helping a Gypsy to find land on which planning permission might be granted and assisting him to make an application. Some, however, were told that they should look for land and put in an application which might then be granted but which, in fact, was then refused.

We were therefore faced with a situation where our Gypsy clients were urgently in need of a place to live where they could have security from the increasingly difficult conditions of travelling and could afford to buy a piece of land for that purpose, but not land already scheduled for residential use, which was way beyond their resources.

They had no means of knowing or of finding out whether land which seemed to them suitable would obtain planning permission. Buying land was a gamble and they knew it.

Government policy supported them in their efforts to settle on their own land but gives no practical help except guidance to local authorities which is widely ignored. Local authorities had at their disposal planning policies which were more than enough to justify refusal of every application made to them for planning permission by a Gypsy and these were used by all of them. Our only loophole was to show that there were special circumstances justifying an exception to strict planning policies which at the local enquiry stage might convince an Inspector that he was justified in reversing a local authority's decision to refuse planning permission or to take enforcement proceedings.

Most planners consider that their job relates solely to the land and what its owners wish to use it for, even to the extent of considering that they should protect the land for its own sake, and the special circumstances which might justify an exception to planning policy should also relate to the land and not to people. In Gypsy cases, there was little chance of successfully arguing that land which the planners had decreed was not suitable for residential development was suitable for a Gypsy site, and it was therefore necessary to consider the personal circumstances of the appellant. On our side was Government policy set out in Circulars 20/77 and 57/78 that as Gypsies were entitled to continue their way of life and were not to be forced to move into houses, local authorities should, wherever possible, allow them to live on their own land. Inspectors on the whole were prepared to accept the evidence of a Gypsy that he was born into a Gypsy family, had travelled most of his life and still lived in a caravan.

In the case of John Smith, however, Runnymede Borough Council appealed against the Inspector's decision on the grounds that he was no longer a Gypsy because he was living on his land, and therefore no longer travelling, but the judge found that as Smith had been a Gypsy when he moved on to the land and would be a Gypsy again if he had to leave it, that he remained a Gypsy while he was living there (R v. Runnymede Borough Council ex parte Smith, 1994, 70 P and CR 244, cited in Morris and Clements, 1999: 113).

I never had to deal with a case where the Inspector decided that my client was not a Gypsy, but the fact of being a Gypsy was not enough of a special circumstance to override planning policy. Every case was different, and it was necessary to go in great detail into the lives and backgrounds of each client which would not normally be the case when representing a client at a Planning Inquiry. The fact of being a Gypsy was not in itself a special circumstance or material consideration in planning terms. Under the Caravan Sites Act of 1968, local authorities were required only to make provision for Gypsies residing in or resorting to their area. Although this was not necessarily a requirement of granting planning permission, most local authorities quoted it as one of the reasons for not granting permission. I therefore, as a rule, tried to include in the

Thomas Acton with Tom Lee (right) fighting the eviction of Archie Brown (back to camera) from Half Hyde Lane site in Hertfordshire 1983. *Photograph by David Altheer*

Gypsy's evidence, the names of some places where he had travelled within or close to the area concerned. This was not always easy, as their recollection was often only of a farm or just the name of the owner of a field.

    The planners would also refuse planning permission if they could show that a Gypsy had once lived on and moved off an official site or been offered a place on one, which had been refused for whatever reason. Although most sites were always full and had waiting lists, a pitch would often suddenly become available to cover the time of the Inquiry. Despite the Government's acceptance of the fact that not all Gypsies want to live on sites as a reason for allowing them to live on their own land, many Inspectors would give as a reason for dismissing an appeal the fact that a pitch on a site had been refused. It was therefore necessary to try to find an acceptable reason for Gypsies to refuse official pitches, going beyond a mere statement that they did not wish to live on them. In one case, the Inspector accepted a medical report that a child with heart trouble needed a quiet life and in another case that a woman with asthma needed to live in a mobile home with central heating which was not possible on the site available. It is interesting that in the Buckley case the European Court of Human Rights accepted the UK Government's argument that June Buckley's reasons for refusing the offer of a pitch were not sufficient to override planning considerations, although the refusal to give her planning permission was a breach of Article 8 of the European Convention of Human Rights (Buckley v. UK 23/1995/529/616, 1996 JPL 1018, cited in Morris and Clements 1999: 114).

Inspectors did not always agree with the Government's acceptance that some Gypsies are unable to live in houses. In one case however, where a Gypsy married to a gaujo had moved with him into a council house but had then left him with her children, this was held to be sufficient reason for the husband to buy land to live on so that the family could be together again in a mobile home. This was unusual, but I did find that an increasing number of successful appeals were based on medical evidence, particularly concerning children.

Where children were concerned, I always obtained evidence from the school or the Gypsy Education Service in support of the appeal and this was readily available. This was effective, particularly in the case of children with learning difficulties who had settled well into a particular school but in others the Inspector would maintain that the children could be equally well educated at a school in another area. In one case, where the appellant had been living on a site for twenty years and wished to provide better living accommodation for his family, the Inspector agreed that he had as much right to "better himself" as other members of the community and allowed the appeal.

It was interesting to see the different weight given by both local authorities and Inspectors to objections and support from members of the community. In theory, local authorities represent the community and their decisions in planning matters should presumably, to some extent, reflect their wishes. Opposition varied widely from case to case. At one extreme was the inquiry where a sizable hall was packed with noisy objectors to a site near the sea in a triangle bounded by a motorway on one side, a power station on the second and a mobile home site on the third. The local MP did not appear personally, but he gave an undertaking that he would see the Secretary of State for the Environment to make certain that planning permission was not granted. One of the reasons put forward by the local authority for refusing planning permission, was that there were already over 400 holiday sites in the district. At the other end of the scale, were the enquiries where there was no local opposition at all or practically none. I always advised my clients to take round a petition asking for support and in most cases, they were able to obtain a satisfactory number of signatures. In one case, where the only objectors were the next door neighbours, my client obtained ninety-five signatures in support over one weekend but permission was still refused. Inspectors' reports often quote the amount of opposition to the planning application but seldom the amount of support.

Unfortunately, Gypsies and Planners have very different ideas about what a site should be like. Many sites were small pieces of redundant farm land, which a farmer was glad to sell to a Gypsy for more than he could expect to get if sold as agricultural land, even if it was possible to sell it, but for considerably less than the price of residential land. Often there was an existing hedge of mixed native trees and shrubs often overgrown and providing a natural screen. This is ideal from the planner's point of view but not necessarily from that of the new owners who may see no reason why his dream home should be shielded from view, and whose first instinct may be to clear and tidy the land. They may sometimes remove the existing hedge and replace it with a board fence or conifers, or a low ornate wall along the front. If caught in time we would, of course, advise them to leave the hedge in position with as little pruning and cutting back as possible but often we were too late.

In the end the result of a planning inquiry is a personal decision of one inspector. He has wide discretionary powers and provided the report is written with care and states that all the evidence has been considered, it cannot be challenged.

The majority of inspectors had previously been town planners with a natural bias towards upholding planning policy. Many had no previous knowledge of the special needs of Gypsies and the history of site provision, and some were inevitably prejudiced against them. I needed to make certain that every Inspector was fully aware of the whole Gypsy background and it was not possible to submit this evidence through the Gypsy witnesses. A certain amount could be elucidated from the Council witnesses through cross-examination but not enough. I knew that some people managed both to give evidence and to act as advocates but I personally did not feel that I could do justice to a case by doing this. Eventually therefore, I handed the advocacy to a colleague and became myself an expert witness on Gypsies. I found this satisfying, since not being a planner, I could refuse to get embroiled in details of planning evidence, such as whether the development was inappropriate in the Green Belt. Whether or not the site was intrusive or well screened, could be left to the decision of the Inspector. On everything to do with Gypsies, however, I was better informed than the council advocate and was often given the chance to put in more useful information than was in my evidence, but the success rate for Gypsy appeals was still disappointingly low.

In 1994 the situation changed. Local authorities had successfully refused to carry out their statutory duties because they had found out that the Government had no intention of enforcing the law and the Government in its wisdom decided that the Caravan Sites Act had failed since only three-quarters of the Gypsy population had been provided with sites. The 1968 Caravan Sites Act was repealed by the 1994 Criminal Justice Act. In future the only way forward for Gypsies seeking suitable accommodation was to buy land and set up their own sites, regardless of the fact that only a minority could afford to do so. Circular 1/94, giving guidance on private Gypsy Caravan Sites, has been the basis of all subsequent Gypsy planning decisions.

The Circular has made little difference to the running battle between local authorities and Gypsies over the provision of private sites. It merely provides each side with slightly different material to use at inquiries. It states that the planning system should recognise the need for accommodation consistent with Gypsies' nomadic life style and that their land use requirement needs to be met. It gives excellent advice on how local authorities should set about revising Structure and Local Plans to include Gypsy sites. It assumes, however, that they are only too anxious to do so, which unfortunately is not the case. It then allows them to produce Structure Plans which will make it possible for them to continue to refuse all Gypsy applications. Section 7 states "it will be important for local planning authorities to be ready to discuss Gypsies' accommodation needs with the Gypsies themselves, their representative bodies and local support groups". I have yet to come across a case where this has been done by any local authority. Under the new regime local authorities remain as hostile to Gypsies and as determined to refuse all planning applications as they always were. They have been left completely free to interpret the advice to include Gypsy needs and plans in their own way with no checks or supervision.

The Circular says that provision for Gypsies should be on locational, but if that is not possible, on criteria-based grounds. As a result County Structure Plans now normally include a vague reference to Gypsy sites stating that local plans (to which the details are left) have the option of including either locational or criteria-based plans for Gypsy sites. That is to say they can either specify the actual map references that would be best for a Gypsy site (a location-based plan such as is generally used where housing is being planned) or they can specify criteria for some imaginary site. Invariably they choose the criteria-based policy. This gives them the opportunity to produce a list of criteria which makes it impossible to gain planning consent planning consent.

Local plans vary from risking making no mention whatsoever of Gypsies, to producing criteria which include a number of vague environmental requirements which will always, as has been shown in a number of cases, give them grounds for refusing a Gypsy application, and as a result the refusal rate remains high as before. On the Gypsies' side the Circular does provide room for argument. National policy, if not always local policy, provides for exceptions to strict planning policy in special circumstances. Where Green Belt is concerned the circumstances now have to be very special, where before they were only special. It is encouraging that at the Planning Inquiry stage, Inspectors are still prepared to accept that the needs of Gypsies can override planning policy even when they find that the development does intrude into open countryside or is in inappropriate development in the Green Belt. In fact, statistics drawn up by ACERT show that the number of successful appeals in the Green Belt has remained the same as it was before the 1994 Act and the new Circular (Williams, 1999).

There has also been encouraging help from the High Court in cases where an appeal against the Inspector's decision has been possible. In particular, it was judged in the Hedges' case that Inspectors must take into account not only the individual need of the Appellant whose case they are considering, but the general need for more Gypsy sites. In my experience this is extremely valuable and has been directly responsible for several successful appeals. Many Inspectors are also taking note of the ruling in the

European Court of Human Rights that to refuse planning permission to a Gypsy is a breach of Article 8 of the European Convention of Human Rights in that it interferes with family life and privacy. It is not a general precedent, in that they also found that the rights of the community, as laid down in planning law, could override the right of an individual Gypsy and did so in Buckley v. UK (23/1995/529/616, 1996, JPL 1018, cited in Morris and Clements 1999: 114). Nonetheless, it does open up the possibility of future successes. There has been a very slight rise in the percentage of successful appeals, although unfortunately there has been a fall in the actual number of appeals against refusals by local authorities (Williams 1999).

Although Government guidance recommends that planning permission should be permanent Inspectors not infrequently give only temporary permission, which can be for anything from one to five years. This decision is often based on assurances by the council that within the time allowed, they will be able to offer the appellant a place on an official site. No councils and few Inspectors have any regard to guidance by the Government that a Gypsy's preference for living on his own land to being on a site should be taken into account. At the end of the temporary period, a council will almost invariably refuse an application for renewal so that after living in a state of uncertainty about the future and not feeling justified in carrying out improvements the Gypsy is faced with having to go through the process of appeal and enquiry once again, and not always successfully.

Even when a local authority has won an inquiry, they still have not got rid of the Gypsy and this as they well know, may present problems. They may be involved in the very considerable expense of resisting an appeal to the High Court, although this is seldom possible because of the limited ground on which such an appeal can be made. They know that any attempt to get legal enforcement will be contested. If they issue a summons in the Magistrates' Court for breach of planning conditions the Court will be asked to consider that no alternative accommodation has been offered or is available and also the personal circumstances of the appellant which should almost certainly include the needs and rights of children under the Children' Acts and possibly medical needs. Courts sometimes indicate their dislike of the case having been brought by imposing a very small fine, and in some cases a Gypsy is happy to stay on his land and pay the fine when required to do so and regard it as rent. But in a significant number of cases the local authority has taken no enforcement action, possibly having regard to Government guidance in circulars, before and after the repeal of the Caravan Sites Act, and in the more recent Government publication "Managing Unauthorised Camping: A Good Practice Guide" (DETR 1998). They are also aware that displacing Gypsies from their own land only means increasing the number of unauthorised encampments, probably in their own district. In these cases we generally put in further planning applications often based on a change of circumstances, or for different requirements, which are duly refused, after which there is a yet further enquiry.

One client for whom we are re-applying has been on his land for twenty-four years. We also have a client who has been on her land for fifteen years, during which there have been three inquiries and against whom action is at present suspended because her case is being considered by the European Commission of Human Rights and is due to come before the European Court. There are a number of other cases where clients who have been living on their land for several years and are well settled into the community with their children attending school, who have not yet managed to obtain planning permission. They are never free from the anxiety of knowing that eventually they may have to move and in several cases, this has led to members of the family, generally the wife of the applicant, suffering from depression.

Not surprisingly, many local authorities have complained that what we regard as upholding Gypsies' human rights and they describe as delaying tactics, makes it difficult for them to 'get rid' of Gypsies who should exercise their rights to accommodation, which are not disputed, somewhere else. They are increasingly applying to the High Court for injunctions on the ground that Gypsies living on their land without planning permission are breaking the law. There is no legal defence to such an application. The first hurdle we face is that because there is no defence in law, legal aid is generally refused. It may be possible to obtain legal aid for an application for Leave to Apply for Judicial Review of the decision to evict, but so far such applications have been unsuccessful. Some Judges in High Court appeal cases are showing concern about the situation and in one case, although an injunction was granted, it was suspended for a year.

If an injunction is granted the next stage is an application to commit to prison and under this threat most Gypsies give up and move off their land. In one of our cases, however, an application had already been made to the European Commission of Human Rights, and is now waiting to go before the European Court. Although the local authority has threatened Committal proceedings, it has not as yet started them and the case remains suspended. I have not heard of any case of an actual committal to prison so I do not know whether such an application would succeed especially in cases where there are children involved. It remains to be seen what effect the Human Rights Act will have both on court decisions and planning inquiries. I fear there is little hope that it will influence decisions on planning applications.

What then is the way forward? The present Government are broadly sympathetic but so far it is not prepared to go back to the 1968 Caravan Sites Act of placing a duty on local authorities to provide, or even to encourage them by payment of grants for setting up sites. It has merely confirmed the guidance given by the last Government that authorities should set up sites where needed and incorporate a policy for official and private sites in their structure plans. As there are no grants available and no sanctions if they fail to observe this guidance, most local authorities are continuing to ignore it as blatantly as they have been doing for many years. Some of then are now beginning to close down sites. No help is given to Gypsies who are looking for land where they might obtain planning permission. As before practically every planning application is turned down, enforcement notices are served on Gypsies who move on to their own land and

Diana Allen
Photograph by Stefano Cagnoni

appeals against refusal of planning permission or enforcement notices are strongly opposed on grounds of planning policy. Most, though not all, new Structure and Local plans include a policy for Gypsies but most of them are worded in such a way that they can be used to oppose any planning application made by a Gypsy to live on his or her own land. A way must be found without any further delay to compel authorities to accept that all Gypsies must be enabled to obtain accommodation appropriate to their needs.

Recently a substantial lobbying alliance bringing together many organisations, and underpinned by the Traveller Law Research Unit at the Cardiff Law School of the University of Wales, has led to the publication of *Gaining ground: Law reform for Gypsies and Travellers* (Morris and Clements 1999). This report into all areas of discrimination against Gypsies, based on the research and experience of many people working in various fields, has put forward a number of proposals as to how the situation can be remedied for the government's consideration. Some involve legislation, others merely recommend stronger guidance to local authorities. It is to be hoped that planning policies will be adopted which will bring Gypsy applications in line with all other planning applications, where the presumption is in favour of granting rather than refusing. The biggest problem, however, is that the planning committees of local councils which make final decisions on applications reflect the widespread prejudice and hostility against Gypsies which unfortunately, cuts right through society at all levels. Unless we can in some way educate the non-Gypsy majority about the culture and needs of Travellers, then opposition at a local level might make even the most reasonable of reforms unworkable in practice. I see no way in which what is frequently referred to as the 'Gypsy problem' will be solved and Gypsies given the equality before the law to which they are entitled, as long as the much greater problem of intolerance and prejudice against them remains acceptable in all ranks of society from Government ministers downwards. As someone who has continued to work for this into her ninth decade, I hope that as a vigorous young man of seventy, Donald Kenrick will continue for many years his invaluable work in the battle for the right of Gypsies to live on their own land.

References

Cripps, Sir J., 1976 *Accommodation for Gypsies* Department of the Environment/HMSO, London.

DETR (Department of Environment, Transport and the Regions) with the Home Office, 1998 *Managing unauthorised camping: a good practice guide*, DETR, London.

Hawes, D. and Perez, B., 1996 (2nd Ed.) *The Gypsy and the State*, The Policy Press, Bristol.

MHLG (Ministry of Housing and Local Government/Welsh Office)), 1967 *Gypsies and Other Travellers*, HMSO, London.

Morris, R. and Clements, L. eds. 1999 *Gaining ground: law reform for Gypsies and Travellers*, University of Hertfordshire Press, Hatfield.

Todd, D and Clark, G., 1991 *Gypsy site provision and policy*, Department of the Environment/HMSO, London.

Wibberly, G., 1986 *A Report on the analysis of responses to the consultation on the operation of the Caravan Sites Act*, duplicated by the Department of the Environment at the request of the House of Commons Select Committee on the Environment, London.

Williams, T., 1999 *Private Gypsy site provision*, ACERT, Harlow.

Wilson, M.,1998 *A diirectory of planning policies for Gypsy site provision in England and Wales* Policy Press, Bristol.

CHAPTER TEN

THE BLONDE BANDIT ARTHUR THESLEFF:
COMMITTED SCHOLARSHIP IN EARLY ROMANI STUDIES AND TODAY

Gunilla Lundgren

"There is a nation on this earth with a language of its own, and with manners and customs of its own, homeless and without a native country, poor and miserable, roving about the world. The subjects of this nation are called 'Gypsies'. All over the world these Gypsies have caused fear but likewise they have been exposed to a persecution that could not possibly have been more cruel." (Thesleff 1904)

ARTHUR THESLEFF was born in Finland in 1871 to a middle-class family. His father was a colonel in the army and then a state official. Even as a young boy, he was intensely interested in science and all branches of knowledge. He became an amateur naturalist, exploring fungi, plants and trees, and while still young wrote a guide to the edible mushrooms of Finland (Thesleff 1893). He also devoured travel literature and in his imagination explored unknown parts of the world: Tibet, the Sahara and Madagascar. His dreams filled him so totally that his friends nicknamed him 'Madagascar'. Later he was given other nicknames such as 'Mushroom-Thesleff' and 'The Gypsy Baron.'

From his earliest youth as he roamed the countryside, he began to meet the Finnish Roma, who call themselves 'Kaale'. Without bothering to ask permission, he collected their songs, stories and words and published a dictionary of their dialect (Thesleff 1901). He also went on walking tours of Austria, North Africa, the south of Spain and later in his life extended his trips to Russia, Poland and the Baltic and Balkan countries, taking photographs, collecting songs and stories. He travelled not as a privileged scholar, but on foot, often seemingly without any plan. He ate, drank and slept with the people he met. His clothes were often shabby to the point of raggedness, and he gained another nickname: 'the blond bandit' (Nummelin 1993, Lundgren 1996).

In spite of his serious studies he never gained any real academic recognition in his lifetime. This paper seeks to answer two questions. First, why nowadays do we acknowledge Thesleff as an important anthropologist and linguist? Secondly, is it pos-

Romani children photographed by Thesleff in the hills outside Serajevo.
Photograph from the Royal Library, Stockholm

sible nowadays to carry out such work without encountering the political upsets and personal frustrations that he met, and actually use our knowledge to do something about the persecution of Roma that Thesleff recognised? The events that led to my own discovery of Thesleff help provide an answer.

A young teacher seeks help

As a newly qualified teacher I came to Stockholm in 1968 to work in a school class for children with special problems. I was young and idealistic, filled with passion for my work, inspired both by the revolutionary Black Panther party in the United States, and the peace-loving bishop Paulo Freire from Brazil.

My classroom was filled by nine lively children in vivid clothing, aged between seven and fourteen. They were newly arrived in Sweden from Spain and they had never been to school before. They were Kalderash Roma. I was facing a task which my teacher training had not prepared me for at all.

My work as a teacher trained for special education was to help the children to obtain basic knowledge and support them socially. The aim was to help them to cope with ordinary Swedish school life among children of the same age. It proved to be a more difficult task than I had ever expected. I had to reconsider my political, ideological and religious sources of inspiration.

Racism, prejudice and historic suppression were, of course, the roots and still part of the situation, but my main pedagogic problem was to be found on a much more trivial level: my pupils arrived at the school late every day or did not show up at all. If they were not sick or tired themselves, they had to stay at home to help sick little sisters or tired rheumatic grandmothers. If they were not selling carpets, they had to go to the laundry, to the police, to the health insurance office, to the lawyer's office or to the child welfare clinic. My pupils quite simply had not enough time for school.

I appealed to them and their parents. I bought alarm clocks. I called them by phone in the mornings. I went to their homes and woke up whole families. I talked to the older family members. Everyone agreed: of course the children had to attend school! That was the main reason why the families had come to Sweden. "But unfortunately," said the mothers, "today the children can't come. Tomorrow!"

So there I was, stuck with my good intentions. I was very fond of my pupils, but how could I help them, and how could I explain to the school principal that my pupils were always missing?

Then, one day I read an article in *Dagens Nyheter* (the leading Swedish daily newspaper). It told the story of Donald Kenrick, a dedicated doctor of philosophy educating Gypsy children in caravan schools in Britain. If the Romani families were evicted, or moved for other reasons, the school and its volunteer teachers followed them. Here, for once, was a school adapting to the needs of its pupils and not vice versa!

Fired with enthusiasm, I wrote to the *Dagens Nyheter* and they helped me to contact Donald Kenrick. One week later I got a letter from London: "You are welcome! I can show you around. Don't worry about money, you can stay with me in my small apartment if it's OK for you to sleep on a mattress on the floor."

A visit to London

Next summer I came to England, to a new world of knowledge, unconventional working methods, anarchy and humanism. Since those days, Donald has been a friend of mine and a colleague.

In Freire's (1970) book *Pedagogy of the Oppressed*, he impresses on the reader the risk of the helper becoming a suppressor. Even well-intentioned teachers, social workers and researchers easily develop into instruments for the authorities. Freire is constantly stressing that all education has to aim at democracy. He wants to stop the use of ready-made models. Instead, teachers should construct patterns and useful models *together* with their students. School should not provide the students with incomprehensible books, but books which teachers and pupils write together, and these books should reflect the pupils' own reality.

Donald brought me to caravan schools in Britain where I could see how these ideas were practised in reality. When I returned to Sweden, I brought with me a photocopied handlettered book in the mixed English-Romani dialect. A typical page showed

Gunilla Lundgren with Romani children – outside a Roma run day care centre in Rinberg near Stockholm in 1988. *Photograph by Elly Berg*

a man next to a boy carrying a pole towards a horse and cart, with the words "Mandi jells to buti with mo dad to kur saster from the gaujo, and ker luvvu for hobben". The English was also on the page: "I go to work with my father to get iron from the gaujos, and make money for food" (Acton 1971).

A reflective Donald Kenrick photographed during a visit to Sweden

Donald Kenrick in Stockholm in 1986 after he and Gunilla Lundgren had laid flowers on the spot where Olaf Palme had just been assasinated
Photograph by Gunilla Lundgren

Donald Kenrick and Gunilla Lundgren holding their god daughter, Katy Reinhardt, niece of Django Reinhardt, outside a café in Paris after her baptism in 1970.

The text of the book used the mixed English-Romani dialect actually spoken by English Romanichal Gypsies. But it had a foreword written in an internationalised version of Romani, with translation in English:

"Kana ame sikiarasas an e Romani Krisake jiapen-vardona, but-var diklyam te nai but lila kai kamena len e tikne Roma. Akava lil, chindo and e tiknenge lava kokero, si so manglemas kana sikiardem and o nilai."

"While we were teaching in the Gypsy Council caravan schools, we often felt that there were few books which appeal to Gypsy children. This book, written in the words of the children themselves, is what I would have liked to have had, while I was teaching last summer" (Acton, 1971).

Writing books – the present and the past

At the beginning of the next school year I started to write a book together with my pupils. And in 1972 *Maritza en zigenarflicka* (Maritza, a Gypsy girl) by Gunilla Lundgren, Nina Taikon and Zenia and Gina Tan-Mercowic, was published. This book became the start of my writing. Now I have written around twenty children's books including several others written with Roma (e.g. Lundgren 1991, 1998).

Later I travelled with Donald all over Europe. Like Thesleff, we visited Romany families in big cities and in villages; we talked to professors and beggars, musicians and teachers, flamenco dancers and seamstresses, building workers and composers. Donald could talk to everyone in any dialect or language and he showed the same amount of respect to everyone. Nothing seemed to surprise him and no problem seemed too difficult for him. Unforseen setbacks were handled with his sense of humour.

During the thirty years since we met I have constantly turned to Donald for help and advice, and as Donald even understands Swedish, he has corrected many of my errors. And he has also found errors about Roma or the Romani language in encyclopaedias and even information booklets from the Swedish Department for Immigration. He has published articles in Swedish about Roma (Kenrick, 1992a, 1994d) and written in English about Romani in Sweden (Kenrick 1989d).

It was also Donald who brought me to the Royal Library in Stockholm and told me about the invaluable documents in the Arthur Thesleff files there. Thanks to Donald I have been able to use photographs from this collection both in books and magazines. But today we can do what Thesleff could only dream about.

Thesleff in Finland and Sweden

Before 1906 the Grand Duchy of Finland was still a province of the Russian empire, although with some autonomy, and its own parliament and constitution. When Thesleff wrote some early papers on the Kaale Roma (Thesleff 1899a, 1899b) he came to

Thesleff on one of his adventures.
Photograph from the Royal Library, Stockholm

the attention of the authorities and was appointed before the age of thirty as the principal member of a government commission to investigate "the Gypsy Problem in Finland" (Black, 1914:170). This was published in both Finnish and Swedish, the two official languages of the Grand Duchy (Thesleff 1901b), in the same year as his dictionary of Romani (Thesleff 1901a).

These achievements did not bring happiness, however. His Romani friends resented the publication of their language. Because of his eccentric lifestyle and unconventional character he was not regarded as a scholar by the academic world and his report was not a political success. He regarded himself as uninterested in politics and when people tried to discuss politics with him he would quote Nietzsche: "The earth's skin suffers from a kind of eczema: human beings." When he became a victim of political slander he decided to leave Finland altogether.

In 1904 he immigrated to Sweden. Not long after, however, he set off on a venture to create a colony in Misiones, a fertile part of Argentina. He was paid by the Argentine government to take part in an expedition as a researcher into the geography, animal and plant life of the area. The whole idea proved unrealistic, however, and became a catastrophe. After a few years Thesleff was back in Sweden, now totally ruined. He left behind in Argentina both his wife and the farm on which he had risked all his money. Back in Stockholm he seemed to become a laughing-stock, the subject of malicious gossip about "the Gypsy Baron" in the newspapers.

The Gypsy Lore Society to the rescue?

Just when Thesleff seemed at his lowest ebb, help came from an unlikely source. In England a Gypsy Lore Society had been founded in 1888, and published a journal on Romani folklore, anthropology and linguistics, bringing together wealthy amateurs, like the Archduke Joszef of Austria, artists and writers like Arthur Symons and Theodore Watts-Dunton, and academic librarians like John Sampson, Eric Otto Winstedt and George F. Black., Although it had collapsed in 1892, just when Thesleff was becoming first active, it was revived in 1907, under the patronage of a wealthy sugar refiner in Liverpool, R.A. Scott Macfie, who became both secretary and editor of the journal.

Thesleff's 1901 dictionary was one of the first works reviewed in the revived journal. It was useful in clarifying an early list of fifty-three words noted down at a trial of Gypsies in the early sixteenth-century. They had first been discovered among the papers of an old Dutch family, and published by Professor A. Kluyver in 1900. With the help of Scott Macfie and Thesleff, Kluyver revised his work substantially and republished it in the Journal of the Gypsy Lore Society (Kluyver 1910). The Gypsy Lore Society then invited Thesleff to work for them.

This recognition gave him a fresh wind. He began to make enthusiastic plans. He immediately wanted to make the Gypsy Lore Society into an institute not only for collecting facts about Roma but also for supporting, protecting and educating Roma throughout the world. He supervised the English translation and re-publication of his Finnish Report in the Journal (Thesleff 1911, 1912) and helped Black (1914) prepare the first major bibliography of Romani studies. Once again he felt his knowledge appreciated as he was interviewed seriously by newspapers and invited to give lectures.

At the same time Thesleff had another project; he wanted to study 'thieves' slang' in Stockholm. He did his research for this in the same way he had always done, by living with the people he wanted to study. Sometimes he was even arrested with his new friends for bad behaviour in public. His book on Stockholm's criminal language and lower-class slang was published in 1912 but it brought him many enemies among his friends in bars and pubs in the same way as his Romani dictionary had given him enemies among the Kaale Roma.

This work was not what the Gypsy Lore Society considered part of their study of the 'True Romanies'. Thesleff gave a copy of his 1912 book to Scott Macfie which eventually formed part of the Gypsy collection at the University of Liverpool but it was pointedly omitted from Black's (1914) bibliography. Thesleff's hopes for the Gypsy Lore Society were a complete mismatch with that body's upper-class amateurism. They were not interested in social reform, as he was, but pursued a romantic ideal of knowledge for its own sake.

Although Thesleff served a term as a president of the Gypsy Lore Society, his grandiose plans for it collapsed. The society had no money to pay him a salary. In 1914 its wealthy patron Scott Macfie volunteered for the army at the age of forty-six and served four years in the trenches. The publication of the journal became more and more belated during the Great War, and Thesleff became disillusioned. A further setback was that his request to become a Swedish citizen was refused. Unemployed and short of money, he declined into alcoholism.

He died a bankrupt in Stockholm in 1920. His home was a mixture of a museum and an antique shop. Hippopotamus tusks, ostrich eggs, deer-teeth and the tongues and legs of wild boar hung in strings from the ceilings. The walls were decorated with Lapp and Gypsy knives, and poisoned arrows and spears from Paraguay. There were also the skins and horns and teeth and claws of mysterious animals, and birds as small as butterflies and butterflies as big as birds, and all this mixed together with pictures of the Madonna, piles of manuscripts and relics from the pyramids (Lagerborg 1921).

Much of Thesleff's written material remains unpublished and when he died his library, his photographs and documents were donated to the Royal Library in Stockholm, where they can still be found (Svanberg 1984). Although his discourse is often schematic and old-fashioned and today even seems racist, Thesleff nonetheless had a warm sympathy for the Romani people. He often supported his friends down to his last coin, and he used to say that the happiest time of his life was when he was travelling with the Romani people.

Committed scholarship, then and now

Some of the parallels between Thesleff and Kenrick are striking. Both started as young men with a thirst for knowledge, both were entranced by the situation of the Roma, and dumbfounded by the way Europeans regarded the persecution of Roma as normal, both were enthusiastic linguists and great travellers, who learnt languages by living with the people they studied. Both tried to work with the Gypsy Lore Society. Although Kenrick was born fifty-nine years after Thesleff, he collaborated with those, like Dora Yates and Bernard Gilliatt-Smith who had once worked alongside Thesleff in the Gypsy Lore Society. And yet their lives are so different they could be inhabitants of two different worlds.

Thesleff had no network of Gypsy organisations and teachers and social workers, as exists today, to turn to when the passive scientism of the Gypsy Lore Society failed him. He had no theory of anti-racism to draw upon, painfully learned through the lessons of the Nazi holocaust, the anti-colonial struggle and the civil rights movement; indeed, like most of his contemporaries he accepted 'scientific racism' as truth without really considering any alternative. The objections of his low-life friends to having their languages set out for the reading public took him by surprise.

Today the relation between non-Gypsy scholars and Romani people can be much more equal. There are Romani organisations at whose service they can put themselves. There are many scholars themselves Romani, who do not see lack of formal education as an essential part of Romani identity, and who are re-theorising the history of European policy to Roma, even as Europeans have continually re-theorised Roma. Donald Kenrick did not just visit Finnish Kaale Roma to take information about them; he has also been an information resource for them when they visit London (Kenrick 1973a).

Even as we make use of Thesleff's legacy of history, description and photographs, we can be grateful that there is today a community of Romani intellectuals and their friends committed to equality, democracy and progress which means we do not have to fall victim to isolation and disillusion as he did.

References

Acton, T. 1971 *Mo Romano Lil* Romanestan Publications, Oxford

Black, G 1914 *A Gypsy bibliography* Gypsy Lore Society/ T&A Constable/Quaritch Edinburgh and London

Freire, P. 1970 (English translation 1972) *Pedagogy of the oppressed* Penguin, London

Kluyver, A. 1910 "Un glossaire Tsigane du seizième siècle" *Journal of the Gypsy Lore Society* 2nd Series, Vol.4 (2) pp.131–142

Lagerborg, R. 1921 "Artur Thesleff: En minnesteckning af Rolf Lagerborg" in Artur Thesleff 1921, *Bibliska Naturbilder* Holger Schildts Förlag, Helsingfors

Lundgren, G., Taikon, N., Tan-Mercowic Z. and Tan-Mercowic G, 1972 *Maritza en zigenarflicka* (Maritza, a Gypsy girl), Gebers (Almquist and Wiksell) Stockholm

Lundgren, G. and Tan-Mercowic, Z. 1991 *Zenia en zigenarska* (Zenia a Gypsy woman), Alfabeta Bokförlag, Stockholm

Lundgren, G. and Demeter A.N-E. 1998 *Aljosha zigenarhövdingens pojke* (Alyosha, the son of the Gypsy chief) Bonnier/Carlsen, Stockholm

Lundgren, G. 1996 "'Cikanský baron' Arthur Thesleff" *Romano Dzhaniben* (Prague) Vol.III (3)

Nummelin, S. 1993 "Zigenarbaronen, Artur Thesleff – Bland Tattare och Adel" *Tidningen Vi* (Stockholm) häfte nr. 39

Svanberg, I. 1984 "Artur Thesleffs efterlämnade zigenarmaterial på kungliga biblioteket" *Svenska landsmål och svenskt folkliv – Dialekt-och Folkminnesarkivet I Uppsala* pp.18–123

Thesleff, A. 1893 *Finlands förnämsta ätliga svampar*, Tryckt: I Simelii Arfwingar, Helsingfors

Thesleff, A. 1899a "Zigenarnes utbredning i Finland" *Meddelanden af geografiska Föreningen i Finland*, Vol.4 (6)

Thesleff, A. 1899b "Finlands Zigenare en etnografisk studie" *Finsk Tidskrift* Vol. 46, pp 386–98, 466–77.

Thesleff, A. 1901a *Wörterbuch des Dialekts der finnländischen Zigeuner*, Finska Vetenskaps Societeten (Acta Vol. 29 (6)), Helsinki

Thesleff, A. 1901b *Keisarilliselle Majesteetille, maame mustalaiskysymyksen tutkimista varten asetettu komitea / Till Hans kejserliga Majestät från komittén för pröfningen af zigenarfrågan i landet* Keisarillisen Senaatin Kirjapainossa/ Kejserliga Senatens Tryckeri

Thesleff, 1904 *Zigenare: En inledande öfversikt till det af författaren vid Skansens vårfest 1904 anordnade Zigenarlägret* Centraltryckeriet (The Nordic Museum) Stockholm

Thesleff, A. 1911,1912 "Report on the Gypsy Problem" *Journal of the Gypsy Lore Society* (2nd Series) Vol.5 (2,3 & 4) pp. 81-7, 218–24, 255–69 (Note: This is a translation of the main parts of Thesleff 1901b).

Thesleff, A. 1912 *Stockholms förbrytarspråk och lägre slang*, Albert Bonniers Forlag, Stockholm

CHAPTER ELEVEN

"OH, THIS RUSSIAN SPIRIT ABIDES EVERYWHERE":
A DIALOGUE OF THE IMAGINATION WITH DR DONALD KENRICK

Valdemar Kalinin

THE IDEA THAT "this Russian spirit abides everywhere" sometimes appears as a positive affirmation by exiles, sometimes as a more negative attempt to denounce the ubiquity of Russian influence, sometimes just as mystification. Oh! These Russians! How can we be objective about their influence on Romani culture?

At the time of the collapse of the Socialist Bloc people in the newly independent countries idealised Western life and had a fantastic and unreal view of life in England. Similarly, the believe that whatever comes from these vulnerable places must be primarily Russian, even sometimes only Russian. Such commonplaces as the seven-string guitar, vodka, borscht, blinis and the Cyrillic alphabet are all mistakenly attributed to the Russian culture.

It is true, however, that Russia was the biggest nation in the former Russian Empire, and later on in the Soviet state, and predominated in all spheres of life. Russian culture therefore had a significant influence on the Romani culture. Romani music in the Russian language has become internationally renowned and led to a unique style of singing known as the "Gypsy Romance" (Anon. 1993). Dr Donald believes that the Russian language has influenced the Romani dialect worldwide. Being a Rom from Belarus, rather than Russia, I try sometimes to disagree with him on this point and I would like to draw your attention to our discussion.

It is little wonder that I am so ambivalent! The Western world is obsessed with Russophobia, but it was Russian soldiers who rescued, half-alive, the prisoners of Auschwitz, among whom there were Roma on their last stop before the gas chambers in 1945. Ponder upon this for while, and understand why the feeling of thankfulness to the Russians is still vivid among Roma in north-eastern Europe, and especially among the Russian Roma, the ones who, like Russians themselves, are fond of playing a seven-string guitar. Furthermore, do not forget that Russian Roma are a symbol and model for all Roma in their Romani commitment and dedication to the Romani customary code.

Oh, I seem to hear some Roma from elsewhere mouthing, as if to contradict me, the name *Xaladytka Roma*...

Do not dare to pronounce these words in the presence of true Russian Roma; they will flog you with their whips! It is a term of derision to those who think themselves genuine Russian Roma. They want to be called *Rassejska Roma* or *Ruska Roma* – these are the names they call themselves. Forget about *Xaladytka Roma*, thought of as Russian Gypsies in Poland. They are a far cry from these genuine Russian Roma, both in language and in religion and in customary code. They originate from the Eastern part of the former Polish Empire as it was from the sixteenth to the eighteenth century (Druts and Gessler, 1989, 1990). When in 1944-5 *Xaladytka Roma* found themselves locked within the new borders of Poland, they were identified as Roma from Russia. (Whoever comes from the East is often labelled Russian!) Since *Xaladytka Roma* were not in touch with the genuine Russian Roma, they did not resist this label, even though it was slightly pejorative. *Xaladytka Roma* from Poland are actually Lithuanian Roma; many live in Belarus and Russia where they call themselves Lithuanian Roma (*Litoûska Roma*) while the local Roma call them *Bezhantsy* [Refugees] or *Lipientsy*. So their roots are in Eastern Poland, Western Belarus and Lithuania, but not in Russia. Is it true? Definitely!

Whenever my highly respected supervising translation consultant Dr Donald Kenrick comes across a new word in my Romani translations of the bible, there comes a smile and he says: "This is Russian." I become awfully bored with this remark and respond: "It's not Russian, why do you keep saying this?" and, with a raised voice, answer, "This is a Romani word, not Russian!"

During my last return visit to Belarus I was struck by an idiosyncratic label used by my fifty-four year-old kinsman, Jagorka Pasevich, for the Russians. He called them the *Bare* (the great, or big ones, a term used in some dialects to indicate chiefs, or perhaps a real old Romani word for Russians). It puzzled me and got me thinking... this was a residue of history. Not too many people in the West are aware of the past relations between Roma and these hideous and hilarious Russians, when the leading men of the nobility started to set up Romani choirs in the eighteenth century. They drank hard, debauched and finally married Romani women, former daughters of steppes and forests, who were born in the open air and knew little of high culture, or even how to write and to read, but ended up as Countesses and even Princesses. Families who did this included the Apraksins, the Golitsyns, the Lanskoys, the Obolenskis, the Orlovs and the Zabelys and others. Even relatives of the great humanist and writer Count Leo Tolstoy followed the fashion. His brother, Sergei, and his son, Leo, married Romani women. The new book by Alaina Lemon (2000) gives some details of this period, but Dr Donald Kenrick's reading of Russian literature has informed his understanding of northern Romani culture for a long time.

In the Russian Empire Romani musicians were always around the Russian writers, singers and composers. They created the new "Gypsy Romance" style in perform-

County Leo Tolstoy holding the hand of his Romani sister-in-law, M. Siskina in 1907. *Photograph from the Tolstoy Archive*

ance. Roma inspired famous Russian poets and writers who used Romani images in great works, which have become treasures of the world culture: A. Pushkin, L. Tolstoy, A. Blok, A. Grigorjev, N. Nekrasov, S. Jesenin, V. Brusov. Also there were composers: A. Dargomizhski, I. Glinka, P. Tchaikovsky, A. Alyabyev, N. Rubinstein (Maxwell, 1962: 213, 580, 727). In their music we seem to hear the kindling dancing steps, the unique genius of Russian Roma. Their dancing, accompanied by sharp shouts, is so vivid and so athletic and energetic that people who see them think the Russian Roma originate from another planet. Russian tradition (c.f. Bobri 1961: 119) is that the famous Hungarian composer Franz Liszt, who drew on Romani musical traditions, was only completely captivated by the dancing and singing of the Russian Roma of Moscow. When he visited the rest of the Russian Empire and toured across the places where Roma lived in the south and in the Ukraine, he heard and watched the music and dance of Vlach and other Roma and found them boring and dull compared with Russian Roma. His own work (Liszt 1859, 1926), as discussed by Fraser (1995:205), may have stigmatised the Romani art of the capital as decadent or artificial, but perhaps we may see that as professional jealousy.

I ran the Romani folk group *Belvelitko* ('evening party') in Belarus from 1988 to 1991. I had aspirations to the highest standards of the Russian Roma but was always mocked by our local Belarus Roma. It was a Russian Rom from the *Murashki* ('ants') tribe, the respected counsellor Kolya Jefimenkov (known as *Zyamka*) who went about with me while setting up the group and even abandoned his other Romani activities trying to help me. When the Russian Roma sing or dance, they do not simply perform, they compete with each other to the utmost.

The Russian Roma have long been Russian Orthodox in religion. There is no overt trace of the Hindu beliefs of their ancestors, or of pagan festivals. They do not worship the Kali Mura or Sara, attributed to other Roma by Gypsylorists. Despite this, many people believe that in Moscow there exists a collection of interesting notes on the mysterious Romani philosophy, upon which the brother of the writer Leo Tolstoy, Count Sergei [who was married to the Romani Glasha], started to make notes. A. Dobrovolski is also supposed to have contributed to this collection at the end of the nineteenth-century. I was once told some of this material was in the hands of the leading Romani poet, translator Nikolai Pankov (1895–1959) and that my friend, the brilliant and prematurely deceased poet and linguist, Alexander Belugins (1942–97), who wrote under his Romani name, Leksa Manush, tried to have it published, and that it was partly due to this research that Manush was confined to a mental asylum by the KGB.

In 1990 I visited Pankov's daughters: Doctor of Biology Lyuba Pankova (b.1930) and Doctor of Chemistry Natasha Pankova (1926–96). They were then both retired, two modest scholars who never married, but dedicated all their lives to the research sciences and to looking after their mother, Slava Pankova (b. 1903). The sceptic might find it strange that two Russian Romani women, might spend their lives ploughing a monotonous furrow in laboratories, without men. Were they so ugly?

On the contrary. They were very beautiful, demure, and of classic Romani appearance. Everything in the flat reminded me of the fruitful life of their father Nikolai Pankov. They hinted that I might be able to find the Tolstoy/Dobrovolski materials. There were piles of material on Roma, but try as I might, I could not find any trace in the limited time at my disposal. Mr Rudevich, a Romani MP from Riga and son of the notable artist and poet K. Rudevich, later told me that a Latvian Rom possesses the material in full. I have my doubts, however, whether, even if I track this collection of papers down that it will be prove to be the definitive collection of arcane folk Romani philosophy of myth.

We have to consider the real philosophy of a people as that by which they live and practise, and understand the Russian Roma as they have actually lived over the past two centuries. The Russian Roma, for example, revere the profession of doctor, though there is a taboo on this profession among other Romani groups. One of my friends is a consultant surgeon, Professor V. Matusevich, a Russian Rom from Moscow. Hundreds of Roma across the countries of the former USSR spend a lot of time trying to get an appointment with him. Another Romani medical doctor, Maxim Lukyanenko from Bryansk (born 1940) also achieved some fame (Crowe 1989:152–192).

They are a people who believe in free will and condemn any pretensions to authority of a *Shero Rom*, or Gypsy King, especially if the position is claimed to be hereditary. There are, however, councils of the Romani elders, who take turns to chair the meetings. Such elders were not without broader political influence. Between 1970–80 the notable Romani playwright and poet Nikolai Satkevich (1917–91) served as patron of Roma and Adviser on Romani affairs for the former Soviet Government. His poetry (Satkevich 1974, 1977) is still read.

Satkevich graduated from the Romany Teachers' Training College in 1938. When he was called up to the army, from 1940 to 1945, he was at the front during the Second World War, where he was known for his strictness once promoted sergeant. He embodied the new Soviet Romani ideal. During the 1960s he managed to re-open some Romany Schools, first in his own local area in Tula and Bryansk and later in Siberia in Irkutsk for a while. In Siberia he used the police to monitor school attendance, which made some Roma angry with him. He wrote to me twice in 1983, inspiring me to open Romani classes in two schools of my native city, Vitebsk. In the most extraordinary handwriting, very artistic, with subtly curved, shapely letters, he urged me fervently to action. I rushed around the Romany families and began to make preparations.

Then, one winter day, while my wife was serving me with lunch and we were discussing the Romani classes, there arrived a letter from Moscow, from, Leksa Manush, mentioned above, which strongly recommended me not to do anything together with Nikolai Satkevich.

Leksa Manush and Nikolai Satkevich had very little in common. Manush had a non-Romani appearance – it was his grandfather on his mother's side who was a Rom. He was a deep, intelligent man of high principles and morals, a musician and a charming conversationalist. Though he spoke Romani with an accent, he learned many dialects and wrote stunning poetry. Nikolai Satkevich was a born orator with an outstandingly Romani appearance. He was very abrupt and bold to excess. During his last years he turned to God and began to translate the New Testament. Once Leksa Manush and Nikolai Satkevich had been very close. When the young poet Alexander Belugins, then known as Sasha, and later as Leksa Manush, arrived from Riga to Moscow, he had recently finished four years army service in the Kazakhstan desert. Satkevich took him up and introduced him to a golden-haired Romani girl, Nadya (or Nadezhda) Shnurkova (born 1946), who worked as a manager of a Post Office unit in Moscow. They got married and Nadya later took a doctorate in Hungarian Studies.

Now a widow, she runs the private 'Luludji' ('Flower') studio-school together with another Russian Romany intellectual, Mrs. Ganga Batalova.

By 1983, however, Nikolai Satkevich and Leksa Manush had quarrelled over a poetry book. Leksa Manush alleged that Satkevich had plagiarised from himself and other Romany poets, like Dzheki Zaparozhanu (b. 1949), a Moldavian Romany poet and guitar player at the Moscow Romani Theatre (Rom-Lebedev, 1990). Manush derided Satkevich's appeals to my intelligence, and wrote that he had been going around boasting that he was the Romani *Führer*. Because of my great respect for Leksa Manush, I slowed down my preparation work for the Romani classes. Almost immediately Satkevich sent me another immaculately penned letter, this time a rebuke: 'Your heart is not on fire for Roma. It doesn't suit you, so forget about your humble fellow-tribesman'.

Tell me please, Dr Donald, where this strange spirit of the Russian Roma comes from? You wrote about the flowering of Romani education and culture during 1925–38 when there were state-run Romani schools (Kenrick 1998a: 174). That was a massive undertaking: compulsory Romani schools! But then there was no need for some Romani scholars to rack their brains over words like, 'book', 'notebook', 'school', 'crèche', 'teacher', or 'authority'. They always existed in the Russian Romani, *lylvary, patryka, sykliady, unta, sykliakiribnaskiro, baluni*.

There was a problem, however: the Northern Russian dialect (from the Baltic Romani Language group, essentially *Xaladitko*) was given the status of a standard language in Romany schools of Russia and Ukraine. It was compulsory in the spirit of the Soviet state at that time: no alternatives, no comments, unless you wanted to be sent to Siberia. The 1925 decree had to be carried out not only by other Baltic Romani dialect speakers (Polish, Lithuanian, Estonian and Belarus groups), but also other rather different dialect groups, such as Vlaxh Roma (*Kalderari, Lovari, Katunari, Chokanari, Churari*), Balkan Roma (*Ursari, Krymean, Drindari*), Ukrainian Roma (*Servi, Charnobylci, Chergari, Plashchunuja, Voloxuja, Galichiyaki, Karamichi, Richarja*), German-influenced dialect speakers (*Sinti, Fliuki, Esterajxi, Pliuniaki, Sasytka*), and Scandinavian, Finnish and Karelian Roma (*Kaale, Shvieditka*, and *Manjur* or *Shamhaychi*). Adult Roma and Sinte and their children from all of these groups strove hard to learn standard Northern Russian Romani (Kalinin, 1994, Ventsel and Cherenkov, 1966).

But it was not only those who called themselves Roma or Sinte who were covered. Gypsy groups from the Caucasus and Central Asian who also spoke Indian derived languages, but from a different family to European Romani, were counted as Roma for this purpose, such as speakers of *Bosha, Karachi, Domari,* and *Suzmani*. Moreover, even nomads who can only be described as "Gypsy-like", Iranian dialect speakers like *Liuli* learnt the standard Romani like a foreign language.

The Russian Roma dominated in this matter, just as Russians themselves did in the Soviet empire as a whole. Only in Azerbajdzan did one Domari Romani Muslim clergyman and teacher Hassan Kyamal Ogli Niyazov (b. 1881) dare to oppose the line that all pupils must be taught from the standard Romani ABC of N. Dudarova and N. Pankov. To great surprise he was not arrested but managed to start to compile his own small books. He gave up his religious profession, (as many others did at that time), and dedicated himself entirely to completing a Domari ABC "*mektuby*" in Latin script and to start teaching Doma children. This unique book was even printed in small numbers but it is difficult to track down. However, the episode was recorded in the Azerbajdzhan encyclopaedia of 1949. About two hundred boys and girls had gone through his home-based schools by 1938. In 1942, however, Niyazov was arrested but, luckily for him, he was expelled to Iran, not exiled to Siberia, because he was an Iranian according to his passport. The Azerbajdzhan encyclopaedia does not tell us what eventually happened to him but he had a following.

The standard Russian Romani was also the business and administrative language of the 53 Romani collective farms (*Kolkhozi*) that were founded in that remarkable era. Some of these farms, or successor communities, still exist, as for example in the village of Alexandrovka in the region of Smolensk, or the Hungarian Romani Christian collective farm in Koroliovo in the Ukraine, or a Ursari Romani collective vineyard in Moldova, whose chairman is the notable Romani folklorist G. Kantia (b. 1940).

It is hard for Roma from other countries to realise what Roma have achieved in Russia. Do you remember, Dr Donald, when you and I were talking to the German Sinto leader, Romani Rose, and astounded him with our talk of Russian Romani generals? Although they did not publicly identify themselves as Romani (unlike the paratrooper Timofy Profokiev (1913–1944), Hero of the USSR, and Order of Lenin) there were two of them: Admiral I. Kozlovski (1904–79) and the legendary Commander of the Ukrainian Partisan detachments, twice Hero of the U.S.S.R., General Sidor Kovpak (1887–1967). Oh, it's too much for some Roma ... generals! But, yes! Many were the Roma among the warriors who joined his partisans, and many the Romany families whom they saved from extermination at the hands of the German Commandos and ferocious Ukrainian collaborator police and the joint German-Ukrainian Punishment teams (Kovpak 1946). Even today old Romani women still light candles in churches with a dedication saying: "To Uncle Sidor".

There was even a film about Kovpak's heroic deeds, *A Diary of the Partisan Marches*, made in 1966. Under the Tsars and under the Commissars alike the *Ruska Roma* prospered and made their mark and became part of civil society as in no other country. All the migrant Roma who passed through the communist bloc and left for Western Europe have some knowledge of this at the back of their minds. Throughout the world they know that in one country at least it was possible for Roma to penetrate the highest levels of non-Romani society. But did they keep their Romani spirit in the communist era?

It is true that during the Communist times quite a few Roma were Communists.

Some Roma, like people from other groups, just wanted to be promoted in their careers but some believed in the ideas of Communism. The Chairman of the Romany Culture Union of the former Soviet Union, Professor Georgi Demeter worked as a party secretary at his former institute for many years. Then the former director of Agriculture Department in Novgorod, E. Sukhobski (*Grafo*) was also a senior member of the Communist Party of the Soviet Union.

The chronology in the PEN anthology of Romani Poetry (Hancock et al., 1998: 78) gives a misleading impression when it baldly states "1938: Stalin bans Romani language and culture". It is true that Romany schools were closed in that year, alongside many other minority nationality schools: Jewish, Finnish, Polish, Latvian, Chinese. The Romani closures were, however, not exceptional in those troubled times; in fact they were the last to be closed, perhaps because their attendance was low. Some Romani literature appeared even after 1938 (Brodski, 1941, Sholok, 1940). The Pan-Russian Romani Union, led by Alexander Taranov, had been in fact closed earlier in 1929 (Hancock 1991: 140). Stalin probably restrained the effects of this change of policy on Roma. It is widely believed that Josef Stalin always tried to cool down ministers who wanted to settle Roma by force. People say that when such forms were put before him the old monster used to say; "Let my horses run across my fields" or "Let these children of nature live in their natural way, they are special people." In the 1930s if a non-Romany person humiliated a Romany or insulted Roma publicly such an offender could be subject to five years imprisonment. It is a mystery why Stalin was so tolerant and soft with Roma. Actually it was his successor, Nikita Khrushehev, cursed by Roma, who authorised a Soviet State Act on 5 October 1956 "to enlist Travelling Gypsies in full-time jobs". This menacing decree was later followed in all other Socialist Bloc States in the period up to 1964.

Many Russian Roma loved and some still adore Josef Stalin. I was a small boy, seven years of age when on a frosty, sunny day, 5 March 1953, I saw Roma weeping and mourning together with other people when the official radio and press announced the death of this bloodthirsty tyrant. During 1999 I was able to interview Ivan Tumasevich (b. 1925), a distant relative who is one of a very few surviving graduates (class of 1938) of the Romani boarding school in Grishkova in Russia (near the border with Belarus). He was Commander of a Tank Unit, then bodyguard of a Soviet General. A twice-wounded veteran of the Second World War, he adores Stalin and made me feel uncomfortable about discussing Stalin by telling me sharply: "Stalin was cruel but fair. It was he who saved mankind from the Nazi plague." It is difficult to argue with one's older relatives.

A notable English balalaika player, and collector of Romany songs, Bibs Ekkell (b. 1946) confirmed to me that the Russian-Romani Romance singer of the 1930s, Vadim Kozin (1905–92) sang personally for Stalin in the Kremlin at his request. Vadim Kozin was a Rom who sang mostly in Russian. Like many other intellectuals in 1937–8, during a notorious period of purges, he was imprisoned in the far north of Siberia in

Magadan. On the eve of big party festivals or celebrations, Vadim Kozin, at the command of Stalin used to be delivered from his cell by a special plane to the Kremlin to sing for Stalin and his élite. He was treated like a special guest but then later on he was returned to prison or exile, which lasted many years. He never returned to Moscow and eventually died in Magadan.

Roma played every role in Soviet society, from general to prisoner of conscience. As I wrote this paper, a telephone conversation with the notable Moscow Romani studies scholar, Lev Cherenkov (b. 1936), told me about a now retired Soviet Colonel, a Rom by the name of Alexei Danchenko (b. 1934). For many years he was in charge of an Intelligence Service unit which dealt with certain Middle Eastern countries but he was best known by his friends as an excellent dancer – another example of how the Romani spirit survives, no matter what.

What do you think, Dr Donald? Perhaps we have had enough discussion of these difficult matters. Let us go outside and make a fire and maybe invite some Russian Roma to sing or dance around it. Russian Roma are obsessed with making fires. They have a sort of special spirit of fire. But don't forget that generations of the Russian Roma grew up and matured around fires, especially in Siberia. Fire gives Russian Roma not only warmth but something more spiritual. They yearn to use this spirit of fire like their inner prayer. This is also the food of their spirit. The spirit of the Russian Roma while dancing and singing is a unique phenomenon; it is still a mystery. Maybe it bears also the imprint of the combination of the Russian and Romani souls. You are right again, Dr Donald, Russian spirit abides also here. But let us not think too hard about it; let us listen to the music.

References

Anon., 1993 "Gypsies" in the *Great Soviet Encyclopaedia*, 3rd. Edition, Collier Macmillan, New York, Vol.28, pp.607–9, (originally *Bolshaya Sovietskaya Entsyklopediya*, 1978 (3rd Edition) State Publishing House, Moscow).
Bobri, Vladimir, 1961 "Gypsies and Gypsy Choruses of Old Russia" *Journal of the Gypsy Lore Society*, Series III, Vol.: pp.112–20.
Brodzki, D., 1941 "Cyganski je stikhi" *Oriol*.
Crowe David, 1989 *A History of the Gypsies of Eastern Europe and Russia*, Taurus, London.
Druts, Yefim and Gessler, Alexei, 1989 "Tsiganski Mir" in *Druzhba Narodov*, No.2, p.81.
Druts, Yefim and Gessler, Alexei, 1990 *Tsiganie* Sovietski Pisatel, Moscow.
Fraser, Angus, 1995 2nd Edition, *The Gypsies*, Blackwell, Oxford.
Hancock, Ian 1991, "The East European Roots of Romani Nationalism" in Crowe D. and Kolsti J. *The Gypsies of Eastern Europe*, M.E. Sharpe, New York.
Hancock, Ian, Dowd, Siobhan and Djurić, Rajko, 1998, *The Roads of the Roma* PEN/University of Hertfordshire Press, Hatfield.
Kalinin, Valdemar, 1994 "Tsigani na Belarusi" in *"Z historyi na vy"*, Mastats Literary Press, Minsk, pp.330–49.
Kovpak S., 1946 *People with a Clear Conscience*, State Publishing House, Moscow.

Lemon, Alaina, 2000 *Between Two Fires: Gypsy performance and Romani memory from Pushkin to post-Socialism.* Duke University Press, Durham, North Carolina.

Liszt, Franz, 1859 *Des Bohémiens et de leur musique en Hongrie,* Bourdilliat et Cie., Paris, tr. E. Evans, 1926 as *The Gipsy in Music,* Reeves Music Publications, London.

Maxwell R., 1962 *Information:USSR* Macmillan, New York.

Rom-Lebedev, Ivan, 1990 *Ot Tsigansko Khora k Teatru 'Romen'* Iskusstvo, Moscow.

Satkevich, Nikolai, 1974 *Kostry,* Sovietskaya Rossiya, Moscow and Archangel.

Satkevich, Nikolai, 1977 T*siganskiye Mirikle,* Sovietskaya Rossiya, Moscow and Archangel.

Sholok E., 1940 "Literatura Tsigani" *Literaturnaya Gazeta,* 1940, 10 (iv).

Ventsel T., and Cherenkov L 1976 "Tsiganski Izik" in *Yaziki Narodov SSR* Volume II, State Publishing House, Moscow.

CHAPTER TWELVE

DONALD KENRICK AS POLYGOT:
COULD HE BE REPLACED BY A MACHINE?

Erik V. Gunnemark

ACCORDING TO the information available to the association *Amici Linguarum*, Donald Kenrick is probably now 'Polyglot No.1'. In the age of information technology we have to ask whether this is still a model to which to aspire, or whether it is a talent superseded by the computer.

The Association *Amici Linguarum* was founded in 1964 as a Scandinavian association of people interested in languages and culture. In the late 1970s Donald Kenrick joined the circle collaborating with me on the production of a general directory of countries, peoples and their languages, and was listed as co-author of the first two editions, published under the title *A Geolinguistic Handbook* in 1983 and 1985. In 1985 the association began collaboration with the American Society for Geolinguistics and by the end of the twentieth century it had members in about thirty countries around the world, particularly in Europe and North America but also in Latin America and East Asia. A mixture of amateurs and professionals, it has thirty-five professors among its members but also writers, librarians, translators, journalists, teachers, doctors, diplomats, civil servants and restaurateurs. A few of the members describe themselves as linguists but the interest of the group is not so much in linguistics as in the languages themselves and the use to which multilingual competence can be put.

Every year that passes sees a greater accumulation of knowledge and experience within the ranks of *Amici Linguarum*. However, as well as deriving pleasure from this treasure-house, many members have been able to make use of it in a direct practical way in the course of their work in schools, universities, libraries and various types of enterprise, and as authors or translators.

There has been considerable correspondence within the Association about remarkable polyglots of the past, and many stories – or perhaps we should say, legends – exist, but I know of only two cases where information which may be considered factual and reliable exists about such 'superpolyglots' of the past: Pent Nurmekund (Gethin and Gunnemark 1996: 317-9) and Emil Krebs (Matzat 1999).

Dr Emil Krebs (1867-1930) was a professional interpreter and translator for the

Donald Kenrick with leading American linguist, Professor Victor Friedman, and Kosovo Romani poetess, Lumia Osmania.

German Ministry for Foreign affairs. Matzat's (1999) pamphlet concentrates on the period of the German colonies in Peking and Tsingdao (where they founded the famous Chinese brewery which thirsty scholars still have cause to praise), and shows that Krebs was quite a character. His obituaries in newspapers and journals in 1930 celebrated the fact that he could translate from over 100 languages and spoke around sixty of these. The exact number of languages given depends, of course, on what is counted as a separate language. In this paper we are erring on the cautious side by not counting as separate languages dialects which are generally considered to be 'the same' language.

Professor Pent Nurmekund (1905-97) was founder of the Oriental Department in the University of Tartu in Esthonia. He could translate from about eighty languages and also spoke many of them.

Among living European polyglots Donald Kenrick is pre-eminent, able to translate from over sixty languages, and speaking around thirty of them, mostly fluently. Others include: Eugen M. Czerniawski in Moscow, who can translate from about forty-five languages and is a fluent speaker of nearly twenty of them, and Arvo Juutilainen from Helsinki in Finland, who can translate from over fifty languages and speaks a dozen of them, more or less fluently. The greatest American polyglot is probably Georges Schmidt who was born in Strasbourg in 1915, but moved to New York. In his heyday he could translate from about sixty languages and speak over twenty of them.

So far only one book on polyglottery has been published which I can recommend, that by Dr Dmitri L. Spivak (1989). He based his work on interviews with polyglots in Russia and other parts of the USSR. The most striking fact he claimed to discover was

Donald Kenrick recording Romani songs in Eastern Europe, 1967

Donald Kenrick responding to questions in many languages at a conference on the Holocaust.
Photograph by Frantšek Toth

that most of these polyglots agreed that they did not know more than about seven foreign languages 'completely', in the sense of being able to speak them fluently and read new and differing texts without any difficulty. He presented this as 'The Law of Seven.' This is a very provisional and approximate 'law', of course, but an interesting point of departure for further research – when he and I are able to resume the collaboration we put on hold in 1993 because we had too much other work to do.

Another unexpected finding of Spivak's (1989) research was that all the polyglots interviewed preferred to learn languages *on their own.* So, polyglottery may well be called 'a profession for autodidacts.' Furthermore, like most polyglots in other countries, (c.f. Gethin and Gunnemark, 1996: 50-1), the Russian ones regard today's language-teaching industry as a glaring scandal. But should we be worried about this? Is the example of Kenrick irrelevant in the modern world ? Could he be replaced by a machine – not now, of course, but say in about another twemty years?

The Fata Morgana of machine translation: "Just wait for another twenty years!"

It is sometimes argued that machine translation will make polyglottery redundant but it seems to us that the development of information technology will make competent multilingual translators more and not less necessary. The history of machine translation has been one of recurrent enthusiasm followed by disillusion. The initial burst of enthusiasm in the mid-1950s predicted that within twenty years most scientific, technical and other non-fiction would be machine-translated. In the mid-1960s, however, the US Department of Defense pulled out of financing research. As this experience was forgotten however, advances in computing brought forward a new wave of enthusiasm in the mid-1970s, suggesting that, if not now, at some time in the next 20 years machine translation would be used to save time and money in all non-fiction fields. As time progressed the claims became more extravagant. At a translation conference in Lund in Sweden in 1985 Professor B. Sigurd predicted that – again within the next twenty years – machine-translated texts will be read in our newspapers like sympathetic voices. In the 1990s, with the spread of the Internet to millions of people without the knowledge and experience which are necessary to be able to distinguish between true and false statements, the danger of misinformation has become rather more serious. There is an acute need of an information counter-offensive.

In my view the claims of various corporations offering machine translation are dangerously overstated, but meet with relatively little protest, perhaps because even academics have relatively little understanding of how machine translation 'works'. The necessary post-editing is not mentioned at all, or only in passing. In fact, the term 'machine translation' is actually misleading, for as a rule it has to be combined with post-editing, even for rough translations. For professional standards of translation, competent translators are still needed.

Sometimes pre-editing may be necessary or preferable; that is to say, if computer manuals or such are put into a very standard form, machine translation may give better results. It is possible that some time and money has been saved by giant corporations using such techniques but they would still be wise to have a professional review of the result! One should therefore always take a sceptical attitude to claims that money is saved by using machine translation instead of traditional translation.

We need people to make sense of the things other people say or write. The development of computing and the globalisation of information technology make polyglots like Donald Kenrick more and not less necessary. They can form their own assessments of what is meant by, and what the importance is, of information in another language. The priorities programmed into machines can only ever be a selection of human concerns. A broad human vision must stay in charge of technology. As a language teacher Donald Kenrick has been in the forefront of using new technology to promote language learning, but not to replace it. Information technology will make multi-lingualism easier, rather than redundant.

References

Gethin, A. and Gunnemark, E.V., 1996 *The art and science of learning languages* Intellect/EFAE, Earl Richards Road North, Exeter EX2 6AS.

Matzat, William, 1999, *Dr Emil Krebs*, The Association for German Life in East Asia, Bonn.

Spivak, Dimitri L. 1989 *Kak stat' polyglotom*, [How one becomes a polyglot], private, St.Petersburg.

CHAPTER THIRTEEN

TO EAT IS TO HONOUR GOD:
XHABEN – PAT'IV LE DEVLESKE

Milena Hübschmannová

Among all Romani people food has a multi-dimensional value, not only biological but also social, cultural and even spiritual. everything connected with it, its preparation, its serving, consumption and catagorisation, is governed by customs which have to be observed, and all

Gazhé who work with Roma have to some extent to be aware of these customs. Donald Kenrick himself when organising summer schools had to write a little guide for student volunteers showing how English Romani customs protect the purity of food (Kenrick 1971e).

I came to know Donald in Prague in 1968 – just when 'our Russian friends' occupied the former Czechoslovakia. At that time Donald was a pleasant young fellow who played the recorder. Today maybe he looks a little different in reality to his picture from the year 1968, but the same vitality is always present in his speech, behaviour, in his sarcastic humor, in his energy – and he himself knows best in what else. Whenever I needed some information or some publication, in a week's time it safely reached Prague, especially surprising under communism when it was so difficult to get literature from abroad. He has always been a selfless friend, in all the dimensions of humanity, scientific brilliance, and love for Roma.

When I was thinking what to write for this *festschrift,* an old Romani csardász came to my head and was humming in my brain:

Pheñe, miri pheñe,	Oh sister, my sister,
tav mange haluški,	cook haluški for me,
xochá len tu na makhlâreha,	you needn't put any fat on them
cha len lodhareha.	just put a little salt.

This inspiration, which came from God knows where, led me to cook up this article, about food and *haluški,* from which, maybe, fat is missing, but I hope, that there is at least some salt in it.

Donald Kenrick with Roma in Eastern Europe in 1967

Roma views on food

Below are five statements which I have selected from fieldwork notes to show what supreme significance was ascribed to food in the traditional community of the *Servika* ('Slovak') Roma.

"O Del chidha manušes pre koda baro svetos, bo kamel, kaj manuš te dzhivel. Ale našt'i dzhivas bixhabnaskero. Mušinas te xhal, te kamas te dzhivel. Kajcha – 'Hop!' – avka vakerlas miro papus: 'Na dzhives, kaj te xhas, mro cho! Xhas, kaj te dzhives! Soske dzhives? Kaj te sikhaves pat'iv amare gule Devleske. Ta dzhanes, soske xhas? Kaj te sikhaves pat'iv le Devleske, bo jov kamel, kaj manuš te dzhivel'"

"God has thrown man into this great world, because he wants man to live. But we cannot live without eating. We have to eat, if we want to live. But – 'Ha!' – that's the way my grandfather spoke: 'You do not live in order to eat, my boy! You eat in order to live. And why do you live? To show respect to our sweet God. So, do you now know why you eat? To give honour to God, because he desires that man should live.'" Jozef Mirga, aged 72, Rakúsy, Poprad, Slovakia (recorded Rakúsy, 1969).

"Xhaben esas ko Roma baro. Bo Xhaben hin le Devlestar. Vašoda xhaben mušinel t'avel zhuzho. Te taves, mušines t'avel zhuzhi, o pira, o kucha, o tepši, sa sa sa – mušinel t'avel zhuzho. O gadzhe phenen, hoj o Roma hin melale. Amen phenas, hoj o gadzhe hine melale degeša! Bo dikh: gadzhi lel piri, tavel andre zumin, chino xhelavel avri u rajbinel andre gada! Jaaaaj! Te oda kerdhahas romañi dzhuvli, ta la tradlehas – mi dzhal peske, kaj la na prindzharen ñi Roma ñi gadzhe – sar pes phenlas. Mi dzhal peske te rovel, kaj la ñiko na dikhela!"

"Food (eating) was something very important for Roma. Because food is from God. That is why food must be clean. When you cook, you have to be clean, the pots, the cups, the pans, everything has to be clean. The gadzhos say, that Roma are dirty. We say, that the gadzhos are dirty. Because, look: a gadzhi takes a pot and she cooks soup in it, then she rinses it a little and she washes her laundry in it. Yuck! If a Romani woman did something like that, she would be driven out – she would have to go somewhere where neither Roma nor gadzhe know her – as we used to say. She should go and weep where nobody sees her!" Vojtêch Fabián, born 1918, Kurima, Bardejov, Slovakia (recorded Prague, 1984)

"Dzhanes, hoj Roma nane jekh. Hin zhuzhe Roma, hin degeša. Zhuzhe Roma xhan zhuzho xhaben, degeša xhan grastano mas, vaj rikonen. Jekhgoreder degeša hin gadzhe. O gadzhe xhan savoro. O gadzhe xhan the mukhlo chaben, achel zumin, aver dhives tat'arel, xhal, mek achhel, pale tat'arel, xhal. Trin, štar dhives tat'arel jekh zumin. Amen phenas: 'gadzho xhala the khul, te leske na khandela.'"

"You know that all Roma are not the same. There are clean Roma and there are *degeša* (impure, ; not observing *romipen*). Clean Roma eat pure food, *degeša* eat horse-meat or dogs. The worst *degeša* are the gadzhos. Gadzhos eat everything. Gadzhos eat also the food which remains uneaten, some soup remains uneaten, the gadzho will warm it up next day and eat it, if still some of it remains, he will again warm it up and eat. A gadzho is able to eat one soup for three or four days. We say: 'A gadzho would even eat excrement if it wasn't smelly.'" Margita Miková aged 50, Babin Potok, Prešov, Slovakia (recorded Rokycany, Czechia, 1976)

"Kana e romñi tavel, ta sa andal late avel andre koda xhaben. Vaš oda mušinel te taven na cha zhuzhe vastenca, ale the zhuzhe jileha. (Ma ruš, sopat'iphenav angel tiro mujoro somnakuno, kana romñi dzhanelas peskerestar, ta na šmejinelas te taven. Ta kaj!) Miri daj furt vakerkerlas peskera borake, mira romñake: 'Mri chaj, tu sal adadhives varesi cholamen! Dzha het! Tavava me! Me tiri choli na dzhav te xhan! O texhanoro mušinel t'ven zhuzhoro, na cholamen' Te e romñi tavelas cholamen abo apsenca, ta pes phenlas: 'Me tiri choli, me tire apsa na xhava! Mi xhan o rikone!' Mro dad šoha na xhalahas peskere borijendar, cha mira datar. Bo dzhanelas, zhe e daj hiñi zhuzhi."

"When a woman cooks, everything that is in her is apparent in that food. That is why she has to prepare food not only with clean hands, but also with clean heart. (excuse me, I apologise in the presence of your golden face, when a woman was menstruating, she never was allowed to prepare food. In no case!) My mother was always saying to her daughter-in-law, to my wife: 'My girl, you are somehow angry today! Go away! I shall cook! I am not going to eat your anger! This humble thing we are about to eat has to be humbly clean, and not angry!' If a wife would have been cooking angrily or while weeping, Roma would say: 'I am not going to eat your anger! I am not going to eat your tears! The dogs should eat them!' My father would never eat the food prepared by his daughters-in-law but only what my mother prepared. Because he knew that my mother was clean." Andrej Tokár, aged 70 or more, Humenn, Slovakia (recorded Humenn, 1974).

"Kana terñi bori avla te bešel ke peskeri sasvi, ta takoj peršo dhives la thode le Romenge tel o jakha – savi hiñi, chi hiñi zhuzhi. Kerlas ajsi sar maturita – "skúška dospelosti" chi imar hiñi suco sar romñi – vaj mek hiñi cha limali, khandiñi chaj. Ešeb la bichade ke chañig pañeske. Savore Roma dikhenas, sar phirel – chi phirel sar lubñi, chivkerel kofenca, vaj chi hiñi khandiñi, darangutñi, ladzhangutñi – ada tizh na has lacho le Romenge. Dikhenas, sar pherel pañi, chi khosel o vedros, vaj thovel o vedros chikalo andre chañig. Kana lachhes thodha tele kadi skuška, mušindha te tavel. Kana me tavavas miro peršo xhaben ke sasvi, oda has goreder sar kana gejlom te thovel "pohovory" pre Karlova univerzita. Bešenas odoj miro rom, leskero phral o Jañi, leskere bratranci, asanas mandar, prasavenas man, dikhenas, chi anglo taviben thovav o vasta, chi phandav o khosno pro šero, chi plukinav avri o pira, sar randav o gruli pro haluški, sar ušanav, na tromavas te phenel pale o lav, mušinavas man te likerel, te tavel asabnaha – e choli andre mande tadholas, peravas pal o pindre andre ladzh – ale mušinavas man te likerel. Palis imar sar xhale, ašarde mire haluški – a me somas barikañi, hoj kerdhom maturita te dzhal te sikhlol dureder andre mira saskeri škola."

"When the young daughter-in-law came to live in her mother-in-law's house, she was the very first day put under the eyes of Roma to test her what was she like, whether she was clean. She had to pass a sort of matriculation exam – whether she was capable to be a wife or still a snotty, lazy girl. First of all she was sent to bring water from the well. All the Roma were looking how was she walking, whether she was not moving her hips like a whore, or whether on the other hand she was not too much afraid and shy – neither this was approved by Roma. They were observing how she took water from the well, whether she first wiped the bucket or whether she plunged it into the water still dusty. When she passed this exam well, she had to cook. When I had to cook my first meal in my mother-in-law's house, it was worse for me than later when I had to pass my entrance interview at the Charles University. In the room were sitting my husband, his brother Jañi and his cousins and they were mocking me, ridiculing me. They were looking whether I washed my hands before going to cook, and whether I put the scarf on my head, whether I first rinsed the pots, whether I was grating the potatoes for haluški in a proper way, how was I preparing the dough – and I had to keep my mouth shut, I had to cook with a smile on my lips – anger was boiling inside me, I was fainting from shame – but I had to stand all this. Then when they had eaten my haluški and praised my cooking, I was proud that I had

Milena Hübschmannova and Ilona Lacková at a working lunch in 1984

passed my matriculation and was able to proceed my further studies in the school of my mother-in-law." Ilona Lacková M.A., born 1921, Velkì Šariš, Prešov, Slovakia (recorded Prešov 1986)

The statements above show how people, especially women whose *dharma* was to care for food and its preparation, were judged according to how they observe all the rituals concerning food. (I used the Sanskrit word *dharma* because it connotes all the important meanings relevant in this connection: commitment, duty, obligation and religion.)

Many studies refer to the theme 'food' in the traditional culture of Roma. Hancock (1991, p.1) concentrates on food ways among various Roma groups in USA. The very first sentence of his article, however, points to the fact that "there is no single, cohesive Romani culture but instead many, and while all the Gypsy populations retain more or less of a shared cultural and linguistic core, the fragmentations of the population after reaching europe seven centuries ago has led to the emergence of many distinct groups since. That being the case, no description of the life and customs of any one group can possibly hold true for the entire Romani people."

It may be interesting to compare the food ways of the Vlaxi Rom in the USA and the habits of the Servika Roma who have been settled in Slovakia for at least three centuries (and one third of whom has been recruited to repopulate the vacant areas of Czechia and Moravia after three million Germans had been deported to Germany during 1945-8).

Food as the marker of social distinction

Within the Indian caste system the distinction between purity and impurity of food for each *jati* (caste-group) is the most important marker of their status. Although the Sanskrit term *jati* is not used in Romani, the model of *jati*-identity, of overt manifestations/markers of *jati-dharma* and of inter-*jati* relations has been in operation since Roma left India until today.

Among the Servika Roma horse meat is considered to be 'impure'. Those who consume it are scornfully called *degeša* (pl.). *Degeš* (sing.) is the worst possible insult. However the 'horse-eaters' have a higher status than the *rikoñara* (dog-eaters, from *rikono/rukono* –dog) whom the *degeša* call *dupki* (from Polish: dirty people). The ethymology of the word *degeš* is interesting: it is derived from the Hungarian word *degö* (carrion). However, it is considered less contaminating to eat meat of edible animals who died a natural death then to eat meat of butchered horses or dogs.

The enlightened Slovak scholar Samuel Augustini ab Hortis (who was plagiarised in virtual entirety by Grellmann, 1783) wrote in his chapter *Von den Speisen und Nahrung der Zigeuner*:

"Sie essen das Aaß von Schafen, Schweinen und allerhand Geflügel ...ohne der geringsten Verletzung ihrer Gesundheit. Und wenn ihnen dessentwegen ... Vorwürfe gemacht werden, so antworten sie darauf und sprechen: Daß das Fleisch eines solchen Thieres, welches Gott schlachtet, nothwendig besser seyn müße, denn eines solchen, welches nur von der Hand eines Menschen stirbt..."

"They eat carrion sheep, pigs and all sorts of poultry ... which is not at all harmful to health. When they are reproached because of this ... they answer and say: The flesh of such an animal, which was killed by God, is definitely better, than of the one which dies by the hand of man ..." (ab Hortis 1775/1995, 122-286)

Would it be too far-fetched to say that this habit might be an echo of *ahimsa*, the order not to kill any living being? According to Dr Dharmapal Goyal, a homeopathic doctor, (personal communication) even a *Brahman* is allowed to consume flesh of an animal deceased naturally if his life is endangered by hunger. (Even if it turns out, as with English Romanichals, that willingness to eat braxy meat was an image cultivated to cover up the practice of secretly poisoning farmyard animals with witherite in order to beg their bodies from the farmer (Myers, 1909), this is still an indicator of the complex historical interaction between ideology and practice.)

It is in the nature of human beings to consider their own habits better than the habits of others, to glorify their own ideologies and beliefs and disdain those of others.

If we want to get out of the prison of atavistic stereotypes we should accept the fact that eating flesh of deceased animal in some Roma *jatis* is just another of the numerous culinary habits existing in various cultures of the world. There were specific ways how to prepare such meat and ab Hortis is correct saying that it "is not at all harmful to health". The more 'sanskritized' *zhuzhe* Roma, however, that is, those who had internalised the ideology and habits of a 'higher *jati*', would not accept the eating of meat of carrion animals and would on the contrary declare how dirty it was to demonstrate their social difference and social distance from the *degeša*.

The social distance between the *zhuzhe* (clean) Roma and those whom they consider 'unclean' is manifested in the very same way as in India: by endogamy and prohibitions of comensality. A *zhuzho Rom* would never eat in the house of a *degeš*. If the hierarchical distance between the groups is not so high, a *zhuzho Rom* might take *šuko xhaben* (lit. 'dry food', i.e. food bought in a shop, which has not been contaminated by touch of the *degeš* while cooking). The *šuko xhaben* corresponds to the Indian *kachchá kháná* (raw food, fruit or biscuits). If the difference between the *feder* ('better' in the social and cultural sense) and the *choreder* (lit. poorer, but 'poorer' also in observing *romipen*, the cultural tradition of Roma) is great, then a *zhuzho Rom* will not take any sort of food in the house of a *degeš*, and would not even enter his household.

Ilona Lacková, the oldest Romani woman writer in the Slovak and Czech Republics was born in 1921 and grew up in a Gypsy settlement. In her native settlement Velký Šariš there were two Gypsy settlements (Lacková 1997, 2000). One of them, where she was born, was inhabited by *zhuzhe Roma*: most of them were musicians, two were blacksmiths. In this settlement located (of course) at the end of the village, Roma have been settled for many generations. After the First World War the village authorities brought another group of Roma into the village, the *valkara* (sun-dried brickmakers), and allotted them a place to live at the opposite end of the village. In some regions of Slovakia including Velký Šariš the profession of *valkaris* was also considered 'unclean' (as in India where professions in which one has to touch earth are considered 'unclean', like *kumhars* – potters, who also produce pots and bricks). Lacková reports that Roma from the *lavutariko vatra* (settlement of musicians) would never enter the house of the *valkara*. The contacts between these two groups of Roma were limited to business. If some *zhuzho Rom* from the *lavutariko vatra* wanted to have bricks made for building a new house, he would either visit or invite a *valkaris* and settle the deal. If the *valkaris* was offered water to drink in the *zhuzho Rom*'s household, the cup from which he was drinking was afterwards thrown away.

The *zhuzho* status of the family was declared in a formula with which food was offered to a guest – even to a guest who knew the family well: *Xha, xha, ma dara, amen sam zhuzhe Roma* (eat, eat, don't be afraid, we are clean Roma). The guest had to take at least a bit of the offered food to show that he did not suspect the hosts of eating horse-flesh.

If by chance a *zhuzho Rom* should visit a family of those who ate meat from horses or dogs, food was not offered to him: the hostess would not want to run the risk of being refused, even though failure to offer food in such a case would clash with the requirement to offer food to a guest.

The offer of food represents an offering to God

To offer food to anybody *kas o Del andro kher andha* (whom God brought into the house) was a holy command: *sar te dehas Xhaben le Devleske* (as if you were offering food to God.) Offering food to a guest (known or unknown) was in fact an offering to God.

In old days, writes Lacková (1997) a stranger who stood in front of the entrance to the house was addressed by a sentence: *Te sal lacho, av andro kher* (if you are good, come inside the house). Sometimes, in traditional tales, another formula is added: *Te sal bizhuzho, našluv* (if you unclean, run away).

As soon as the guest has entered the sanctuary of the inside of the house (*andro kher*), he becomes the one 'whom God has brought' and is treated as God's representative. The house-wife – even if it was midnight or four o'clock in the morning – immediately cooked 'fresh' food (usually the 'national dish' of *Servika Roma*, the *haluški*). She never would ask before: "Are you hungry? Do you want something to eat?" That would be highly impolite. The poetess Margita Reiznerová put it to me this way: *"Phuches le grestar: graja, xhaha dzhov? Des les te xhal a imar!"* (Do you ask the horse: horse, will you eat barley? You give him something to eat and that's it). Nowadays most of the Roma have adopted the *gadzho* habit of offering coffee. The difference, however, is that a *gadzho* host would ask whether the guest would like to have coffee while a Rom hostess will prepare and serve coffee without asking.

The formula for offering food was as I mentioned before: *Xha, amen sam zhuzhe Roma*. If a stranger came into a family that ate horse-flesh but the hostess was sure he would not refuse her food, she would still say: *"Xha, me som zhuzhi romñi"* (Do eat, I am a clean woman.) This meant that she was observing all other rules of purity: washing hands, wearing a scarf while cooking, using the cooking pot only for cooking and for nothing else, cooking with a smile on her lips, not coming near food while menstruating and so forth. The offering of food was accompanied by a theatrical performance of *šukar lava* (beautiful words) and actions: *"Sal bokhalo/bokhali, choro/chori, jaaaj! Cha xha, xha chaluv, ma ladzha, xha Devleha, xha pro sast'ipen!"* (You are hungry, you poor thing, eh! just eat, eat to your full, don't be ashamed, eat with God, eat for your health!) Afterwards the housewife would usually enumerate all the ingredients which she had put in the offered dish with the same theatricality.

A polite guest was also obliged to observe a ritual: he or she had to refuse the food two or three times – not more – with words such as: *Na som bokhalo, cha akana xhalom* (I am not hungry I have just eaten). The guest would be demonstrating she or he was not greedy. Greediness and stinginess are condemned as the worst human qualities and they are ascribed to *gadzhé*. It is said: *Bokhalo jilo goreder sar bokhale goja* (a hungry, or greedy, heart is worse than hungry entrails). The guest also had to demonstrate his lack of greed by another manifestations: he had to leave a bit of food on his plate. This habit is also mentioned by Hancock (1991). Young girls and women were especially prohibited from eating too much. If a *terñi bori* (young daughter-in-law) ate too much she was ridiculed with a rude song:

Chaje ma xha but:	Girl, don't eat too much
bo xhineha tut.	or you'll soil yourself
Avla khere tro romoro	When your dear husband comes home
maj marela tut.	he'll immediately beat you

It is not polite to thank the host for food. "*Ma paliker, ma paliker, na sal ko gadzhe*" (No need to say thank you, you are not in a *gadzho* house) was said to me whenever I forgot and behaved according to the *gadzho* stereotype. If one is aware of the significance of offered food being an offering to God, it is clear why thanks for food is not required: it is a blessing to be allowed to offer food to God and thereby wipe away some of one's bad deeds; in fact the host should thank the one who enables him make the offering.

A pregnant woman is a special manifestation of God's blessing. Offering food to a pregnant woman is a special case of making an offering to God. A pregnant woman has to be given food anytime and by anybody – whenever she *kijavindha* (felt a desire to have some special food). I myself witnessed several times situations which would not have happened in the gadzho society. Once a pregnant friend and I passed a household of Roma with whom her family was on 'terms of war'. It was early autumn, the door of the flat was open and there was a pleasant smell of plum-dumplings. The pregnant lady *kijavindha* and so she just stood at the doorstep and waited. The lady of the house eventually saw her, and brought out a plate with dumplings and passed it to her without a word. My friend invited me to share the food with her and then, after I declined, she ate two dumplings, standing in front of the house. Then she returned the plate without a single word and we went away. "We don't talk to each other," she explained to me afterwards, "otherwise she would have invited us in." Then she apologised to me that I was not treated properly – but she had to be offered the food and she had to receive the food otherwise she might have lost the baby.

Food was always offered. The social context of this habit was the general poverty of most of the Roma. In the past Roma – with exception of the *rajkane lavutara* (musicians playing for the gentlemen) were rewarded for their products and services with goods and not with money. Food was not stored long, and the wife would go every day *pal o gava* (through villages) and exchange her family's products (metalwork or basketry or whatever) for potatoes, curd, flour or some fat. In winter when there were no weddings at which musicians could play, and less work for a blacksmith and no seasonal work in the fields, then hunger set in. Sharing and offering food was then essential to avoid starvation.

The social context of hospitality

Many proverbs touch on the social context of hospitality: *Bokhaleske de te xhal, te lacho vaj nalacho* (Offer food to a hungry person, may he be good or bad). *Sakoneske kampelas bokh te prindzharel* (everybody should recognise what it means to be hungry).

The command of sharing food was also articulated in another ritual: when a woman cooked her first meal after she had returned *pal o gava* (from the villages), she would send one of her children with a dish to some poorer family with words: *mi xhan lakere chave* (her children should also eat).

It was the custom at festivals like Christmas to invite a beggar (even, sometimes, a *gadzho* beggar) and treat him with food. Margita Reiznerová told me how her father used often to go out to the cross-roads and wait for some beggar or vagabond to invite him to eat. These tramps would pay back the hospitality with news from the wider world. In the old days when there was no television, no radio, and when Roma did not read newspapers, itinerant vagabonds were a precious source of information: *Ko but phirel, but dzhanel* (He who wanders a lot, knows a lot) – and they would inform people, *so šundhol andr'oda baro svetos* (what is to be heard in the great world outside).

Pat'iv *at the feast as the affirmation of family ties*

Although food is offered in every social situation, there are situations when it is offered with special ritual solemnity, as *pat'iv*. The expression *te del pat'iv* literally means 'to give respect' but has acquired a secondary meaning: to make a feast, to treat someone with special food and drink. To make a feast is an obligatory manifestation of kinship solidarity and a declaration of family ties and mutual responsibilities. When *familija avla te dikhel* (relatives came to pay a visit) the visited member of the extended family had *te del pat'iv* even if the arrival was at midnight.

Familija (the extended family) is another *baro lav* (great word), in Roma society. Primary socialisation, professional skills, social welfare and education in *romipen* were all provided by various members of the kinship group. *Roma likernas familija dzhi pandzhto, šovto paraput'a* (Roma pay respect to family ties to the fifth or sixth degree). That is why a visit of any relative had to be celebrated with *pat'iv* and the hosts would have *te thovel skamind* (to prepare a table), which means to cover the table with the best food.

The visits of relatives, and indeed visits in general, were often unexpected. Visitors might appear at any time during the twenty-four hours of the day. The welcoming ceremony for relatives was a sort of cultural *hors d'euvre* of events to come. *Familija rovenas pre peste* (the relatives would weep in each other's arms), *chivenas prachos* (they would throw ashes) in front of the door to see the blessed footprints of their relative. After that the head of the family would serve alcohol and the housewife would start preparing the banquet table. At such occasions meat was usually served, as these were markers of prestige, food of high status, which was consumed only occasionally on Sundays at parties for *bašaviben* (playing music) and *mulatšagos* (singing).

If there was no money saved in the family the housewife would go and borrow money from anybody who had it, run to the shop and buy what was necessary. The requirement to affirm family solidarity, *te del pat'iv, te thovel skamind* was so imperative that any violation of it would have been a *bari ladzh* (great shame). One of my good friends in Prague had a visit from her father's brother from Slovakia. As she had no money at home, she ran the risk of stealing four pounds of meat and a bottle of vodka in a supermarket. She was caught and the visit of her uncle resulted in half a year of prison for her. This, however, she considered 'normal' while not 'giving respect' to her uncle would have been a *bari ladzh,* and a matter of everlasting gossip in the Roma public.

The mule *(the souls of the dead) police the kitchen*

Cooked food had always to be fresh. To offer re-warmed dishes was a sign of terrible *degešipen* (that is, *degeš* behaviour). Left-over food was demonstratively thrown away to dogs or to the pigs of the *gadzhe* neighbours who would rebuke Roma for being spendthrift and not knowing how to economise. Roma on the contrary would despise the *gadzhé* for eating anything 'dirty' which came into their hands. The prohibition of eating re-warmed food – which has parallels in Indian culture – is also mentioned by Hancock (1991).

When I tried to find out the ideological justification of this habit, often no special reason was given – just: *avka ko Roma hin* (it is a habit of Roma) or: *kada dzhal papi pre papende* (that comes down from our great-great-grandfathers). Some of the knowledgeable old women, however, gave a more specific reason: *rat'i, phiren o mule, habrinen, a te manuš xhal, šaj merel* (at night the spirits of the dead walk around and meddle (with the food) and if a person eats it, he or she may die).

Traditional oral folklore contains all sorts of semi-formalised *vakeribena* (narratives) which show how violation of *romipen* can be dreadfully punished. One story I recorded from Verunka Goralová (then about sixty years old, born in Levocha, Slovakia) told of an uncle who died because he had eaten *muklo chaben* (left-overs). His daughter was too mean to throw away some pork and cabbage, and left it in the pot overnight. During the darkness some malicious *mulo* came and meddled with it. The next day her father ate the food and died.

On the other hand *mule* have to be offered food but the food is special and prepared specially for them and a living person would never even think of tasting the food for *mule*.

Food is offered to *mule* at certain formal occasions (like Christmas) or to satisfy their 'hunger' and thus divert them from reappearing. The food for *mule* never consists of meat, it must be some kind of *chumer* (dough or pastry). Meat would turn the *mulo* ferocious or even turn him into a vampire. At Christmas-time special cakes are prepared called *bobalki*. They are served *le vodhenge* (dative pl. of vodhi, soul) to the souls of deceased relatives. *Bobalki* are put into the corner of the room or on the window ledge. Otherwise *haluški* are often prepared for a *mulo* who returns either because the soul cannot find peace or because his living relatives have not paid some debt to him.

Offering food to a *mulo* is, of course, only one of many practices to divert him from returning to haunt the house. Food which is put on the window ledge or on the threshold (only the Christmas *bobalki* are served inside the house) is usually eaten up by some dog, cat, bird or another animal – which of course, can be the *mulo* himself, as a *mulo* can appear in a human form or animal form as it likes. If the food remains uneaten, it is burned, as fire purifies everything.

Food, ritual and the ideal of zhuzhipen (cleanliness)

As food is *le Devlestar* (from God), it is holy, it is an offering and a 'sacrifice': it makes God happy because he created man to live and man eats to live and thus to fulfil God's wish. It is imperative to handle food with the highest respect, which means with the highest purity and cleanliness.

Another reason why everything which comes in contact with food had to be clean was the *chachipen* (truth) that whatever comes inside into the body with food affects not only its physical parts but the whole phenomenon of the person – their psychology, mood, destiny and everything. Food can also be misused for witchcraft and therefore every woman had to demonstrate by deeds and proclamations that she was *zhuzhi* to show that 'her' food and her cooking cannot harm anybody. Women are considered 'unclean' in general – at least from their first menstruation till their menopause. That is why they have to observe all regulations of cleanliness so strictly.

Women who were cooking had first of all to wash their hands. Ilona Ferková remembers how once when she was fifteen years old she had to cook when her mother was ill. She was wearing red nail-varnish. Her father saw it and ordered her to take it off immediately. She had no nail polish remover so her father took a knife and scratched it off, which was very painful. Her father claimed that vampire-like qualities would go inside the food if she had cooked with red nails

Another things which was obligatory while cooking was a scarf on the head. A hair found in food was not only disgusting but might have meant that the person who found it had become an object of witchcraft. An accusation of witchcraft was something terrible. Roma would avoid all contact with such a family, which was the worst punishment possible, afflicting people socially, culturally and morally. The famous self-taught painter Ruda Dzurko recollected to me once how once his uncle Janchi found a hair in soup served to him in the household of a distant relative. He never visited this family ever again and to the end of his life was trying to guess who wanted to bewitch him and why. He blamed the hair and the woman who cooked that soup for all the mishaps of his life.

Women were not allowed to cook in the six weeks after giving birth or while menstruating. In traditional Gypsy settlements there were always enough sisters, sisters-in-law, daughters-in-law, aunts and other relatives, who could prepare the food instead of the one who *dzhanelas peskerestar* (lit. 'knew her own business', i.e. was menstruating).

It was not only the physical cleanliness which was required but also psychic or spiritual purity. If the woman was not able to control her anger or her sorrow she either herself refused to cook or was not allowed to cook by her mother-in-law or some other elder woman. If still she was cooking without having *zhuzho jilo* (a pure heart), then she was blamed for anything improper which might have happened two three days after 'putting her *ñecuchos* (evil spirit, bad temper) into the food'. This, of course, was an ideal norm and the conditions of real life do not always allow people to follow the norm in every respect.

The ingredients prepared for cooking had to be protected from any 'evil eye' of somebody who might enter the kitchen. Therefore dough which was put aside to rise was always covered with a piece of clean linen so that no evil eye might affect it. Also pots, plates, cups, utensils and everything used for cooking and eating had to be clean. It is unthinkable to wash dishes in the same sink as laundry, as gadzhe housewives often do, for which they are considered to be *melale degeša* (dirty carrion-eaters).

"Chirla o Roma sastes xhanas, sastes dzhivenas"
In the old days Roma ate healthily and lived healthily

Hancock (1991) discusses *baxhtalo xhaben* (blessed food) in the community of Vlaxi Roma in the USA. No special food is denoted as *bachtalo* by Servika Roma. Nonetheless, the *chirlatune pat'ivale chache Roma* (the old Roma worthy of genuine respect) knew much better what was good for their health than the 'modern' Roma of today. Their diet was influenced by the simple (and often poor) living conditions of most Roma, and by the traditional way of exchanging their products with the *gadzhe* peasants for what they were growing in their fields and gardens or the products of their cattle. The most common payments in kind were potatoes, curds, sour milk, cabbage, beans, peas, corn, grain or flour, eggs and fat. This kind of nourishment contained all the important vitamins, proteins, minerals, calcium and other stuff which human organism needs. Ab Hortis (1775) describes Roma as being thin but healthy. Mortality of newly born babies was high and accidents were frequent but those Roma who survived all the early dangers, often lived to a ripe old age. When I was collecting folk-tales up to forty years ago I met many famous *paramisara* (story-tellers) who were over eighty or even ninety years old.

Adadhives o Roma meren terne (today Roma die young) is a current saying. Meat which formerly was eaten only once a week or even once a month – and was a food of 'prestige', is being consumed three times a day today, to demonstrate that *amen Roma sam raja – šaj xhas mas, keci kamas* (we Roma are gentlemen now and can eat meat as much as we want). To discuss modern food ways of Roma, however, is a different theme which would require a deep analysis of the pervasive changes which Roma have undergone during the past fifty years.

When today political leaders, cultural workers, writers and thousands of unknown, anonymous Roma try to reaffirm their identity, and the genuine *romipen*, worthy of respect, then they try to revive the precious values which have always helped Roma to survive, and to live in harmony within the family, community and the world, to live 'with God'. While they are trying to draw out the essentials of their traditional culture it always is food with all its cultural, social, ethical and spiritual, as well as dietary implications that is discussed.

Just as many Roma families are coming back to the Romani language which they had deserted under heavy assimilatory pressures, so they are also coming back to traditional Romani meals such as *haluški, pišota, marikla* and others. They contrast this with what they say was the situation twenty or thirty years ago when communist social workers were organising 'cookery classes' for women of Gypsy origin, where Roma women were taught to cook fried steaks or fat pork with heavy dumplings – while the traditional *haluški* were constantly ridiculed. Today there are classes organised by Roma women where Czechs are enthusiastically learning to prepare *haluški, pišota* and other simple and healthy Romani dishes. The perfect cook Verunka Goralová, for whom cooking is a prayer of delight, said to me: *"Te amen o Roma tavaha the chaha avka sar chirla, kaj te sikhavas pat'iv le Devleske, o Del amen arakhela. e baxht amen na omukela."* (If we Roma will again prepare and eat food as before, to show respect to God, God will protect us. And happiness and blessing will not abandon us).

References

Ab Hortis, Samuel Augustini, 1775 *Von dem heutigen Zustande, sonderbaren Sitten und Lebensart, wie auch von denen Übrigen eigenschaften und Umständen der Zigeuner in Ungarn*, in Kaiserlich Königlich allergnädigst privilegirte Anzeigen aus sämtlichen Kaiserl. königl. erbländern, V. Jahrgang, XXII Stück den 31. Mai, (New edition, študion dd, Bratislava, 1995).

Grellmann, Heinrich, Moritz Gottlieb, 1783 *Die Zigeuner*, priv. Dessau/Leipzig.

Hancock, Ian, 1991 *Romani foodways, the Indian roots of Gypsy culinary culture*, The International Romani Union and The University of Texas at Austin, Austin.

Kenrick, Donald, 1971 "Some points to watch when visiting a Gypsy Site" *Temeski Kris te Romengo Jinapen Lil. National Gypsy education Council Newsletter* No.1, pp.6-7.

Lacková, Ilona, 1997 *Narodila jsem se pod šťastnou hvězdou*, Triada, Praha. (published in english, 2000, as *A False Dawn: my life as a Gypsy woman in Slovakia*, University of Hertfordshire Press, Hatfield).

Myers, John, 1909 "Drab" *Journal of the Gypsy Lore Society*, New Series, Vol.2 pp.199-207.

APPENDIX

The recipe for *haluški* as recounted by Verunka Gorolová

"Haluški hin chirlatuno Romano xhaben. Haluški hin le Romengero sast'ipen. Hin but sorti haluški: chuchimen, vastengere, pharade, ciraleha, arminaha, the pro gules – phenav tuke but, but sorti haluški, save kames.

    Jekhbuter kerenas o romňija churde vaj chuchimen haluški. Kušes tuke gruli, randes pro sano tarlos. Chives jaro, grisovo – vareko phenel "thulo" jaro. Chives lon. Mišines. Keci jaro? Keci tuke o vast – kaj o chumer te avel zoraleder. Te ela kovlo chumer, ta pes tuke o haluški rozdzhana. Thoves pañi te tadhol. Sar imar o pañi tadhol fest, thoves tuke o chumer pre lopatka, vaj pro tañiricis, chures andro pañi la rojaha vaj churaha. Furt tuke cindhar e churi, kaj o chumer pes tuke te na lipinel. Kampel the churel sanores, sanores. Kana o haluški aven opre, mišin jekhvar, duvar, pre tritovareste imar šaj les avri varechaha. Chives andro charo, sisig plukines avri pañeha te pes na lipinen jekhetane. Chives ciral, opral chives bilardo khil – a imar. šaj xhas. Xha Devleha, xha pro sast'ipen."

Haluški is traditional Romani food. *Haluški* is the health of the Roma. There are many kinds of *haluški*: sliced, *'vastengere, 'pharade'*, with curds (soft cheese), with cabbage, you can even make them sweet – I tell you there are many, many sorts of *haluški*, whatever you want.

    The commonest type prepared by the women, however was ''cut' or 'sliced' *haluški*. You peel the potatoes, and grate them on a grater with thin holes. You add roughly ground flour – some call it "thick". You add salt and you mix all together. How much flour is needed? As much as it takes to feel with your hand when the dough is getting stronger. Your dough must not be too soft, or your *haluški* will dissolve. You put water to boil. When the water is boiling properly, you put the dough on a cooking board or on a plate and you slice the dough and put into the boiling water either with the knife or with a spoon. Make the knife wet again and again, so that the dough does not stick to it. You have to cut tiny, thin pieces of dough. When the *haluški* come up, stir once, twice and the third time you make take them out with a wooden spatula. You put them into a dish, and rinse them with water so they do not stick together. Then you can put cottage cheese, or butter on them and they are ready. You can eat. eat with God! eat for your health!"

A SUMMARY BIBLIOGRAPHY OF WORKS BY DONALD KENRICK

1956-9 (joint editor with Bente Kenrick) *Odin – The London Scandinavian Journal*.
1965 *The Portrayal of the Jew in Scandinavian Fiction and Drama (1700–1940)* MA thesis, University College, London.
1966 "Some notes on the Gypsies in Bulgaria" *Journal of the Gypsy Lore Society* (3rd series) Vol. XLV (3–4) pp.77–83.
1967a "The Romani dialect of a musician from Razgrad" *Linguistique Balkanique* (Bulgarian Academy of Sciences, Sofia) Vol.11 (2), pp.71–8.
1967b (with T. Pobozniak, H. Mikolos and G. Meszaros) "Présentation de nouveaux travaux sur la langue tsigane" *Études Tsiganes* Vol.13 (3) pp1–6.
1967c "Three Gypsy tales from the Balkans" *Folklore* Vol.78, pp.59–60.
1969a *Morphology and lexicon of the Romany dialect of Kotel (Bulgaria)*. PhD thesis, School of Oriental and African Studies, University of London.
1969b (ed. with G. Meszaros) "Four Hungarian songs" *Journal of the Gypsy Lore Society* (3rd Series) Vol. XLVII (1–2) pp.55–7.
1969–1973 (with Ronald Lee) *Learn Romani – a correspondence course in 20 lessons* Romani Institute, London (afterwards serialised in *Roma* 1974 Vol.1 (1) p.58 – 1983 Vol. 7(1) p.54 and published in book form, 1985 as *Learn Romani Lessons*, Roma Publications, Chandigarh (India).) Also Sinte edition, 1984, Romani Institute, London.
1970a "Greek coppersmiths still in England" *Journal of the Gypsy Lore Society* 3rd series) Vol.XLIX p. 152.
1970b "The new Sites Act" *Romano Drom newspaper*, April, p.3.
1971a "Sociolinguistics of the development of Anglo-Romani" in T. Acton ed. *Currrent changes amongst British Gypsies and their place in International Patterns of Development*. National Gypsy Education Council, Oxford.
1971b "The sociolinguistics of Anglo-Romani" Paper to the annual conference of the British Association for the Advancement of Science, Swansea.
1971c "The World Romany Congress – April 1971" *Journal of the Gypsy Lore Society* Vol.L, (3–4) pp 101–8.
1971d (editor, with Venice Manley) *Amaro Lil – Temeski Kris te Romengo Jinapen Lil – The National Gypsy Education Council Newsletter* Numbers 1–3.
1971e "Some points to watch when visiting a Gypsy Site" *Amaro Lil – Temeski Kris te Romengo Jinapen Lil – National Gypsy Education Council Newsletter* No.1, pp.6–7.

1971f (with T. Acton) "News from the London Borough of Newham" *Amaro Lil – Temeski Kris te Romengo Jinapen Lil – The National Gypsy Education Council Newsletter* No.2, p.10.

1971g "News from Hounslow, Newham and Wandsworth" *Amaro Lil – Temeski Kris te Romengo Jinapen Lil – The National Gypsy Education Council Newsletter* No.3, p.18.

1971h "News from Yugoslavia" *Amaro Lil – Temeski Kris te Romengo Jinapen Lil – The National Gypsy Education Council Newsletter* No.3, p.30.

1972 (with G. Puxon) *The Destiny of Europe's Gypsies*. Chatto Heinemann/Sussex University Press, London.

   1974 repr. 1995 *Destins gitans* Gallimard, Paris.

   1975 *Il Destino degli Zingari* Rizzoli, Rome.

   1981 *Sinti und Roma: die Vernichtung eines Volkes im NS-Staat*, Gesellschaft für Bedrohte Völker, Göttingen und Wien (tr A.Stegelmann).

   1990 (though dated 1988) *Berša Bibahtale* Romanestan Publications, London (Tr. G. Puxon).

   1997 *Bibaxtale Berša* Editorial Presencia Gitana, Madrid (new tr. M.Cortiade). (This has also been translated into Japanese.)

1973a "Finnish Gypsies visit London" *Journal of the Gypsy Lore Society* (3rd Series) LII. (1–2) pp.50–51.

1973b "Notes from Dorset" *Traveller Education* No.1 (inc *The National Gypsy Education Council Newsletter* No.4) p. 9.

1974a "Calo borrowings by an English Gypsy family" *Journal of the Gypsy Lore Society* (4th Series Vol.1 (1) pp.45–7.

1974b *The Gorgios come on Mondays* Thameside Adult Education Centre, Gravesend, Kent.

1975a "Progress under the 1968 Caravan Sites Act" *Traveller Education* No.4, pp.1–3.

1975b "Gypsies: the need for a new initiative" *Traveller Education* No.6, pp.13–15.

1975c "Les terrains de stationnement en Grande-Bretagne – Progrès réalisés depuis la loi de 1968" *Études Tsiganes* Vol.21(1) pp.38–39.

1976a *The date of origin of Shelta* Occasional Paper of the Romani Institute No.2, London.

1976b *A contribution to the early history of the Romani people*. Occasional Paper of the Romani Institute, No.3, Romani Institute, London.

1976c "Romanies in the Middle East Part One" *Roma* Vol.1(3) pp. 5–8.

1976d "Romanies in the Middle East Part Two" *Roma* Vol.2(1), pp. 30–36.

1976e "The Banjara", "Lore and Language", "The Dom in Europe" "Romanies and the Burushashki" *Journal of the Gypsy Lore Society*, (4th series) Vol.I (2) pp. 150–152.

1977a "Romanies in the Middle East Part Three" *Roma* Vol.3(1), pp.23–39.

1977b "Eilert Sundt and the Norwegian Travellers" *Roma* Vol.3 (2) pp.23–5.

1977c "Criminal Trespass provisions of the Criminal Law Bill" *Traveller Education* No.10 pp.38–39.

1978a "Études sur le vocabulaire des Voyageurs en Grande Bretagne et ailleurs" *Études Tsiganes*.(March) Vol.26 (1) pp. 21–5 (originally delivered to Études Tsiganes seminar in Sevres, 1977.)

1978b "Romanies without a road" *Contemporary Review* No.232 pp. 153–6.

1978c "Shelta" *Traveller Education* No.12 p.7.

1978d "The Dom in Europe" *Journal of the Gypsy Lore Society* (4th Series) Vol I (4) pp. 287–8.

1978e (with R. Wells) Letter to the Editor – a response to Beresford-Webb *Journal of the Gypsy Lore Society (4th Series)* Vol I (4) pp. 289–291.

1979a "Romani English" *International Journal of the Sociology of Language*, No.19 pp. 111–120.

1979b (with T. Wilson) *An English Romani word book* Romanestan Publications, London.

1980a (with G. Puxon and T. Zülch) *Die Zigeuner: verkannt, verachtet, verfolgt* Niedersachsische Landeszentrale für Politische Bildung, Hanover.

1980b "England's other Romanies – the London Kalderash" *Roma*, Vol.5 (1) pp.39–43.

1980c "New books in Romani", "Neue Bücher aus Deutschland" *Traveller Education* No.18, pp.28–9.

1981a "The development of a standard alphabet for Romani" *The Bible Translator* Vol.32 (2) pp. 215–219.

1981b "Die Vernichtung der Sinti und Roma im NS Herrschaftsbereich" *Zeitschrift für Kulturaustausch* (Institut für Auslandsbeziehungen, Stuttgart) Vol.31 (4). pp 393–7.

1981c "Der Völkermord an deutschen Sinti und Europaischen Roma im Dritten Reich" Paper to Deutscher Evangelischer Kirchentag, Hamburg.

1981d "Romano alfabeto" *Loli Phabaj* (London) No.1, pp.3–4.

1981e "The World Romani Congress" *Traveller Education* No.16 pp. 7–10.

1981f "Romani education in Norway" *Traveller Education* No.16 pp. 26–8.

1982 "A further note on the secret languages of the musicians of Iran" *Journal of the Gypsy Lore Society (4th Series)* Vol II (1) pp.84–5.

1983a "Reparations for Gypsies" Paper to the Warsaw Conference on Nazi War Crimes.

1983b "Die britischen Roma heute" *Pogrom*. Vol.12 No.80/81. March/April. pp.14–17.

1983c (by E. Gunnemark in collaboration with D. Kenrick) *What language do they speak – a geolinguistic handbook*, private, Gothenburg and London. (New, editions revised by E. Gunnemark, 1985, 1986 and 2000 as *A geolinguistic handbook*).

1983d "A bridge too far – a walk along the Thames" *Bush News* May-June pp.6–7.

1983–1990 (contributor) *Atlas Linguaram Europae* Vol.I (1–4) Van Gorcum, Assen (Netherlands).

1984a (with G.Taylor) "The portrayal of the Gypsy in English schoolbooks" *Internationale Schulbuchforschung – Zeitschrift des Georg-Eckerts Instituts* Vol.6 (1) pp. pp.38–48.

1984b "Gypsies, why learn about them?" *Bulletin of Environmental Education* No.161 (October) pp.4–19.

1984c "Risarcimento agli Zingari" *Lacio Drom*. Vol. XX (2–3) p.38–40.

1984d (ed. with T. Acton) *Romani Rokkeripen ToDivvus. The English Romani dialect and its contemporary social, educational and linguistic standing*. Romanestan Publications, London.

1984e "New books from Germany" *Traveller Education* No.19 pp.33–4.

1984f "West London waterway walk" *Bush News* July/Aug. pp.6–7

1985 "The oral tradition among the Romanies in Bulgaria" *LacioDrom* Vol. 22 (6 – supplement) pp.71–76.

1986a "Die gemeinsame Geschichte von Sinti, Roma und Juden" *Pogrom* No.123.p.9.

1986b "Gypsies and Jews" *Jewish Socialist* No.5 pp.8–11, translated in German in *Pogrom* No. 123 pp. 33–5.

1986c (with G. Taylor) "Gypsies in Cyprus" *Roma* (New Numbering System) No.24, pp. 36–38.

1987a (with P. Mercer) "Roma und Fahrende in Grossbritannien" *Pogrom* No. 130.

1987b "Irische Fahrenden in Grossbritannien" *Pogrom* No. 130.

1988a "La scolarisation des enfants tsiganes au Royaume Uni" Paper to the Montauban conference on the Education of Gypsy Children.

1988b (with S. Bakewell) "'They call me Shaikh' – the Odyssey of a Yugoslav Rom" *Roma* No.28, pp. 9–14.

1989a "L'evolution d'une langue litteraire romani: ou en sommes nous?" in P. Williams (ed.) *Tsiganes, Identité, Evolution* Syros, Paris pp.395–401 (originally delivered to Études Tsiganes

seminar in Paris, 1986.)
1989b "Why the Jews and the Gypsies are enemies – a Bulgarian Romani folktale" in D. Tong ed. *Gypsy Folk Tales* Harcourt Brace Jovanovic, San Diego and New York.
1989c "Letter to the Editor" *Holocaust and Genocide Studies* Vol.4 (2) pp.251–254.
1989d "Romani in Sweden" *Traveller Education* No.24 p.23.
1990a (with S Bakewell) On the Verge: the Gypsies of England Runnymede Trust, London. 2nd. much enlarged ed 1996 University of Hertfordshire Press, Hatfield. (See also 1999d.)
1990b "Sar te standardisaras o keripe Romano". Paper to the Linguistic Conference at the Fourth World Romani Congress, Warsaw.
1990c "Romani at the crossroads" Paper to the Gilze-Rijen colloquium.
1990d "Private Sites – a step backwards" *Traveller Education* No.25 p.10
1990e "Eastern Europe – brighter prospects" *Traveller Education* No.25 p.16
1990f (with M. Karpati and members of the kibbutz Lohamei ha Ghettaoth) "Ricordo di Miriam Novitch" *Lacio Drom* Vol.26(5) pp.37–39.
1991a "Gypsies in East Europe since the changes" *Europinion* (Oslo) No.3.
1991b "Gypsies, criminalized from birth" *Criminal Justice Matters* No.6.
1991c (with T. Acton) "From Summer voluntary schemes to European Community bureacracy: the development of Special Provision for Traveller Education in the United Kingdom since 1967" *European Journal of Intercultural Studies*. Vol.l (3) pp.47–62.
1991d "The Gypsies in Bulgaria before and after 10th November 1989" Paper to the Gypsy Lore Society Annual Conference, Leicester.
1991e "The Irish Travellers – a unique phenomenon in Europe?" Paper to the Anthropological Association of Ireland conference on Irish Travellers, Dublin.
1991f "Time of the Gypsies" *Catalyst* No.6 and *Traveller Education* No. 26 p.15.
1991g "Report on the Dublin Conference on Travellers" *Traveller Education* No.26, pp. 20–22.
1992a "Zigenarna" *Invandrare och Minoriteter* (Stockholm) No.1992/5–6.
1992b (ed.) *Report of the Working Party for Gypsy Education Conference at Burwell* East Anglian Gypsy Council, Peterborough.
1993a "Romani at the crossroads" in: G. Extra and L. Verhoeven *Immigrant Languages in Europe* Multilingual Matters, Clevedon (UK).
1993b "The Romany Gypsies of Europe" *Jewish Quarterly* No.152.
1993c "Language contact – the case of Drindari" Paper presented to the Hamburg conference on Linguistics.
1993d "La scolarisation des enfants tsiganes au Royaume Uni" in *Les enfants tsiganes a l'ecole*. (Report of a conference in Montauban). Strasbourg.
1993e "Response to Cohn and Lipa" *Nationalities Papers* Vol.XXI (2) pp. 288–290.
1993f "New books from abroad" *Traveller Education* No. 27 p. 16.
1993g "Gypsy poetry" in: *The New Princeton Encyclopedia of Poetry and Poetics* Princeton University Press, Princeton.
1994a *Gypsies: from India to the Mediterranean*. Interface Collection, Vol.3. Centre Régional de Documentation Pédagogique Mid-Pyrénées, Toulouse.
    1995 *Los Gitanos: de la India al Mediterráneo*. Interface Collection, Vol.3. Presencia Gitana, Madrid.
    1995 *Les Tsiganes de l'Inde à la Méditerranée*. Interface Collection, Vol.3. Centre Régional de Documentation Pédagogique Mid-Pyrénées, Toulouse.
    1996 *Zingari: dall'India al Mediterraneo*. Interface Collection, Vol.3. Anicia, Rome.

1998 : Τσιγγανι απο Ινδιες σιη Μεσογελο Interface Collection, Vol.3. Editions Kastaniotis, Athens.

1998 *Tsiganite: ot India do Sredizemno More.* Interface Collection, Vol.3. Litavra, Sofia.

1998 *Rromii: din India la Mediterana*. Interface Collection, Vol.3. Editura Alternative, Bucharest.

1998 *Sinti und Roma: von Indien bis zum Mittelmeer*. Interface Collection, Vol.3. Edition Parabolis, Berlin.

1998 *Ciganos: da India ao Mediterrâneo.* Interface Collection, Vol.3. Entreculturas, Lisbon.

1994b "Foreign Gypsies in England" Paper to the Economic and Social Research Council Seminar on Romani Studies, University of Greenwich.

1994c "The Irish Travellers – a unique phenomenon in Europe?" in M. McCann et al. (eds) *Irish Travellers: Culture and Ethnicity*. Institute of Irish Studies, Queen's University, Belfast. pp.20–35. (paper orginally delivered at Irish Anthropological Asssociation Conference, Dublin, 1991).

1994d "Zigenarna inte Valkomna (Gypsies not welcome)" *Invandrare och Minoriteter* (Stockholm) No. 1994/5–6.

1994e "Romani: on the move". *Index on Censorship* (London) vol.23.

1994f "Romanies in the Nazi Period – Romak a naci korszakban – E Roma Tela e Nazisti, so Zhanas, so na Zhanas" in: Z. Bodi (Ed) *Cigány Néprajzi Tanulmanyok*. II (Papers from the First International Conference on Gypsy Ethnography, History, Linguistics and Culture1993 Budapest) Magyar Társaság, Budapest. p.69–78.

1994g "A legend about Gypsy origin" in E. Mariushakova and V. Popov eds. *Studii Romani* (Club 90 Sofia) Vol.11: 62–64.

1994h translation of W. Shakespeare *Romeo and Juliet* First performance May 7th 1994, Theater an der Ruhr, Mülheim, Germany.

1995a "The Nazis and the Gypsies" *Jewish Quarterly* No. 156.

1995b "Uj bunbakok Kelet-Europaban" *Amaro Drom* (Budapest) January.

1995c "The Roma in Eastern Europe since the changes". *Roma* No. 42–43, pp. 35–48.

1995d "Gypsies threaten our trees" in: A. Sebasteyen ed. *Casablanca*, private, London.

1995e "The Roma in Eastern Europe since the changes" *Roma*, no.42–43, pp. 35–48.

1996a (with G. Puxon) *Gypsies under the Swastika*. (heavily revised ed. of 1972). Interface Collection, Vol.8. University of Hertfordshire Press, Hatfield.

1997 *Gitanos la Cruz Gamada*. Interface Collection, Vol.8. Presencia Gitana, Madrid.

1997 *Les Tsiganes sous l'oppression nazie*. Interface Collection, Vol.8. Centre Régional de Documentation Pédagogique Mid-Pyrénées, Toulouse.

1998 *Hitlerismat i tsiganite*. Interface Collection, Vol.8. Litavra, Sofia.

1998 *Os Ciganos sob o dominio da suástica*. Interface Collection, Vol.8. Entreculturas, Lisbon.

1996b "Romani literacy at the crossroads" *International Journal for the Sociology of Language* No.119, pp.109–123.

1996c "Come gli Ebrei hanno onorato le vittime zingare dell'olocausto" *Lacio Drom* Vol.32(3) pp.21–2.

1996d "Ztracena princezna" (The lost princess) *Romano Dzjhaniben* Vol III.

1996e "Les Chants Tziganes dans les Camps de Concentration" in Federation Nationale de Deportées, *Créer pour Survivre* (Report of a Conference held in Rheims, September 1995), CFND., Paris, p.167.

1997a "Foreign Gypsies and British immigration law after 1945" in: T. Acton (ed.) *Gypsy Politics and*

Traveller identity. University of Hertfordshire Press, Hatfield.

1997b (ed. & tr.) "Once upon a time there were five brothers", "Once upon a time there were twelve brothers", "Twelve brothers", "The story about Pavel" in: E. Mariushakova and V. Popov eds. *Studii Romani* Vol.II-IV, (Litvara, Sofia) pp. 55–60.

1997c (translator) K. Fings, H. Heuss & F. Sparing *The Gypsies during the Second World War, Vol.I From "Race Science" to the Camps*. Intereface Collection, Volume 12. University of Hertfordshire Press, Hatfield.

1997d (contributor) *Atlas Linguarum Europae* Vol I (5) Istituto Poligrafico, Rome (Italy).

1998a (with GillianTaylor) *Historical dictionary of the Gypsies (Romanies)* Scarecrow Press, Lanham, Maryland, USA.

1998b "How many roads?" *Index on Censorship* No.4 pp.55–69.

1998c "Shakespeare a Romové (Shakespeare in Romani)". *Romano Dzjhaniben* Vol .V. (1–2), pp. 90–95.

1999a (ed. and tr.) *The Gypsies during the Second World War, Vol. II In the Shadow of the Swastika* University of Hertfordshire Press, Hatfield.

1999b "Romani (Kalderash)" in: M.R. Key (ed.) *Indo-European Languages – a computer database*, University of California, California.

1999c "The image of the Gypsy in German Christendom: a commentary" (Response to G. Margalit) *Patterns of Prejudice* Vol.33 (2) pp.84–5.

1999d (with C. Clark) *Moving on: the Gypsies and Travellers of Britain*, University of Hertfordshire Press, Hatfield. (Much enlarged 3rd edition of 1990a).

1999e "What is a Gypsy" in: R. Morris and L. Clements eds. *Gaining Ground: law reform for Gypsies and Travellers*, University of Hertfordshire Press, Hatfield, pp.64–9.

2000a "Towards a typology of unwritten languages" in: T. Acton and M. Dalphinis eds. *Language, Blacks and Gypsies*, Whiting and Birch, London.

2000b (with Peter Bakker, Milena Hübschmannová, Valdemar Kalinin, Hristo Kyuchukov, Yaron Matras and Giulio Soravia) *What is the Romani language?* Interface Collection, Vol.21. University of Hertfordshire Press, Hatfield.

(forthcoming) "Groome, Francis Hindes" Revised entry for *New Dictionary of National Biography* Oxford University Press, Oxford.

Note

All citations of Kenrick's work in this volume are referenced in this bibliography, and are not listed in the individual lists of references given at the end of each paper.

Donald

CHARLES SMITH

Through thick and thin there's always been
A man called Donald K
That's K for Kenrick not Kendrick
As you may have heard him say

Abused, accused and often used
But with Gypsies he still stays
Often defamed, even remembered:
"Academic Crackpot: comes to mind

He's been served writs
By the King of Gypocrites.
Yet he fights the fight that he knows is right
And calmly proves his case.

At conferences here and conferences there
From Russia down to Spain,
The history of our people
In fifty languages he can explain.

He's an author, linguist and spokesman,
An educator, scholar and grafter,
A fighter, advisor and confidante
Even a Doyen

But to the Gypsies he's a friend
Held in respect and love
This all round guy Donald Kenrick
Is to us
A romani Rai.

BRIEF INFORMATION ON CONTRIBUTORS

THOMAS ACTON is Professor of Romani Studies at the University of Greenwich.

DIANA ALLEN was a founder member of the Hertfordshire Federation of Gypsy Support Groups, and works as a Solicitor, mainly with Gypsy Travellers.

PETER BAKKER lectures in linguistics at the University of Aarhus and has published extensively on the Romani language.

PAUL ELLINGWORTH is a Methodist Minister, and was for many years the United Bible Society Consultant on Romani, and Professor in the Department of Divinity with Religious Studies at the University of Aberdeen.

ELI FRANKHAM is President of the National Romani Rights Association and has published poetry and short stories.

ANTHONY GRANT lectures in linguistics at the University of Southampton, and advises the United Bible Societies on Romani translations.

ERIK GUNNEMARK translates from forty-five languages and is Chief Editor for Eurasia of the Intercontinental Dictionary Series. He is the co-ordinator of Amici Linguarum.

IAN HANCOCK is Professor of Linguistics at the University of Texas at Austin and has been appointed by President Clinton to the US Holocaust Commission. He represented the International Romani Union at the United Nations for many years.

HERBERT HEUSS works for the Project Bureau for the Promotion of Roma Initiatives in Eppelheim, Germany, and has written extensively on the history of Roma.

MILENA HÜBSCHMANNOVÁ reaches and researches Romani culture and language at Charles University, Prague, and edits the journal Romano Dzhaniben.

VALDEMAR KALININ works as an Educational Welfare Officer with Roma refugees in the London Boroughs of Camden and Hammersmith, and is translating the Bible into the Romani language.

GUNILLA LUNDGREN has published around twenty widely translated children's books and made several short films. She chairs the Swedish Academy of

Children's Books, and won the Gulliver Award in 1994.

ELENA MARUSHIAKOVA and VESSELIN POPOV both work as Anthropological researchers at the University of Sofia, and have published extensively on Roma in Bulgaria.

GRATTAN PUXON founded the Gypsy Council in England in 1966, and organised the first World Romani Congress in London in 1971. He was General Secretary of the International Romani Union till 1981. His paper is extracted and adapted from an unpublished history of the Romani movement.

CHARLES SMITH is Chair of the Gypsy Council for Education, Culture, Welfare and Civil Rights and has published two volumes of poetry.

SUSAN TEBBUTT lectures on German at the University of Bradford, and has edited a collection in English on German Roma and Sinte.